VENDETTA

VENDETTA

**TURNING YOUR BACK ON CRIME
CAN BE DEADLY...**

PAUL FERRIS
&
REG McKAY

BLACK & WHITE PUBLISHING

First published 2005
by Black & White Publishing Ltd
99 Giles Street, Edinburgh EH6 6BZ

ISBN 1 84502 061 8

Copyright © Paul Ferris & Reg McKay 2005

A CIP catalogue record for this book
is available from The British Library.

Cover photograph courtesy of Brian Anderson

Printed and bound by Creative Print and Design

CONTENTS

For my father,
William Chalmers Packer Ferris
(17 May 1927–9 September 1993)

Wish you were here.

1

GROUNDHOG DAY I

13 June 2002

The big dog stared up at me with cold eyes. Was he looking at a target? Begging me to move too quickly so he could spring and snap? Or was it familiarity? Was he saying hello? I'd met that dog before.

We were moving slowly through Frankland Prison – me, three screws and the big dog tethered on a lead but ready for action at the most trivial excuse. I wanted to get to that gate as soon as possible but no way was I hurrying. The dog's pace would suit me just fine.

Why the security? I was a Category-A prisoner, deemed to be an escape risk and a threat to the community – even when locked up.

Why the procession? I was being released but, until the exact moment I stepped through the gate to freedom, they would continue to treat me as a public enemy. Some said Public Enemy Number One. Then again, maybe they knew about something at the other side of that gate that I didn't? Fat chance.

The judge at the Old Bailey had described me as a very dangerous man and a threat to society. I'd been caught in London with three Mac-10 sub-machine guns, three silencers and ammo – one thousand rounds of subsonic bullets, standard issue for guns with silencers. For some reason, the court didn't believe me when I swore those weapons had been a big shock to me. Maybe they didn't like the company I'd been keeping. Paul Massey and the Salford Gang were good mates. The Adams Family in London were good friends. I'd met the Arifs and not for tea and cakes. Joey Pyle, London's Don of

1

Dons according to the New York Mafia, was a friend. I hadn't been on a tourist day trip when they caught me with those arms.

Whatever. I'd been arrested on 23 May 1997. To start with, they'd held me at Islington cop shop. I laugh now when I hear about Islington being full of swanky bistros and wine bars and the place where the new upper class lives. All I saw of the area was the four walls of my cell, the interview room and the back door.

Then they moved me to Pentonville Prison. Christ, that was a move downwards on the social scale of incarceration. Don't let anyone fool you that all jails are just four high walls, crowned with razor wire and a thick locked gate. You get better and worse. Pentonville was a cockroach-infested sewer of a place.

There, they kept me in the block – a segregated unit within a unit. It was all twenty-three-hour lock-ups and no association. A couple of days of that and you're almost grateful when the cops come to grill you again. I said almost.

Thank God I was deemed too much of a risk for that stinking hole of a jail and soon they whisked me off to the secure unit at Belmarsh. It was a prison within a prison and meant to be the most escape-proof jail in England. Some outsiders describe Belmarsh as hellish but at least prisoners get to move around and can talk with each other. And what people you meet – big-time mobsters, murderers by the score, drug traffickers, serial killers, poisoners, armed robbers, IRA, kidnappers, airplane hijackers, blackmailers, on and on. Get the jail and you meet interesting people, that's for sure.

It all kind of started in Belmarsh for me – this time – and ended up in Frankland. I'd sworn to do my time as peaceably as possible and get back out there to be with my partner and my kids. I was missing out on too much of their lives. But you can't be dumped in that company and those places without events taking on a life of their own – no matter how you try.

In Frankland, they were going to set me free. We edged, step by slow step, towards the big gate that would allow me through to reception for a shower and a shave. Then, dressed in my civvies again, I would be ready to step out into the free world. But that's how they were going – step by slow step. I knew their game. Three screws and a dog were taking me through one of the most secure jails in the country – bombproof, tank-proof and impervious to attack from the air. Should war ever break out, Frankland Prison is no bad place to take shelter but war hadn't broken out and I was about to be freed. Why the show of strength and the snail's pace? The system takes you in against your will and it frees you according to its will. It was their final show of strength. That slow procession through the jail was sending the message to me and to every con watching – we are in charge. Even now, when Ferris is about to be freed, we are still in control and there's nothing he or you can do about it. It's the same principle as 'dead man walking' except with a happier ending – or so I hoped.

I knew their game. I wasn't about to grumble or complain or suddenly go stir crazy. Why should I when, within a few hours, I would be home, drinking a glass of wine, holding my woman's hand and playing with my youngest boy? I knew their game and I would play it.

As the gate loomed closer, the sense of déjà vu became stronger and stronger. It didn't spook me at all. Why should it? I had been here before.

I looked down at the big dog and smiled. He didn't smile back. Two feet in front of me, the gate remained firmly shut. The bastards were taking their time, making me sweat out long, unnecessary seconds in that place. I knew they would. I'd been here before in every sense. I smiled again at the big dog, staring him straight in the eyes, daring him to blink, and I remembered why all of this felt so familiar.

2

FORTUNES
1998

'I sentence you to fifteen years.'

I've been sent down often enough – though some say not nearly enough – to know you can catch an underlying tone in the judge's voice. This one, a life-sized stuffed toy in his paraphernalia in Number One Court at the Old Bailey, had a hint of satisfaction. Clearly he didn't like gunrunners or bad men from the north coming down to his neck of the woods and making trouble. I'd news for him – I'd been hanging around Manchester, Liverpool and London for years and I wasn't sightseeing.

But I should have seen it coming – when an armed National Crime Squad ambushed my car, I should have known then that something stank. I'd gone with my friends Arthur Suttie and Connie Howarth to the London house of a bloke called John Ackerman – big mistake. Ackerman was a trader in illegal arms and had been providing most of the major teams in England and farther afield with weapons for years but Ackerman was also known to dabble in other scams like counterfeit money. In 1997, he'd invited me to invest in a big deal. Ackerman claimed to have high quality printing plates that could produce banknotes that were indistinguishable from the real deal. It was tempting – too bloody tempting.

For about two years, I'd been going straight – more or less – and doing very well, thank you, but this counterfeit dough lark offered the chance to produce massive sums. The counterfeit notes would

4

be laundered through large companies that were carrying out work, backed by EC funding, in places like former East Germany. The Berlin Wall coming down had opened up personal freedom of all sorts. If the plates were as good as I'd been led to believe they were, I could skin a couple of million in about a year – enough to retire on. Do one last job and then retire. That's what most street players want – out.

Trusting those you don't know is fatal in this business. I didn't know Ackerman so an arrangement was made that I would pick up the plates and some sample notes, test them out at leisure and then make my mind up. In a counterfeit money job, you obviously need top quality notes but effective distribution is also paramount. I could take care of the latter but it would be no good without the former.

I duly arrived at Ackerman's and lifted a box he said the plates were in – it felt the right weight. Outside Ackerman's flat, I put the box of goodies in Connie's car boot. Ackerman wouldn't have known this. If he was setting us up, the cops would follow me, not Connie. You can't be too careful – or so I thought. Ackerman didn't know about Connie's car but the MI5 spooks who were keeping the house under surveillance did. A short drive away, my car was hit in an armed ambush by the National Crime Squad, known as NCS. It was a recently formed national team of detectives who had been hand-picked from every police force. They were the cream of the cream and their role was intended to be the UK's equivalent of The Untouchables. When their first director, Roy Penrose, a cop with many years distinguished service, announced that arresting me was the pinnacle of his career, I had to laugh.

For years, Glasgow police had blamed me for everything, including a great deal that hadn't even happened yet. I'd done time inside all right – too much in my book but not enough in theirs. So they were out to get me big time – whatever it took. The Glasgow bizzies had planted heroin on me. They had accused me of robberies where witnesses had described the perpetrator as a tall, dark-haired man despite the fact that I'm a short, fair-haired bloke. They had bribed street players to set me up and threatened them with all sorts – going down for smack, getting a good kicking etc. – if they didn't do it. The guys agreed and then came straight to me revealing all. We managed to tape the cops not just trying to set me up but talking about killing me – we still have the tapes.

In 1992, they charged me with attempted murders, kneecappings and the killing of Fatboy Thompson, the son of Arthur Thompson, Glasgow's so-called Godfather. It was the longest criminal trial in Scottish history and I was found not guilty on all charges. That was in spite of the police and prosecution arranging for an infamous, professional informant by the name of Dennis Woodman to claim I had confessed all to him. Aye, right – like I would do that.

As I strolled, smiling, out of Glasgow High Court, the cops weren't best pleased. In fact, they were bloody furious and intent on getting me one way or another. I'd had enough experience of being set up by the blue serge mob and was certain they'd raise the stakes. There was no time in my life for that hassle.

While I was cooped up in jail waiting for the 1992 trial, my two pals, Bobby Glover and Joe Hanlon, had been shot dead when they were meant to be under twenty-four-hour police surveillance. The cops had 'lost' Bobby and Joe that night. That's what they were capable of. Screw that game. I headed out of town – Manchester and London would do me nicely.

If the world is shrinking, Britain is a tiny postage stamp. I knew I'd never be beyond the reach of Strathclyde Police, the force that covers Glasgow and one of the biggest cop outfits in the world. As I read the words of Roy Penrose, director of NCS, about my arrest, I laughed out loud. Who had been listening to the Glasgow polis then?

During the gunrunning trial, the Crown Prosecution proposed building a special witness box from which the MI5 undercover agents could give their evidence without being seen from the public benches. I didn't like the sound of that one bit. What sort of message would such cloak-and-dagger stuff give to the jury? Guilty as sin, that's what. When the Crown then offered a deal, giving my defence team surveillance files compiled by MI5 and NCS in return for the spooks being excused giving evidence, we grabbed it. As the Crown's representative was leaving the meeting, with the deal agreed, he hesitated and added, 'Oh, we might not call Ackerman either.' That seemed like even better news to me. What else would he be saying as a prosecution witness except that I'd bought those Mac-10s from him knowingly? If only I'd known what else he was getting up to.

3

FAKES

1998

Ackerman had been dealing in death for twenty years. You'd expect the guys in the white hats to want to nobble him good and proper. His name came up in all sorts of major cases in the UK and even Ireland. Caught out by Operation Shillelagh, which was run jointly by NCS and MI5 in 1998, Ackerman was the armourer who provided the weapon that was used on the outskirts of Dublin in 1996 to kill the Irish journalist Veronica Guerin whose story was made into the film *Veronica Guerin* (Joel Schumacher, 2003), starring Cate Blanchett. This guy had a lot to account for. Ackerman – a bad man who was going to be locked up forever? Don't you believe it.

Behind the scenes, Ackerman sang like a bird and was given only six years in jail for trafficking in death for two decades. Later he appealed and had that reduced to eighteen months. Result? He never spent one day proper in prison and worse was to follow. His family were told by the authorities that he'd died of a heart condition. Natural justice? No chance – last seen, he was having a great time living in Amsterdam, under a different name and, no doubt, on a UK pension funded by the police. Some grasses get more than thirty pieces of silver.

Years later, I'd learn that Ackerman had many reasons to turn informant. He had fallen out big time with long-term business associates Bob Bowen and Anthony 'Machine Gun' Mitchell. As his nickname suggests, Mitchell's speciality was reactivating deactivated

Mac-10s and he was Ackerman's main supplier for years. Then Ackerman paid Mitchell some money he owed him and the two fell out. The lowlife had tried to pass off some counterfeit £20 notes that had been made using the very plates he'd proposed to sell to me. The notes were such poor quality they were soon sussed as fakes. Ackerman was in big trouble and turned supergrass.

While we waited for the trial, Ackerman was moved from cop shop to cop shop all over England, spending no more than one night at a time in each. At another time, there was a report that he was holed up in a special unit in deepest rural Wales – a kind of hotel for supergrasses run by the screws. They couldn't afford to allow the man anywhere near the prison system. He had sold guns to too many people over the years and they were very nervous now. Instead, he got the five-star version of the protection scheme.

Standing in the Old Bailey, the judge's words rang in my ears – 'I sentence you to fifteen years.' It was a blow – I thought I might be looking at eight at most. Down in the well of the court, the bewigged clerk cleared his voice loudly, blushed and looked up. 'M'Lord,' he muttered. This was interesting. My brief and the prosecution were on their feet trying to attract the judge's attention. There was a kerfuffle, the swishing of black cloaks and much whispering. Then the court was cleared. What the hell was going on?

After an hour in the cells, I was brought back up again. I'd caught the judge's mood and half-expected to be sentenced to life. 'Harrumph,' the judge cleared his throat and the place descended into a deeper level of silence. 'I have been advised that the maximum sentence for such convictions is only ten years,' he said, or something like it, looking down at me. 'Therefore, I have no hesitation in sentencing you to that maximum – ten years' imprisonment.' And he whacked his gavel for the second time. On this occasion, I swear it gave a louder, sharper thump as he crashed it down. The aggression of the blow matched the expression on his phizog and the tone of his voice. Old judgey was well pissed off that he could give me only ten years in the pokey. 'Only'? – I ask you.

'Thank you, Your Honour,' I said from the dock. The beak's face went scarlet – he was probably thinking I was taking the piss – but, hey, I had just been given back five years of my life.

My co-accused, Arthur Suttie and Connie Howarth, got much lighter sentences, just as they should have. Both were absolute stalwarts. Arthur was an old-time boy and moral to the core. No court could scare him. Connie impressed me in particular. Many experienced *male* street players would have panicked at charges of gunrunning – not Connie. Her defence was that her boyfriend, one James Addison, was meant to have carried out the job but, at the last minute, couldn't. No problem – Connie would do it.

When she got nabbed, James Addison visited her in jail, knowing fine well his name was being noted. He even arranged to phone me and spoke about his original plans to be in the job and how his plans included an arms cache. All this was to be made available to the defence. It was finally decided that we wouldn't use it as it portrayed some foreknowledge – fair dos. But NCS also had photos of Addison taken in a bistro in Islington. That was something Strathclyde Police and other forces would be interested in. Not only are there still warrants out for his arrest, Addison is wanted by almost every cop force in the UK. He's either been very active or it's one case of mistaken identity after another.

For grassing on everyone he knew and for setting me up, Ackerman was going to walk away from a six spell and they called that justice. But, even at the time of sentencing, my lawyer was confident I'd get a reduction on appeal. That would have to wait till later. I was about to enter the English prison system for the first time in my life. It was a different system with different prisoners and different politics. How the hell would I get on? If only I had known.

4

FAMILY

1997

'He needs protection, Paul.' It was Arthur Suttie, my friend and co-accused in the gunrunning trial, talking to me privately in Belmarsh Secure Unit. Arthur is a good man who had been around for years, with an old-fashioned ethical approach to life.

'I know, Arthur. Especially with his name,' I replied with understatement.

'He's getting on a bit though he won't admit it.'

'Believe me, Arthur, you don't need to spell that out to me.' I was remembering my old man, Willie, a small guy with the heart of a lion. When I was inside awaiting trial for Fatboy Thompson's murder, my old man tackled his father, Arthur Thompson, Glasgow's Godfather, and did so single-handedly. As if that wasn't enough, my dad was no spring chicken and needed two walking sticks to get about. But Willie Ferris thought that Thompson had set me up and I shouldn't be the one inside for it. So a principle was a principle, Godfather or no.

The Thompsons should have known better than to mess with Willie Ferris. When he was just a teenager, he decided to join the Merchant Navy, see the world, make some dough and avoid the inevitable slip into crime back in Glasgow. Great idea but it turned out to be a bit more adventurous than that. One time, off the Gulf of Mexico, he was on one of those enormous ships that carry huge loads all around the world. Pre-computers, there were hundreds of sailors on board

11

and that meant trouble. One guy – tall, muscled and a bully who'd been on the ships for years – smacked my father's equally young and small pal in the mug with a big spanner. The old man went straight into the arsehole though well out of his weight division. He had seen an injustice and he wanted to redress it – that was just the type of thing he'd do. The scrap was broken up and the two men warned to give it a miss. My old man assured them there would be no more trouble. And, just as he said, there wouldn't be.

Next morning, there was no sign of Jack The Bullying Tar – his bunk hadn't even been slept in. The captain stilled the engines and ordered a thorough search of the ship but Jack Tar was not to be found. Conclusion? He had gone overboard, in spite of calm seas, and would be dead for sure. The old man was hauled in and grilled. He denied tipping the bastard over the rail, of course, and there was no evidence, no witnesses and no body – so no crime and no charge.

A year later on another big ship out in the Far East, a similar set of circumstances occurred and the heavy-handed guy was again lost at sea at night. Again Willie Ferris was dragged in front of the captain and again there were no witnesses, no body, no crime, no charge and word soon got around the merchant ships that you didn't mess with wee Willie Ferris.

However, by 1992, my dad was old and needed sticks just to walk and here he was single-handedly taking on the Thompson Family, the biggest crime crew in Glasgow. My father came off second best physically. He was beaten up by the younger Thompson boy, Billy, and his gang of lowlife mates and slashed by Arthur Senior, The Godfather. Second best physically but the high moral ground belonged to Willie Ferris.

My father died not long after that tussle with the Thompsons. It's impossible to know but I often wonder if his troubles with them hastened his death. I'd been in jail at the time and couldn't help or protect him. Did I feel responsible? No. My dad always made his own decisions right till his dying breath. Did I feel guilty? Aye. I should have been there for him. Had I learned anything? You bet. No one was going to take advantage of any older person as long as I was around.

'So, you'll keep an eye on him?' asked Arthur in Belmarsh in 1997.

'Of course and I'll let it be known but quietly. Don't want Charlie thinking he's not capable of taking care of himself.'

The old man we were discussing was Charlie Kray, older brother of the twins, Reg and Ron, serving twelve years for drug running. The name Kray has become synonymous with organised crime and violence. It might seem strange that we were talking about protecting one of the brothers but Charlie was different from Reg and Ron. He was quiet, almost gentle, and certainly a gentleman. He was also seventy years old and suffering from a heart condition. So who would bother aggressing an old man in bad health? Scalp hunters, young guys with no morals who might want to earn the reputation as the one who killed a Kray. These guys are a danger to any well-known street player and, because the Kray name carried more weight than others, Charlie was more at risk. Mind you, the conversation Arthur and I had was repeated in other groups throughout the jail so, if anyone did come hunting Charlie Kray, they would be in for one big shock.

Charlie Kray's prison time was passed peacefully but, unfortunately, his heart condition deteriorated and he died in 2000. Before that happened, the screws had him transferred to the Isle of Wight. There was no need for that. Belmarsh was a good safe place for Charlie. It was just another example of the system having long, bitter memories.

Thankfully, on the outside, other friends hadn't forgotten either. Paul Massey and the Salford Team were putting word about the system that I was OK. They were also doing more than Glasgow players I'd known all my life to make sure that my partner Sandra Arnott and my young son Dean were looked after. Joey Pyle, London's Don of Dons and a man who carries respect everywhere, was also putting out a good word.

Then there was the family we'll call the A Team because, like so many of my people, they don't like media publicity. Anyone who was anybody knew of the A Team and listened when they spoke. If Joey was the man who spanned generations, they were the new kids on the block and both were saying I was all right. But it could have been so different with the As. It could have turned nasty between us.

5

THE A TEAM

1992–93

It was late 1992 and, earlier that year, I'd walked out of court with a not guilty on the murder of Fatboy. I was down in the Big Smoke chilling out and, one night, when I was in one of the A Team's clubs, I was approached by one of the leading brothers. This guy offered me help to set up in London. What he wanted me to do was act as 'The Accountant' and collect substantial sums of money owed to the A Team. It was a generous offer and well received by me but it would have meant being based there permanently and I wasn't keen as I hadn't decided that London was where I wanted to settle. At that time, I was swanning around between London, Manchester and Glasgow and that suited me just fine.

I explained this and declined the offer with respect but, good men that they were, they created a new post working as The Accountant but based in Glasgow. In street terms, this was a big compliment and it had come from some of the leading players in the country who usually got what they wanted on first time of asking. The idea was that money would be collected from various people throughout the UK, taken back to Glasgow, counted, checked and packaged and then driven south, hidden in the panel of a motor, and handed over to a third party. Perfect.

In a sense it was exactly what I did when working for Arthur Thompson way back when I was a teenager except for one thing – scale. I'd pick up ten grand here, twenty grand there for Thompson but, with the A Team, it was hundreds of grand a time.

One of the younger As was put in charge of this operation but he was attached to a guy we'll call 'Spaghetti' to act as the middleman. Spaghetti was older, more experienced and the young A was going to learn from him. At one time, Spaghetti was investigated by the cops for having killed this guy in a wheelchair but it came to nothing. Apart from that, he was just another player but I reckoned he had to be good and reliable or the Λ Team wouldn't have touched him.

We settled in to the job and, for a while, everything went smoothly. As with everything else, you get better at the job as you learn and I soon sussed that Saabs, with the panels adapted, could hold the most dosh. While the scale of money was impressive, it was a right bastard to handle. The dead part of the process was counting the notes. The blokes would pay it in all sorts of notes, often the smallest denominations, and it could take bloody days to count and package. Bugger that! There was only one thing for it – delegation. I brought in a couple of young pals who were more dextrous than me – quick at the counting, that is, but not quick enough.

One time, there was over £350,000 to handle and it came in all sorts of scabby notes so I left my two mates with the money and went off to do other business. I came back late that night and it had taken them almost twelve hours to count and package £50,000. It would take days to count the whole haul but the delivery was expected to set off the next morning – sod it. We made the count and the money was spot on the button but, instead of packaging it up neatly in our usual way, we just bundled the notes together, wrapped them in plastic and loaded them into the motor – not the tidiest delivery I'd ever made.

Next day, as per usual, the money was delivered to Spaghetti and we thought no more about it until I got a phone call from the A Team a few days later. The money was short by about £50K. Now there was going to be trouble. So, in double quick time, I went off to see the young A brother in charge of the operation. I'd learned long ago that talk is the best way to resolve anything. Believe me, if the As thought someone had ripped them off, hell would pay the thief a visit.

There was no way I had any doubts about any of my people so I chatted about the details of the handover with the young A. It seemed that everything was as normal except he had been away for a few days and had only checked the money when he returned. My people, his people, delivery on time, money never left alone . . . this was looking bad.

'How did the money look?' I asked, having run out of any other questions.

'The usual,' he replied, 'neat bundles, face up.'

'But that's not how we packaged them,' I replied.

'The thieving bastard,' the young A spat.

A couple of weeks later, we had to make another delivery. Given the previous difficulty, I belled the young A and asked if it was to be the usual procedure.

'No chance,' he said, 'just deliver it to me direct.' So that's what I did. The A man might have been young but I was in no doubt who was in charge. A couple of days later, I had Spaghetti on the phone creating a rumpus because he had been bypassed – not my problem. It seems that, when the young A was away, Spaghetti had decided to invest in a wee venture. That would have been no problem if it had gone right but it went well wrong. Now he owed the A Team £50,000 and they wanted paid pronto.

One night, Spaghetti turned up at one of their clubs not looking very well at all and in his mitt he clutched a big holdall. In a private office out the back, he opened his bag and unloaded gold watches, necklaces, pendants, rings and as much bling as you could imagine. Skint and in dire fear for his life, he was cashing in all his and his family's valuables in payment. It was pathetic. The man should never have lowered himself to that but it just shows how much the experienced player feared the A Team.

There was something about that scene that I hated – the breach of trust, the fear of reprisal, the grovelling. It wasn't for me and, shortly afterwards, I ended my arrangement with the As. There was no fall-out, no ill feeling, just a parting of the ways. Looking back, I can see that it helped me realise that that way of life was not for me any more. I didn't have the stomach for the underlying brutality it entailed – not for business and business between friends.

Other top teams might have taken my decision personally but not the As. They remained good friends and saw to it that they did their bit to ensure the English players knew I was OK by them. And, a few years later, when I was held in Belmarsh for the gunrunning charges, the As' support was to do me no harm.

6

NEW FRIENDS

1997

You meet some interesting characters in jail – very interesting indeed.

Charlie Kray had been safe in Belmarsh Prison. Weren't we all? The place was a jail within a jail. Newly built to house the highest risk prisoners such as the IRA, visitors were screened as much as inmates. When friends and families turned up at the main gates, they had to identify themselves not with the usual passport but sanctioned photographs and palm scanners. After that, they were bussed from the gates to the secure unit. Much as I detested being in jail, I could almost understand the security measures. The place was jumping with very dangerous folk. I was Category A but some of my peers were Category AA or even Category AAA and, compared to them, I felt like an upstanding citizen.

One of the big faces in Belmarsh was a bloke called Tommy 'The Boxer' Mullen who must have had one of the least clever nicknames of all since he was a champion boxer, right. Mullen had turned to organised crime and trafficking drugs big time with bases in Ireland, Manchester, Liverpool and London and is reckoned to be the man who sanctioned the hit on the journalist Veronica Guerin. He was one very powerful man in more ways than one.

I used to go to the gym for light workouts. You can get unfit and lazy in jail just at a time you need to keep fit and alert. Taking a breather, I'd watch Mullen train. He'd be gloved-up, thumping this big canvas punchbag with a huge guy holding it from the back. Every punch smashed a big indentation in the bag and lifted the other bloke off his feet. Mullen would go hard at this for maybe half an hour and made it look so easy.

One time, when he'd finished and left the punch bag and the gym, wiping his only slightly moist brow, I decided to have a go. I had decided that fist fighting wasn't for me a long time ago – man, it makes your knuckles raw and your eyes water. So I didn't punch the bag, I kicked it – I gave it a whopper. The bag didn't budge an inch and I hit the deck. I thought I'd broken my fucking leg. My pride shattered and my foot aching, I limped from the gym thanking God I'd never had to take Tommy Mullen on in a square-go.

Belmarsh was full of characters like Edgar Pierce, the Mardi Gras Bomber, and Charles Bronson, the man reckoned to be the most violent prisoner in England. Jailed in 1975 for an armed robbery, Bronson could have expected to be free by about 1980. Instead, he couldn't accept the system and tackled it every time. One-man riots and assaulting the screws all gave him added time. Then he started hostage taking with extras. In 1994, he took a deputy governor of Hull Prison hostage, tied him up and threatened to kill him unless his demands were met. Another time he took three inmates hostage and demanded an Uzi sub-machine gun and, for reasons known only to him, an axe.

Also in Belmarsh was a gentle bloke, an actor by training, called Adnan Hoshnan, jailed for hijacking a Sudanese Airbus a couple of years before. Adnan and his extended family were en route for home where they knew they were going to receive a very hostile reception – jail at least, torture certainly and possibly death. On the spur of the moment, Adnan took over the plane pretending a sauce bottle was a gun. Then he cleared the first-class section and moved his own family in. Well, why not? First class was separated from the rest of the plane by a thick, velvet curtain and this was duly closed to give the family some privacy.

'With the passengers, I was the nasty hijacker but, behind that curtain, I was just another family member, Paul, and terrified of what I'd done,' he explained. 'I couldn't believe what I'd just pulled.'

'I know what you mean,' I added comfortingly. And I did. The buzz you get out of pulling off some audacious job is half satisfaction, half wonder at your own nerve.

Adnan instructed the pilot to head for England where he thought they would be fairly treated. As soon as Adnan and his family hit English soil they were nabbed by the SAS but he was delighted since jail time in the UK was far preferable to what was waiting for him back home. Then he met Charles Bronson and the hijacker became a hostage. Thank God Bronson let Adnan go when his demands were met – ten Big Macs, the edible kind not the shooters – with extra cheese.

In Belmarsh, I met an old friend, Dessie Cunningham. One of Dessie's claims to fame was that he took on Charles Bronson one time – probably the only prisoner ever to have a go. Bronson ended up knifed, hospitalised and almost breathed his last. Dessie was no slouch in other words.

I was even closer to Dessie's brother, Noel, who was with me and a pal, Jaimba McLean, one time in London when a pub got smashed up. The trouble was we discovered that the pub belonged to the Arif Family, one of the big London firms. That was one night out that could have turned really nasty and long term. Noel helped us smooth the troubled waters, good man that he is.

Dessie had advised me to get a lawyer called Paul Robinson from London to fight the gunrunning charges. If someone wanted advice on getting a top Scottish lawyer, I'm not a bad guy to ask for it. When Dessie recommended Paul Robinson I knew his opinion would be sound and it was.

For a hard man, Dessie also had a big soft spot – something that was not unusual in my experience. When he was coming close to the end of his sentence and his girlfriend ended their relationship, he killed himself – it was the loss of a great guy and a good friend.

In Belmarsh, Dessie's brother, Noel, turned up. He was passing through heading to the new prison ship, HMP Weare at Portland, Dorset. The ship had been converted to a jail because all the other prisons were bursting at the seams. It still made me think of convict ships and the old days of sending bad boys and girls off to Australia. My time with Noel was all too brief before he moved on to his watery jail. He would serve his time and be released, only to be nabbed on another robbery – £1.25 million from a Securicor van in Brixton – along with his mate Clifford Hobbs. But the bold Noel had plans other than jail.

In June 2003, he and Hobbs were being driven from prison to London's Inner Court. When the prison wagon pulled up outside the courthouse, two armed men – one dressed as a postman with a mailbag slung over his shoulder – rushed the van blasting away with guns. Along with Hobbs, Noel vamoosed and has never been seen since. Well, at least not by anyone wearing a blue serge uniform. There was me worried about the politics in the English prison system. Nothing to worry about. Guys like Dessie and Noel Cunningham carry great respect in that system. If they say you're OK, you are OK. Simple as that.

My friend and co-accused Arthur Suttie is also well respected. In Belmarsh he shared a cell with an Italian bloke called Angelo Casalli. Angelo was a right character. A smooth talker and card sharp, he'd travelled the world earning a living by his wits. He was good company and could keep you going with stories about his adventures all night, every night.

When I met him, he was awaiting trial on cocaine smuggling. Once that was behind him and he was released, he went and stayed with my sister Cath for a while. Then he popped home to Italy to visit his family. As soon as he arrived, he was nabbed by the cops and put under house arrest as a suspected member of the Mafia. That was a few years ago and, last I heard, he was still there in his house under arrest. For all the stories Angelo told us, he never once mentioned the Cosa Nostra but maybe there was even more to him than met the eye.

As I was about to find out, being stuck in the UK's most secure prison and keeping a clean sheet doesn't stop all sorts of strange things going down. Even in Belmarsh, I wasn't safe from the outside world – quite the reverse.

7

REPORTS OF MY DEATH . . .

'Ferris.'

'What the fuck!' My cell door had been opened. Strangely enough, this was on a Saturday afternoon when it was a total lock-down in Belmarsh but standing there in the doorway was a governor, the head of security, two screws and a big dog. I had to be in serious trouble – the alternative was even worse to contemplate. I was on my feet in a split second.

'Could you phone this number, please?' said the governor, handing me a slip of paper. Written on it was my sister Carol's number. My stomach flooded with acid and a dull ache pressed my chest. 'My mum's died,' I thought to myself with as much certainty as dread. This was the procedure for a close family bereavement for sure. The staff group moved off with me in the middle. With every step, my feet felt heavier and heavier. I wanted to get to that phone yet I didn't want to get to that phone. I needed to know but I didn't want to hear the words. The procession walked at my pace – dead slow – and what should have taken a few minutes seemed to take an age but, inevitably, I was standing there, the phone in my fist, dialling Carol's number.

'Oh, Paul,' Carol said down the line when she heard my voice.

'Carol,' I replied, 'are you OK?'

'Yeah, I'm OK but are you OK?'

'Aye. Aye, I'm OK but are *you* OK?' Certain as I was that my mum had died, I didn't want to ask Carol, didn't want to hear the words that she had passed away.

'Paul, are you OK?'

'I'm OK – are *you* OK?'

It was like some social workers' convention and it felt like this bizarre routine could go on forever.

'I really *am* OK, Carol.'

'Really?'

'Aye, *really*.'

'You sure?'

It suddenly dawned on me that this had nothing to do with my mum. Relief swept through me and I started to laugh, snigger nervously. I was aware that the phone call was being taped. They all were in Belmarsh. I didn't care if I sounded like some blithering idiot to the censor screws – my mother was alive and that was all that mattered.

'Look, what's up, Carol? Why are you phoning?'

It was the power of the press again. In that day's *Evening Times*, one of the local Glasgow papers, there had been an article about me being badly beaten up by Frankie Fraser's mob in the prison. I was meant to be in a hell of a state, in hospital and maybe not going to survive. My mother was very much alive but worried sick for her youngest boy.

The *Evening Times* had been running with quite a number of fabricated stories about me. I knew where they all came from. An ex-friend of my brother Billy, Donnie McMillan from Drumoyne, had a cousin who worked at the paper and he was feeding him tales and probably getting drinking money in return. Donnie was a wannabe of the lowest order. He'd dress in an ankle length leather coat, matching gloves and, for some reason, would carry an attaché case. He was an arsehole but a dangerous one when it came to upsetting my family.

Relief turned to anger. The governor had heard everything between Carol and me. He even asked me if I had been attacked – one of the most stupid questions I've ever heard. Belmarsh was absolutely dripping with cameras. The only thing you could do in private was have a shite and even then they watched you enter and exit the cubicle. Besides, I was standing there whole and well in front of him. If Frankie Fraser's team had done me in, I *would* have been hospitalised for sure. The medical I demanded was carried out the next day and it proved the obvious – that there had been no beating.

My co-accused on the gunrunning, Arthur Suttie, was an old friend of Frankie. At the first chance he got, he was on the bell to him and explained the situation. Frankie was fizzing and lived up to his reputation of Mad Frankie by first offering to phone the paper and then, when he realised how upset my old dear had been, proposing to go up there and sort out the hacks personally. That was taking it too far. The phone call did just fine.

Because of my lawyer, the medical, the call from Frankie and a letter from Belmarsh's governor, the *Evening Times* printed an apology and correction. Later, some scribbler claimed I had forced the apology because of pride because I couldn't let the world believe I'd been beaten up. But I did it for accuracy and, much more importantly, as independent proof to my mum that I was all right. She still half believed I was protecting her by lying but, if the paper said it didn't happen, Jenny Ferris would believe it didn't happen.

Long before, I'd learned that, just because you're in jail, it doesn't mean you can't fight back but sometimes you just get it in the neck, minding your own business and there's sod all you can do about it. My long term pal, Jaimba McLean, was lifted and questioned by MI5 at Glasgow Airport on his way to visit me. The authorities reckoned he had too many connections with Ireland and was too notorious by half to be safe. He had to be planning to break me out. Jaimba had been grilled for hours in some airless room. When they eventually gave in to his demands for a drink, they brought him an open can of warm Coke. Freed an hour later, Jaimba went mad – truly mad. He was hallucinating and saw monsters crawling out the walls to get him. Within a few weeks, he was locked up in the State Hospital Carstairs, a very unwell man. Jaimba is convinced that MI5 drugged him with that Coke. Far fetched? Maybe but it's the one and only time I've heard of anyone in custody getting a Coke – it's usually a cup of tea or coffee. And, of course, you can't see in the can, can you?

Jaimba McLean was a capable player who'd tackle any job and no doubt. Yet even he'd struggle to find a way to break me out of Belmarsh. Obviously the authorities thought differently and flung me into solitary for good measure but they wouldn't leave it at that.

Category-A prisoners get told nothing about the prison service's plans for them. Well, if you're a risk to the community and thought likely to escape, that would be foolish, I suppose. One morning, very early, I was wakened roughly by a screw shaking me. Ordered to dress and pick up my belongings in double-quick time, I was soon led from the block.

What the hell were they going to throw at me now?

8

DANGEROUS NEIGHBOURS
1997–98

Stuck in the back of an armoured van with no windows, I was clueless about our destination till I was marched into a reception area.

'Welcome to Full Sutton,' said the warden behind the desk with a broad smile. 'I trust your stay here will be a pleasant one.'

I was in Yorkshire, in another top-security jail – the one-time home of people like Dennis Nilsen, a serial killer of young gay men, the Moors Murderer Ian Brady and child-killer Robert Black. It felt like I was following these guys about. Of course, they were all in the nonces' and ponces' unit away from the main jail but it was that sort of place with that level of security. What the hell was going to happen here?

'Hello, Mick.' My tone was pleasant enough but my face was poker straight.

'Paul.' Mick or Mickey Healy answered in the same vein.

When I first spotted him, I couldn't believe it. I'd been dumped in a cell in Full Sutton directly opposite his. We couldn't have been placed closer but Mickey Healy and I had differences to sort out. I already knew he would be out to get me because of what he had been told about a recent robbery – the very reason he was in jail. And, what was more, the prison service knew that fine well. Each prison keeps a friends-and-foes file detailing people who are close to others and people, like Mick and me, who are likely to kill each other. Yet they still set us up as neighbours. An accident? I don't think so.

27

Mick Healy was a well-known Glasgow player. He was very capable and had made a big name for himself when locked up in Shotts Prison in the 1980s for an armed robbery. Shotts is a long-term jail and pretty secure. The worst it has suffered is a couple of riots – during the first of which, I acted as the prisoners' negotiator – but few breakouts. Then Mick Healy drove out through the front gates in a butcher's van. That incident and his habit of carrying a shooter were enough for the authorities to dub him 'Most Wanted in the UK'. However, all that was behind him by this time and had nothing to do with the grief between us.

I thought back to last time Mick and I had met.

'It's that flat there, Paul,' said my helper, pointing at a window.

We were in Glasgow, my territory, and I'd a little business to sort out.

'Fine – well, lead the way,' I responded, nodding to the entrance doorway to the building.

'Can I no' just give you the keys?'

'If that was on, you could have done that back at my place,' I barked. I'd only known this man for a short while but I was fast developing doubts about him. He was always big on the talk but, when it came to the action, he was reported missing too often.

'Right then,' he replied, looking cowed, scared.

'Just take me to the door and use your key to let me in, you stupid bugger,' I said as way of reassurance. It was just common sense. He visited that flat a lot, sometimes stayed over and that's why he had a key. His fingerprints were all over the place and legitimately. My paw prints, however, were going to show up nowhere near the place. He was meant to be experienced. He should have understood that.

'It's up here,' he said as if I couldn't work it out for myself. Loud strains of Bob Marley and the Wailers seeped through the front door. Good. My target wouldn't even hear me go in.

I nodded to the guy with the key and he opened the door gently, quietly. A brisk toss of my head told him to get the hell out of the place. Whatever was going down, I could do without a witness.

Especially that guy. Totally unreliable. He was the one who told me that a certain party was putting it about that I was untrustworthy, that I talked to the cops – the same party sitting in his flat listening to some reggae. Being thought of as a trader with the bizzies was the lowest of the low, in my opinion. Any rumours to that effect about me had to be quashed – whatever it took. I checked the gun's weight in my back waistband, walked into the flat, quietly clicked the door shut behind me and headed in the direction of the music.

'Evening, Mickey.'

'What the fuck?' He choked on his smoke and stiffened, ready to rise to his feet.

Too late – I'd pulled my pistol and pointed it at him. 'You and I need a wee chat.'

Mickey Healy had been chilling out – a drink by his side, a long fat joint in his hand and good music. Well, not my taste really. I scanned the room for guns and found none. That was sloppy.

'So, we'll have a bit of quiet, eh?' I turned and fired, blasting a bullet through his ghetto blaster. Suddenly the room was quiet and I had Mickey Healy's full attention.

'What's going down, Paul?' Most guys would have pissed their pants by now. Not Mickey Healy. He was made of stronger stuff though on edge, wary, maybe a little scared. Who wouldn't be staring up the barrel of a loaded pistol?

Standing over him, I kept the pistol trained on his nut. 'I've heard you've been spreading filthy lies about me,' I finally said.

'No.' A hesitation then, 'NO!' Shaking his head, almost swinging it from one shoulder to the other, he screamed, 'No' me!'

'Something about me being worth the watching?' It was the exact phrase used when I was told about Mick and it was my guess that it was the very phrase he'd used. His face went a deep red.

'No, Paul, no' me.' It was half plea, half honest Joe act.

'Worth the watching because I'm supposed to talk to the cops.' I left the words hanging in the air for a while. 'That's what you've been saying.'

Another bout of furious head shaking.

'It's McGraw and Thompson and their filthy crews who play *that* game,' I said as I looked him straight in the eye, watching for signs. I was sure I caught a flicker of electricity when those names were mentioned. My ex-boss Thompson was the so-called Godfather of Glasgow and McGraw was better known as The Licensee for trading information in return for never being prosecuted for his own crimes. Both of them would like to ruin my reputation. For some reason, they felt threatened by me. Healy might well have spoken to both.

'I know,' he muttered.

'And do you think I play that dirty game?'

'Nuh,' another mutter, quiet, tense. 'Thompson showed me a letter, Paul.' Now he was interesting me. 'One from the Crown Office saying you were an informant.' I knew the letter he was referring to. It was one that we had proven to be a forgery by getting the alleged author himself, a Mr A Vannett, to say so in court, under oath.

'And is that what you think?' I demanded.

'No, no' me,' Mickey replied. 'I took it to a pal of mine. Well-educated bloke – uni degrees and stuff. He pointed out all these spelling mistakes. Said it was a fake.'

'And what did you do with the letter?'

'Nothing. Told old Thompson I wanted fuck all to do with it nor should he.' Mick Healy was beginning to grow on me.

'So have Thompson or McGraw been bending your ear? Or maybe Blink?' Blink McDonald was an old childhood friend of mine and a player like me. Up to now, Blink had been OK by me but I'd heard on the grapevine that he was becoming a bit lippy, a bit gossipy.

'No, no,' Mick shook his head emphatically but then I wouldn't expect an honourable man to finger anyone who'd been bad-mouthing me.

'But do you think I play the grassing games? *Do* you?'

'No, I don't,' he said, this time louder and clearer.

'Would I take all this bother in paying you a visit if I did?' I demanded. He looked blank. 'If it was The Licensed One, he wouldn't need to come in here and shoot you.' His dry throat gulped and his fingers gripped the arms of the chair, his knuckles showing white. 'For starters he wouldn't give a fuck about being called a grass. But, if he did, he'd just have a word with his cop pals and you'd be off to jail again – set up with a load of smack or maybe worse.'

He nodded his head.

'Do you get my point?' I asked, still pointing the gun at him.

'Aye! Aye, I do.'

The meeting was short but thorough. I decided – but only then – not to shoot Mick Healy. I knew there was the risk of him tooling up and coming after me – no mean threat – but I'd heard good things about Mick and was willing to take that risk. Little did I know it would explode in my face in an English jail.

'Just one thing, Paul,' Mick called out as I backed slowly out of the room. 'Who pointed the finger at me?'

'You know better than to ask that, Mick.' He shrugged acknowledging that he did know better but was just chancing his arm. Besides, how could I tell him it was his very own pal, the man with the key, William Lobban.

Lobban, also known as Tootsie for his habit of dressing up in women's clothing, was a young guy related to one of Arthur Thompson's long-term loyal supporters who went by the name of Manson. In the late 1980s to the early 1990s, Lobban had been on the run from jail and my two mates, Bobby Glover and Joe Hanlon, and I were asked to shelter him so we did. We put him up in a safe flat for a while and then, for about nine months, he actually lived with Bobby, his wife, Eileen, and their son.

While I was in prison in 1992 awaiting trial for the murder of Fatboy Thompson, Lobban had made a phone call to Bobby's house during which he talked to Eileen Glover first. After the call, Bobby announced he had to go to a meeting and called Joe Hanlon and asked him to drive him. Bobby told Eileen he wouldn't be long but he never came home alive. He and Joe were shot dead that night and dumped in Joe's car outside Bobby's pub, The Cottage Bar.

As you might imagine, I hated William Lobban, now dubbed 'Judas', with a passion. Needless to say, he left Glasgow sharpish as I wasn't the only one who wanted words with him.

Mick Healy, oblivious to that at the time, was pally with Lobban. He agreed to take part in an armed bank robbery in Torquay with that same childhood pal of mine I had suspected of spreading lies about me, Ian 'Blink' McDonald. The robbery went belly up and the gang were soon captured. At their trial, out of the blue, a certain Mr X offered to give evidence to the court, on behalf of the accused, as long as his ID was kept secret. Mr X spun a web of stories about me being the mastermind of the robbery and setting them up to be caught. The poor south-coast judge must have wondered what the hell he had got into as tales of organised crime in Glasgow were woven in his court – tales and fabrications.

Mr X admitted that he had an extensive criminal record himself and had been involved in the Glasgow scene as well as elsewhere. But now he had found God apparently – how that excuse makes me boak and I'm sure it must upset all the real Christians around. Of course, I had sod all to do with the job and Mr X was none other than William Lobban.

After Bobby and Joe had been killed, Lobban, who'd been on the run from a jail sentence for robbery, was arrested. In jail in Perth, his bad conscience got the better of him and he thought everyone was trying to kill him. Poison was put in his food by someone angry about Bobby and Joe's murders but, unfortunately, Lobban had already decided not to eat jail grub. When the screws didn't seem to be taking his plight quite as seriously as he did, he took a hostage using a sharpened silver pen. That did the trick and he was transferred to prison in England for his own safety.

After the Torquay trial, Lobban and Healy ended up in the jail together, co-accused on other charges dating back to the 1980s. Back then, if I had bumped into William Lobban, I'd soon have been digging a shallow grave. Well, how would you feel about the guy who set up your best friends to die?

Mick Healy wasn't to know any of that though and now I expected the worst from a very dangerous man.

9

LONG-TERM MEMORIES

1997–98

'We need to talk, Paul,' Mickey Healy said at that first meeting in Full Sutton Prison.

'All right, Mick.' Talking was the only way I could see of avoiding violence. I hoped Mick Healy wasn't using the word 'talk' as a code for bloodshed. 'We have some air to clear, eh?'

'Aye,' he looked me straight in the eye – no fear, no anger, just man to man. The early omens were good. 'A short while ago, I'd have gladly taken you out.'

'I can well imagine but you need to hear the full story.'

'I know,' he replied, nodding, 'but I've already heard enough to change my mind.'

'Well that pleases me, Mick, because I don't think you and I have any cause to fall out.'

'I believe you. Now, I believe you.'

'How did that happen?'

'When I was holed up with Lobban, waiting for that last trial, he talked.' It was always one of Lobban's problems – talking too much. 'He set Bobby Glover up, you know?'

'Aye, I know.' Even being reminded of that treachery years later, I could feel my blood rise and my soul ache at what had happened to my pals.

'He told me all about it, Paul – making the phone call, being paid by Manson, his uncle – the one that was close to Thompson – even

33

how much he got paid.'

'Bastard.'

'So he is. Bobby and Joe didn't deserve that – especially not from someone they'd taken care of.'

'He's a fucking lowlife, Mick.'

He nodded vigorously and deep thought was etched across his face. 'I don't know if I should tell you this . . .'

'What?'

'I can see you're still hurting, Paul. Fuck sake, who can blame you?'

'Nothing can hurt me any more than I already do about Bobby and Joe. All I need is the whole truth.'

Mick Healy thought about that nodding, imagining being in my shoes with good friends lying in their graves. 'He did it for a few grand – nothing much.'

'Doesn't surprise me,' I said, adding sadly, 'he'd do anything for money and he comes cheap.'

'Filthy bastard moans that it's all spent. All he's got left is a fucking watch.'

'Aye, well he'd better take care of it, eh?' Now my blood was up – angry at the memories. 'His time might be running out.'

Mick Healy and I became good friends. Just how good I was soon to learn.

When I was charged with gunrunning, rumours started circulating the jail system that I'd planned to supply players in Scotland. One other very nasty rumour also spread – that I was planning to supply Loyalist groups with the guns – and there I was in Full Sutton which, at that time, was packed with top IRA men. That rumour was a death sentence and no doubt but I was oblivious to it all.

While I was still in Belmarsh, Mickey Healy picked up the vibes from the IRA. At that time, he was no friend of mine – that would come later – but, honourable man that he is, he went to the brothers and told them the truth that I wasn't associated with the Loyalists or the Republicans.

Earlier, in another jail, Mickey had become good friends with

Dingus Magee and his namesake Patrick, the guy who'd tried to top Margaret Thatcher and her cronies by blasting that Brighton hotel. A personal recommendation from Dingus was all that the IRA needed. They listened to Mickey – thank God.

After Mickey and I cleared the air over William Lobban's tales about the bank job in Torquay, he told me all about the rumours and the IRA threat which was now called off due to his intervention. Even though he assured me that the hit was lifted, I could feel a cold sweat on my brow. These guys didn't mess about.

The rumour must have been circulated by an enemy of mine – either a street player or one of the blue serge mob. Having been brought up in a city that rages with sectarianism just below the surface, I had never taken sides and would never have traded guns to one or the other. The rumour was so far removed from the reality, yet so potentially lethal, it had to have been set off deliberately.

A while after my move to Full Sutton, a high-ranking member of the IRA approached me. 'You might've heard a whisper,' he started off.

'Yeah but I'm more worried about rumours you might've been hearing,' I replied.

He smiled. 'Well, sure you shouldn't believe everything you hear – especially not in these dungeons.'

My turn to smile. 'Nor should you – or your friends.'

'Aye. Well, we don't. We know you aren't one of them thanks to Mickey and a few other contacts on the outside.'

'That's good.'

'Aye, ye're too much of a fucking capitalist to be political at all.'

I laughed out loud. It was the first time my wish to be wealthy had saved my life – or so it seemed. 'Is that a good thing or bad?' I asked, smiling at the guy and thinking he was taking the piss a bit.

He wasn't. 'Well, that depends,' he said with a serious, straight face. 'Depends on what side you're on.'

So everyone had to take a side, capitalist or not.

'Mind, your brother Billy has some explaining to do about that carry-on in Wakefield nick back in 1975.'

Billy was a lifer in the English prison system, serving time for a murder, a crime of passion, he committed when some guy started bad-mouthing his young wife. Later on, I'd find out the whole story of what Billy had been up to back then and why it had angered the IRA so much. But, at this point in time, I couldn't believe it. Whatever it was had happened twenty-three years earlier and still the IRA remembered. 'We never forget,' the IRA man added, as if reading my mind.

With that matter safely dealt with, I was now concerned with my life and getting as much of it back as I could. In other words, I was appealing against my sentence.

It was time for the Old Bailey again and an unexpected delay.

10

SON OF THE FATHER

At the Old Bailey, my appeal was due to be heard after a pleading hearing that featured Russell Grant McVicar, son of John McVicar, an infamous armed robber in the 1960s who escaped from the most secure jails in England and went on the run with the tag 'Most Wanted' plastered under his name. With his successful book, *McVicar*, turned into a best-selling film of the same name, starring Roger Daltrey of The Who, John turned to writing and broadcasting for a living.

At one point in the 1990s, he was the anchorman for a late-night chat show on TV and I was invited on as a guest. As we were chatting before the show, he seemed to be acting the hard man but a very soft, politely spoken hard man at that. I got the impression he was acting the game because of my reputation. Cue for a laugh. McVicar complained of being exhausted because he'd been up half the night before partying and being wild.

'I'm in the same state myself, John,' I said. 'Great at the time but it's a sod when you have to pay the price.'

He laughed and added, 'And we swear we'll never do it again but then we go right out and do it again.' He rubbed his face. He really was knackered.

'Want something to buck you up a wee bit?' I asked in a hushed conspiratorial tone.

'Excellent, Paul. Just the trick.'

'I take these,' I said as I showed him a couple of small white pills and mouthed them.

'Is that . . . ?' He left the sentence unfinished but he meant speed.

'Yeah but they're a bit weak. This is my tenth or something,' I told him, swallowing another one.

'Ten?'

'Aye but I'm hammering them all the time. You maybe should stick to a couple.' He raised his eyes as if to tell me I'd just insulted him. 'Well, try these,' I suggested and I handed McVicar four small white pills.

'Cheers!' He winked, stuck them into his gob and washed them down with a drink. Twenty minutes later, he took another four off me.

As we were set for the cameras to roll, I asked him if he was feeling better.

'Wonderful,' he smiled, giving me the thumbs up.

Five minutes into the interview, his fingers began to fidget, rustling the papers he was holding. His speech was getting faster and faster, his throat was becoming drier and drier and he swigged continuously from his glass of water. John McVicar had overdosed not on speed but on over-the-counter Pro Plus, a remedy designed to aid recovery from hangovers. The stuff was stacked full of caffeine and could give even an athlete the jitters.

Fair play to him, McVicar handled the interview very well and I'm sure nobody else noticed. Off he went at the end of the show, convinced he'd been a naughty boy and done amphetamines live on air. Aye, right.

John McVicar's boy was something else though. Russell Grant McVicar was jealous of his old man's notoriety – well, that's my view having met the man. In 1993, Russell escaped from jail and started his career as an armed robber, following in his father's footsteps. He hit eight banks and foreign exchanges in the most straightforward way. Big time he wasn't since all the jobs together only netted him £120,000. His old boy was scooping more than that back in the 1960s. That's when Russell teamed up with cat burglar

Peter Scott. Scott knew all about fine art and what was worth what. Dressed in the leathers and motorcycle crash helmet, he and Russell hit the Lefevre Gallery in London. Hefting sawn-off shotguns, they went straight in and, after firing one blast in the air, the targeted Picasso, worth £650,000, was whipped off the wall and they were out of there. Subtle? Not.

Russell Grant McVicar had been nabbed and, on the day of my appeal, he was going to plead guilty or not guilty before we could get on with my business. Pleading is usually a five-minute job but McVicar's was going on and on. Inside the courtroom, the clerk of the court read out the first charge which was long and wordy. First charges always are – that's how legal patter is.

'How do you plead?' the official asked.

'Guilty,' replied Russell. There was a silent delay as the clerk made a formal written note of the accused person's plea. The writing done, he looked up and, as he drew breath to read out charge two, Russell declared, 'Not.'

There was a furious look from the clerk and the judge was clearly unhappy. After the record had been changed, the clerk read out charge two and asked Russell how he pled.

He again declared, 'Guilty.' This time the clerk waited a while before recording Russell's plea. That done, he looked up and Russell announced, 'Not.'

Now he really had the court's attention – just as he wanted.

Downstairs, under the court, oblivious to Russell's game, I was beginning to sweat a bit. He should have been in and out of that court in a jiffy. What was it? A judge in bad mood? Not a good omen for me, I reckoned.

Back in the courtroom, as each charge was read out, the clerk delayed longer and longer before recording McVicar's response. Each time, Russell added, 'Not' to his plea. Finally, it got to the last charge and, with Russell having said, 'Guilty', the clerk put down his pen, folded his arms and waited. As the clerk stared at Russell, five minutes passed. Then ten minutes, then fifteen minutes – one hell of a long silence in a court of law. At last, the clerk picked up his quill and started writing but, as soon as he had scribbled a few words, Russell declared, 'Not.'

The man had great face and bottle with it but the bastard had taken two hours to declare a few not guilty pleas. Now that I know how he did it, I forgive him but he had me going for a while.

Later at trial, Russell was found guilty. Judge Geoffrey Grigson gave him a whacking fifteen years and said, 'I sentence you for what you have done not for who you are.' Aye, I don't think so. He was sentenced that hard for taking the piss out of the Old Bailey.

When I was finally allowed to have my appeal heard, my sentence was reduced from ten to seven years. Now that was more like it. Initially, I had calculated eight so it was like getting a bonus of one year of my life back – a good result in anyone's book.

Back in Full Sutton I took stock. The IRA had accepted that false rumours had been spread about me and the Loyalists so the heat was off. Lobban's fantasising in order to raise hell for me following the botched bank job in Torquay had backfired. The prison's plot to sit back and watch Mick and me chib each other had failed. When the authorities eventually sussed all that out, they'd move one of us on in the early hours of the morning, without warning.

It was going to be me. What the hell were they planning next?

11

GRILL PAN SHOWDOWN
1998–99

'Muthafucka muthafucka so she is be it muthafucka whitey.' Well, that's what it sounded like to me. Standing in the kitchen that first morning at Frankland Prison, Durham, I thought I'd scored big time when the ingredients for a first-class full Scottish breakfast were thrust into my paws. Black pudding, sliced sausage, potato scone – I hadn't tasted grub that good since I'd left Scotland two years before. The sausage was sizzling under the grill, the oil in the frying pan popped and spat and the kettle was already boiled. Then the room filled up with big black guys.

'Muthafucka muthafucka so she is be it muthafucka whitey.'

I couldn't understand a single word the brethren were saying. All I knew was that they were angry, very angry – with me.

I know I'm short for a street player but these fuckers were huge, forcing me to crane back my neck as I smiled and offered them some of my bacon or sausage. Fuck me but the growls turned to shouts and what were clearly threats in any language. Okey-dokey, I looked round the room for any kitchen knife that might have been left lying out, all the time knowing fine well they'd all be locked away. Just as I was deciding which one to whack first with the frying pan, one of their number walked forward holding his hands up. The others got the message and shut up.

'How d'ye do, brother?' he asked with a wee smile on his face.

'Aye, fine thanks,' I replied, keeping one hand on the handle of the hefty frying pan.

'My name is Everton Salmon,' he said with a smile.

I smiled back, wondering what kind of a saddo of a mother names her child after a football club and a fish. Later, I'd find out that his street label of ZB, pronounced Zeebee, was just as weird. 'Paul,' I replied, 'Paul Ferris.'

'Ah, the Scotchman.'

Did every bastard know that I was moving here before I did? 'Aye, the Scotsman. And what's the problem with your pals?'

As he spoke to me, Everton smiled with his eyes. Not his face, not his body just his eyes as, behind him, his oblivious mates glowered down at me, desperate for one false move, one signal so that they could have an excuse to happily go in for the kill.

Everton explained that the brothers were all Muslims who didn't touch pork. All the guys were from Jamaica and considered themselves to be jailed in a foreign land. They had fought for a long time to have the right to a pork-free kitchen.

Fair enough – I understood only too well about fighting for your rights in prison – but I wasn't going to leave it at that. 'I'm a political prisoner too,' I said. Everton needed more convincing. 'The Scots and English have been feuding for years. Here I am, miles from home, slung into an English dungeon.' I was getting through. 'It's a William-Wallace type of thing.'

Everton nodded and turned to speak with his mates. Still I couldn't work out much of what was being said except now and then the words 'Wallace' and 'Braveheart' were mentioned. Love it or hate it, that movie and Mel Gibson looked like saving me from a right doing.

Finally, Everton turned round. The brothers had agreed to allow me to use the kitchen, provided I accepted certain conditions regarding the cooking of pork, washing up and so on. Agreeing and thanking them very much, I wondered if they'd won any other special rights for us 'political' prisoners.

Back on the wing with my breakfast, I met Grant Turnbull, the bloke who had given me the grub. Grant was from Edinburgh and he went by the nickname of Basil after he had 'borrowed' the name to con his way out of court one time. I thanked him for the very fine nosh. 'But, for Christ sake,' I added, 'it's the first time I've ever had to negotiate the use of a cooker.'

'What do you, mean?' he asked so I explained. 'Oh, shit, Paul, I should have warned you not to use *that* kitchen – that's the Yardies' kitchen. They're fierce as fuck and have nothing at all to do with the rest of us.'

'Really?' I asked as I stuck another mouthful of bacon into my gob. 'Seemed great guys to me.'

It was the first time I'd knowingly met any Yardies though I knew of their reputation well enough. Who doesn't? Given their media image, you'd expect them to have ripped me apart for invading their space – not fret over a bit of grilled bacon.

In due course, I became friendly with them all, especially Everton Salmon who was doing a life stretch for a shooting. Most of them were in for violence, including murder, and drug trafficking. I often went back to their kitchen but I always obeyed their rules. They also taught me a great deal about the Jamaican style of cooking. Who said prison was a complete waste of time?

Breakfast down and thoroughly appreciated, I was now on the lookout for a certain prisoner. I thought back to a conversation in the textile shop at Full Sutton jail with Mick Healy – the same Mick Healy the jail had set me up with as a neighbour fully expecting warfare between us. Not only were they to be disappointed on that point, Mick also warned me of certain troubles.

I'd been in the textile shop early in my time at Full Sutton when a short, heavy young guy broke away from a work party to speak to me. 'I met a mate of yours in Strangeways,' he said in his thick cockney accent, adding, 'Paul Massey. Said to look you up if we ever crossed paths.'

'Oh, Paul – a good man,' I replied, meaning every word. Paul was the lynchpin of the Salford Team, one of the most respected and biggest gangs in the north-west of England. I'd spent a lot of time with Paul and his people, hanging out at Manchester's Hacienda club and anywhere else there was a party. The last time I'd been there, I was so sozzled I crashed out on a bed and a young nephew of mine, grounded for the night, nicked my shoes and socks so he could go clubbing.

'How's he doing?' I asked.

'You know Paul – he's doing great.'

I certainly did know Paul Massey and couldn't see a bit of jail time getting him down – even though he was serving fourteen years for a stabbing he was adamant he didn't do. If Paul Massey said he was innocent, that was good enough for me.

'I must get in touch with him,' I said.

'Yeah, he'd like that,' replied the cockney stranger. 'Vella,' he added, 'I'm Jason Vella. See you about.' And off he walked back to his work party.

The way the bloke had announced his name, he obviously expected me to recognise it. In truth, I was clueless but Mick Healy was about to put me right in that same textile workshop in Full Sutton jail.

'Do you know who that that guy is, Paul?' he asked, not unreasonably.

'He's a friend of a friend, Mickey,' I replied.

'Do you remember the Essex Boys case?' In 1995, Pat Tate, Tony Tucker and Craig Rolfe, ecstasy dealers and heavies serving the Essex clubs had been found in a remote country lane shot dead. Clearly a hit job, the three had been killed only weeks after young Leah Betts had died after taking E. The dead men had been so involved in the ecstasy market there that the cops surmised there might be a link. Later, I'd find out through police surveillance logs that they had tracked me as a suspect. But that was for later. Right now, I was giving all my attention to Mick Healy.

'Aye, the three boys who got shot up in the Range Rover?' I replied. 'Is he one of the shooters?'

'No, no. He's just an ecstasy dealer with a smack problem. But he likes to play the big gangster.'

'Another fucking wannabe, eh?'

'Nah – worse than that. That man's trouble. Friend to friend, Paul, give Vella a wide body swerve.'

'OK, Mickey, I'll keep that mind.'

Paul Massey would have no truck with some smackhead troublemaker. In Frankland, I quickly looked up two of Paul's mates, Ando and Tabbo, real names Lee Anderson and Lee Taberer, who were serving mega years each for armed robbery along with a Croatian guy called, Parvo Corkovic. It had taken the notorious VO8 Firearms Department, usually deployed on matters of national security, to crack that team.

We were just chatting, reminiscing about the good times in Salford and nearby Manchester. I mentioned being taken along to a Prince Naseem boxing match when, not once but twice, I thought a bomb had gone off in the stadium. They were proper ear-blasting explosions and I don't mind admitting that, for a second or two, I was crapping myself. It turned out the Salford boys had contacted Ando and Tabbo in jail and advised them to watch the gig on TV. The explosions had been set up just for their entertainment – wee messages of solidarity from the outside.

Ando and Tabbo said they had never heard of Jason Vella and were pretty sure that Paul Massey hadn't either. What the hell was Vella up to?

If Mickey Healy said that Jason Vella was trouble, he meant it and no doubt. Vella was now an inmate at Frankland Prison. Just how much trouble he was or wasn't I was soon to find out.

12

CRUISING FOR A BRUISING

You're never too old to get into trouble with your mammy and, believe me, I'm no exception. The very day I was arrested for the gunrunning, I knew I was in hot water with her. It was no laughing matter.

My mum, Jenny Ferris, is one of the strongest people I know. When I was just a nipper, my old man had been jailed – first for not paying tax on a small bus company he ran and then for a bank robbery. Say it quick and it sounds as if I come from some crime dynasty but it was more interesting and messier than that.

We were a well-off family by Blackhill standards. Some might say that wouldn't be difficult and with justification. The tenements at the bottom of the scheme reeked of poverty and the place was so wild repair men wouldn't come near for fear of being mugged, having their vans stolen or stripped of their wheels as they were parked by the kerb. The whole area became more and more rundown. It was a no-man's-land for sure.

The cops' attitude to the scheme was rare. They filled unmarked vans with big bruising polis in boiler suits and cruised the scheme. Pouncing on men and teenagers, they'd drag them into the van and beat the shit out of them. Afterwards, the targets were mostly just thrown out on to the road and no charges were made. The beatings were the point. These were the meat wagons and they dealt in terror.

Then you had families like the Welsh crew, possibly the ugliest bunch of men ever seen anywhere. For decades, they had a feud with Arthur Thompson as they tried to take over his territory. There were stabbings, shootings, slashings, murders, a car bomb that killed Thompson's mother-in-law and a night-time revenge raid led on the Welshes' house by Arthur Thompson's wife Rita.

Poverty and violence – that was Blackhill.

But my dad wanted to make a good, straight living through his bus business. When they jailed him for not paying the tax that was due, he lost all that. So, while he was in Barlinnie – known locally as BarL – he and some cronies planned a bank job, using a school bus full of kids as their getaway motor. And it worked till some loose-lipped gang member started spending the loot like money had gone out of fashion. Pulled in by the cops, he blabbed and that was my old man's Go-to-Jail-Again card.

Billy, my older brother, was already in jail for murder so Mum was left on her own to take care of us kids. Even though I was very young, I could see she was working numerous jobs at once – hard jobs like cleaning or scrubbing pots in a hospital kitchen. For those years of my childhood, Jenny was exhausted but it's just another form of a mother's unconditional love. I owed my mum – big time.

After my pals Bobby and Joe got murdered, I was sick of that whole scene. Too many people now traded with the cops and would stick you in as soon as look at you. I was already turning away from crime, working a number of legit businesses like installing fitted kitchens and the security game and I was doing very well.

One of the reasons I was moving away from crime was to give my mother back some of the loving care she had given me. My old man had died in 1993 so she was on her own and deserved to be looked after a wee bit. Now there I was arrested on bloody serious charges. It felt like I was letting her down and I needed to talk with her pronto – no chance. Arrested and deemed to be a high-security risk, I had to get the phone numbers I wanted to call cleared by the security screws and that took three weeks. So I wrote to my mum but that just wasn't the same. When I was eventually allowed to call, she was quiet, off-hand, a bit hurt. And I felt like shite.

Help was at hand in the form of the bold James Addison, the man who was still wanted on warrant for the gunrunning by the Old Bailey and various courts across the country. My mother knew none of that, of course, but Addie made sure she was OK, helped her understand why I hadn't been in touch and treated her the way she deserved – like a queen. She liked him and there was no surprise in that.

I'd let my girlfriend Sandra down as well – big time. Just three short weeks before I was arrested, she'd given birth to my youngest son, Dean. The day he was born, I was the proud preening father – just another man cradling his wee boy and thinking he owned the world. I did – it was right there in my arms.

It was a time of great optimism as well. My businesses were making good profits. There was the counterfeit dough scam planned and, if it all worked out, Dean would grow up wanting for nothing. Don't we all want that for our kids? It was also a time of determination. One of my great regrets in life was how little time I'd spent with my oldest boy, Paul. In and out of jail, bobbing and weaving, being watched by the cops all the time, I didn't have much time left to be any sort of parent – never mind a good father. That wasn't going to happen again.

Paul's mother, Anne Marie, and I had separated while he was young but we were still together as far as Paul Junior was concerned. At one point, I was to sort them out with a house. Now I was loaded, all ill-gotten gains of course, and I could've bought them any house Anne Marie wanted – except I couldn't. Imagine Paul Ferris buying a massive mansion in Glasgow and paying for it with carrier bags stuffed with cash. Right.

A good council house would have to do. Tam Bagan, my old pal from my Arthur Thompson days, helped me with that. God knows the strokes Tam pulled or who he had influence over but he got Anne Marie and Paul a good house all right and double quick. Helping like that and making sure they weren't short of money were all very well but it wasn't really enough – not in my mind anyway. I wanted to be a dad, to ride that roller coaster of growing up with my kids – me learning from them and them listening to me and then making their own minds up and doing exactly what they wanted. Isn't that always the way?

My life of crime had screwed that up with young Paul. No way was I going to make the same mistake with Dean – except I had.

Three weeks after his birth, I was in the pokey on gunrunning charges. Now in Frankland Prison, I knew that my sentence was seven years. If I kept a clean nose and avoided trouble, I could be out in four and back home with my family. If I was free then, it would mean I'd be with Dean on his first day of school and with Paul Junior when he left. So that was what I was determined to do.

But jails aren't religious retreats – they are social, temptation-ridden holes where violence constantly simmers just beneath surface and I had someone to sort out.

Could I do it without landing in the smelly stuff?

13

STICKS AND STONES

1999

'Fat poof.'

'What did you just say?'

'I called you a fat poof.'

Not that I have anything against anyone who is heavily built and, as far as I'm concerned, consenting adults can get their sexual kicks with any gender that suits them. So 'fat poof' isn't a phrase I'd choose too often and don't see it as an insult. But I knew the bloke I was speaking to would be deeply offended by anyone thinking he was either. That's why I made sure I called him 'fat poof' loudly and in front of a lot of prisoners. I was calling the evil bastard out.

He deserved it. I'd been watching him since my arrival at Frankland jail. Of all the hard nuts there, this was the one guy taking advantage of the weak and vulnerable in the worst possible way. The bloke was a prison dealer. Ever since the government introduced mandatory drug testing, prisoners who liked a bit of weed have had to be careful. Cannabis stays in the human body for weeks so even one joint means you're likely to get caught and lose remission time. In plain English, that means more time in prison and less with your loved ones. If the suits thought they would reduce drugs use in jails by introducing the tests, they were so wrong and I suspect they were deliberately wrong. Many prisoners stopped dope and took up smack instead because it would wash through their systems within hours but leave them zonked, compliant and totally addicted.

It's a policy that has led to guys going into jail clean and coming out junkies. And they call that progress.

Many prisoners take to smack just to get by. Don't ever let anyone tell you that jail time is easy. Those spouting that crap will either be some right-wing fanatic or some former prisoner who wants to look cool and instead looks pathetic. Even some very hard guys need to blank out the monotony of jail and, if you can't use dope, one effective way of doing that is heroin. So the jail trafficker is king to many prisoners and this particular guy thought it was good to be king. He thought he could do whatever he wanted so he did.

Fresh-faced younger prisoners were offered a tenner bag for a shag and, if they refused, they just got raped anyway. Contrary to the mythology, there isn't a lot of this kind of behaviour in jails. There are guys who like guys for sure, just as there are everywhere, but the whoring and raping that the Hollywood movies suggest goes on in jails simply doesn't happen very often.

I'd watched this bloke for a while. Jail is a very good place for sussing people out. He was evil and no doubt and I'd already decided that I would have to tackle him. He had this guy done over because he and his heavies suspected that the man was getting a delivery of smack. But they didn't stop there – they made his life hell every day. It was just too much. I hate bullies so I was going to have to put a stop to it. In a prison full of the toughest nuts you can imagine, why had no one else tackled the man? It's because they believed his own hype – big mistake.

The man in question was Jason Vella, weightlifter, drug dealer, gay sadomasochistic torturer – the man who falsely claimed to be mates with my pal Paul Massey and the same man Mick Healy had warned me about back in Full Sutton. 'That man's trouble,' Mick had said and then added, 'Friend to friend, Paul, give Vella a wide body swerve.' I had promised Mick I would and I had for a while but now I was going to have to break my word. I was sure he'd understand.

Vella was the original Essex boy who was dealing ecstasy in that part of the world before most people knew of the drug's existence.

Es made him rich pretty damn quick and at a very young age and he used his dough to make sure there was no competition. If crossed, Vella's style was to have his team of heavies take the man hostage, lock him in some house, strip him, shave his head and torture him for days on end. He raped his victims and, on one occasion, he shoved a broom handle up his victim's arse and took photographs of him. The obscene pictures were circulated far and wide to make an example of the guy. People thought twice of crossing Vella and his team.

Of course, Vella would let it be known that the rape of his victims was a power thing – just to prove his absolute domination, he'd stick his dick up the other guy's hole. To counter any claims he was gay, Vella always had good-looking, blonde girlfriends – Essex girls, literally. He wasn't gay – of course he wasn't. How could he be since he was so tough and always had a cutie on his arm? Aye, right.

Vella got richer and richer by not only dealing to the thousands of clubbers in that affluent part of the country but also selling huge amounts of Es to a Scottish biker gang, the Blue Angels, who brought it north to serve the young folk of Glasgow and Edinburgh. At one point, Vella needed such a heavy supply of Es that he told everyone he was buying from Kenny Noye. Noye was a big-time moneyman who was well in with the London mobs and some international faces such as John Palmer, known as Goldfinger. Palmer earned his nickname by having been found not guilty of handling gold bullion from the £25m Brinks Mat robbery at Heathrow in 1983. He'd eventually get his comeuppance when jailed for eight years as a massive timeshare fraudster in Tenerife.

Noye was a smart guy who evaded convictions even when he stabbed an undercover detective, John Fordham, to death. But, in 1986, he was sent down for fourteen years for helping to dispose of the gold bullion from the Brinks Mat job. Later, his hellish temper was to get the better of him when he murdered Stephen Cameron in a road-rage incident. In spite of fleeing to Moscow where he had plastic surgery that deliberately made him uglier – that's got to be a one-off – he was eventually nabbed in Spain when undercover cops and the dead man's girlfriend ID'd him.

Whether Jason Vella had done business with Kenny Noye or not is a matter of speculation. Having watched the guy swan around Frankland jail, I reckoned he was all front and no substance. My guess is that he made up the link with Noye because he wanted to be seen to be associating with the big boys – just as he'd lied to me about being a pal of Paul Massey.

Vella was eventually nabbed when one of his victims, Reg Nunn, lay stripped, beaten, bleeding and pretending to be unconscious so that the torture would stop. As he lay there, he listened to Vella telling one of his team, 'The bastard's well fucked. Just leave him there and we'll finish him off good and proper tomorrow.'

It is no surprise that Reg Nunn reckoned he had just heard his death sentence. Naked, he jumped to his feet and dived through the double glazing, falling from the second floor with a hard crunch. Slashed, bruised and battered, Nunn crawled to the nearest house and raised the alarm. Unlike several others before him, Reg Nunn followed through and gave evidence against Vella who was duly sent off to jail for seventeen years, ending up at Frankland.

Kenny Noye and the Essex boys' scene had rubbed off on Vella. He thought he was a big name. To swell his ego further, he was listed in the *Sunday Times*' Young Rich List shortly after he was sent down.

Vella thought he was tall, muscled, hard, popular with the ladies. I thought he was short, fat, nothing without his gang and should come out of the closet pronto and do the world a favour.

'What did you say, mate?' he demanded in the common area at Frankland Prison.

I turned and looked at him again. 'You're a fat poof,' I repeated and stood there staring at him, not budging, not running and perfectly willing to go on insulting him.

The place had fallen absolutely silent. All eyes were on us. It was his call. Now was his chance to live up to his reputation. It didn't take long. Jason Vella turned and slithered away. There would be no more trouble from him for the sweet-faced young prisoners out of their depth or desperate for a tenner bag of smack and easy meat for him and his heavies. And nor would I end up on report and lose time which would break my plan to be home within four years. It had been a risk but some things I just can't ignore.

I hate all bullies – I've despised them since the age of seven when the Welsh Clan decided to make my life a living hell. Every day, they ganged up on me and beat the shit out of me – every day, till I developed psoriasis – every day, till I was old enough to fight back.

As a young man, I picked off the Welshes and their pals one at a time. One was scalped, one had his throat slit, another was given a right doing in the exercise yard at Longriggend Prison. Every time, the locals declared that I was a dead man but it's me here writing this book. Where are the Welshes?

Vella was a bully and he was the only brief fly in the ointment of what was a very civilised, respectful prison term at Frankland. Is there such a thing as a good prison? No but there are better prisons and there are hellholes. I've known them both and I would choose Frankland any day.

But, for some of the good comrades and pals I made there, it wasn't quite as straightforward – not straightforward at all.

14

BAD COMPANY

'Pssst, doc!'

'What're you pssssting at? Think he'll hear you from here?'

'I'm not rattling the window.'

'Why?'

'The medic screw will hear me.'

'So?'

'Well.'

The two men having this conversation were prisoners at Frankland and were queuing up for the morning clinic. There they'd be assessed by a prison officer trained in basic treatments. He was allowed to give out pills but nothing stronger than a paracetamol so most men left the clinic feeling untreated.

'You think they don't know we speak to him? Besides, there's no law about asking another prisoner a question.'

'You try.'

'Yeah, all right. No, look he's spotted us.' One of the men wedged a window open. The pane that ran horizontally at the top of the frame was fixed so that it would only open two inches but it was just enough to whisper out of it if they stood on chairs, which they promptly did.

'Doc, hello, Doc.' The man on the ground looked up. He had spoken with these men often before yet he never smiled or gave any hint of recognition. He was middle aged, bearded, with thick hair pushed back off his brow, and he wore horn-rimmed spectacles.

'How can I help?' asked the doc in a gruff, serious voice.

'I've been getting stomach pains, Doc. Terrible cramps.' The man looked at the others in the queue for the medic screw to see if they were listening. They didn't look as if they were but, of course, they hung on every word. That's prison for you. 'Terrible runs.'

'Runs?' The doc looked perplexed.

'Ye know, skitters.' The con looked around him again but still no one appeared to be paying him any attention.

'Ah, loose bowel movements,' the doc said, pronouncing every syllable. 'How long have you had the symptoms?'

'About two weeks. Well, fifteen days the day to be exact.'

'Not good.' The doc shook his head sympathetically.

'I'm scared I've got that stomach cancer. Or maybe that – what ye call it – Cone's disease.'

'What?'

'Cone's disease. I was reading in the paper that the farther north you go in Britain the more common it is. Well, I'm no' exactly a southerner.'

'Oh, Crohn's disease.' The doc didn't laugh or smile but spoke in an insulted way, like he was lowering himself. One of the things he hated about prison was the scum he had to keep company with and he didn't mind it showing.

'I think it's too soon to diagnose that but make sure the medic gives you . . .' The doc went on to stipulate the drugs the prisoner should insist on as he did with every such consultation. In the queue for the medic screw every morning, at least a handful of cons would seek the doc's opinion. They felt it was much better that a proper doctor made a diagnosis than the hardly-trained medic screw. Besides, even when they relented and allowed you to see the prison doctor, how could you trust them? Why would any employee of the prison system want a prisoner to feel better or even survive? That's what some thought and they would always think that way. They were convinced they were seriously ill and what did they get? Para-bloody-cetamol.

What the prisoner patients didn't know was that, every morning at that time, the doc would make sure he was in the garden right below their window. He enjoyed being consulted. He had been diagnosing and prescribing for years and it made him feel important, like he should. Now he was bound to live in a prison hospital wing along with the nonces and ponces under protection as well as the raving lunatics and terminally ill. Cut off from the rest of the prison, these little consultation sessions were light relief. Every prison has its fair share of hypochondriacs and those were the ones who consulted him most. They appreciated him. What they wrote in the newspapers wasn't true. Not everyone thought of him badly.

He was a good doctor.

A serious man with a sharp brain.

He was born to be a physician and help those in pain.

At least that's what he thought.

The consultation over, Dr Harold Shipman, the UK's most prolific serial killer, turned and walked away.

Inside the jail, it was the turn of Shipman's first patient of the day to see the medic screw.

'No, no,' he insisted, 'I don't need paracetamol. I need Imodium and rehydration granules and extra fluids and . . . What else was it?' He thought along while. 'Oh, aye, and, if it persists more than a week, I demand you test me for Cone's disease. My life might be at risk, you know.'

And he wasn't wrong.

15

POOR TASTE

1999–2002

One hypochondriac who didn't consult Shipman was also the fittest man I've ever met and I've met a few.

Brendan Quinn was an Irish bank robber with an international pedigree. Done for armed robberies in England, he was soon holed up in a top-security prison. Before long, he escaped and took to his heels to the Netherlands.

If you're Scottish, English or Welsh and you're on the run from the law, the Republic of Ireland is no bad place to head but, if you're already well known across that stretch of water, it's a definite no-no. The Netherlands is almost as close as Ireland and a hell of a lot safer. There's also a big Irish contingent in Holland, working in the electronics factories and the like. Away from the city centre, Amsterdam drips with pubs where you can have genuine Guinness and listen to some class Irish folk music. But these places are mostly full of straight Joes and Brendan didn't have much use for them.

Being safe and abroad is one thing but you have to survive and that takes money. Brendan did the type of work he was good at – he robbed banks. After a few successes, it suddenly went belly up. The whole thing was a wee bit messy and ended up with Brendan and his team caught on a tram surrounded by heavily armed soldiers and militia. Back to jail he went and this time it was to Holland's most secure prison – a hellhole of a place. Think of Hannibal Lecter in *Silence of the Lambs* when they kept him in that cage in the middle of a room. Now think high tech, lights constantly on and armed screws walking over as well as around your cage. A series of cells like that were built in isolation, high off the ground with only a small, narrow pathway leading to the main building. It was twenty-four-hours' isolation – no speaking to the screws, never mind other prisoners. Beatings were dished out at random – often for nothing. When he had to leave his cell, Brendan's feet and hands were manacled and he was forced to crawl on his stomach while surrounded by six riot-gear clad screws and a pack of guard dogs.

It really was the prison from hell and it was designed to be hell for the prisoners – the most dangerous in the country. It was also a jail no one could escape from – or so they thought until, one day, Brendan walked out through the main gate with a gun at the governor's head.

The man did it with two cohorts – a Colombian player, one of the biggest drug traffickers in the world, and a man who went by the name of La Torre. He was a member of the Camorra Family who, according to the authorities, were fully paid-up members of the Naples branch of the Mafia. The Italian had relatives in Aberdeen of all places. Up there they ran a restaurant called Pavarotti's – a very good restaurant, by all accounts.

The three comrades led the authorities a merry dance through much of Europe with Interpol on their trail. Interpol came off second best. Then they split up. The Mafia man got caught trying to get to his relatives in Aberdeen. The Colombian disappeared and has never been seen by anyone in authority since. Somehow Brendan made it back to the UK but then he ran out of luck.

When Brendan was lifted, his poor family – straight Joes and Jessies every one – were arrested as suspected terrorists. They weren't – they were just folk who cared for their own, whatever they got up to, much like my own family. With that matter eventually cleared up, Brendan got jailed big time. That's how I came to meet him in Frankland – a cakewalk compared with his Dutch jail which had just lost a case of breaching prisoners' rights under the European Convention. Well, constant solitary for years, with the lights never going off, random beatings, personal indignities and shaming – you wouldn't get off with that during wartime, never mind in a civilian jail.

In Frankland, which he considered cushy, Brendan decided to serve his time and go out to a fresh start which is just as well as I'm sure he could have escaped if he wanted. Now, if he had invited me along for the trip, what call would I have made? Tempting, very tempting.

Fit and healthy, Brendan had lived in a total hellhole and not only had he survived, he had also escaped. So, what had he to worry about? Every-bloody-thing, that's what. The slightest ache, a wee cold, an upset stomach and Brendan had himself down as being mortally ill. I was used to linking such hypochondria with weaker guys – like fat man Jason Vella who was at the doc's every day. He used to come out in these strange lumps on his skull and under his arms. It got to the stage where the medics refused to see him and sent him packing but the bugger bleated so much that, eventually, the prison doctor contacted Vella's lawyer, saying he suspected Vella was working his ticket to get into a general hospital from where he intended to escape. However, I don't think that was right as it would have needed more cunning than Vella possessed.

Nobody seemed to put the strange lumps on Vella's body together with his bouts of bleak depression and mood swings – that and he thought he was some pumper of iron. How long do steroids stay in your system? Besides, this prison dealer had started sampling his own product and it's not unusual for smackheads to get strange ailments.

Brendan Quinn was completely different. Totally fit and utterly courageous, the only thing he was scared of was catching some disease – any disease. So big Grant Turnbull and I decided to set him up.

Early one morning, Brendan and I were chatting about this and that as you do. 'Is there something wrong, Brendan?' I asked.

'No,' he replied. 'Why do you ask?'

'Oh, you look a wee bit pale – that's all.'

'Do you think so?' he muttered, turning to try and catch a reflection of himself in a window. 'I hadn't noticed.'

'It's probably nothing,' I reassured him, 'but are you feeling all right?'

To Brendan this was an invitation to a lengthy self-analysis of every small ache and pain he thought he had. 'Funny you should ask,' he said, now looking worried. 'I've had a right stiff neck for a few days.' He stood rubbing his neck to demonstrate the point. 'And I think my temperature's running a bit high.' Now his hand was on his brow and his expression was a deeper shade of fret.

'You'd better watch,' I added.

'Why?' Brendan snapped.

'That's how it started with big Grant.'

'What started?'

'He's got a nasty virus.'

'No!'

'Oh, aye. The doc says he's never come across it before.'

'Fuck sake.'

'That normal antibiotics will probably not shift it.'

Brendan's face had now turned a puce colour and, for the first time that morning, he really did look sick.

'Some new strain of virus from Mongolia.' I stopped to roll a fag, biding my time, watching the door, trying to catch the right minute. 'Outer Mongolia actually. Seems it killed thousands over there.'

'Killed?' Brendan asked in a low hoarse voice.

I nodded as I licked the gummed paper on my cig.

'Dead?'

Another nod from me then, in a much louder voice, 'Hi, Grant. You feeling any better this morning?'

Grant strolled into the room bang on time and answered in a low, weak voice, 'Mornin', Paul. No, I'm not any better.' He was moving closer to us. 'Much worse if anything.'

As Grant reached a few yards from us Brendan turned and scampered, almost ran, out the door.

'Cracker,' I giggled when Brendan had left the room.

'Ya beauty,' sniggered Grant.

'Did you see the direction he was heading?'

'No.'

'The medical suite.' We both howled with laughter. Once Grant caught his breath he added, 'He'll be up there right now.'

'Jumping the queue.'

'Demanding the medic screw examine him for the dreaded Outer Mongolian flu.'

Brendan Quinn was a top man. Fit and fearless. The guy that no secure prison could hold. The same man that took on the Dutch army and armed militia. The self same Brendan Quinn who led Interpol and the cops of several European countries a merry dance. And that bloke was terrified of a wee virus. A virus that didn't exist.

That's one of the problems with prison. Every weakness you have is likely to be exposed. And a weakness exposed will be a weakness exploited – even if it is by two pals taking the piss.

Every now and then, Grant and I would pull the same scam on Brendan – different setting, different invented illness, different timing but essentially the same scam. And every time it worked with Brendan scurrying away to seek urgent medical attention.

'You'd think he'd suss out our game by now,' I said one day to Grant.

'Aye, you would,' he agreed. 'I mean, he's a bright guy and normally really suspicious of everyone.'

'Maybe he just doesn't want to take any risks.'

'As in one day we might actually be telling him the truth?'

'Yeah and yet he hasn't worked out that it's always you that has the illness.' We both laughed remembering some of Brendan's reactions.

'Maybe he thinks I'm a type of virus carrier,' offered Grant, with a smile.

'Big Grant Turnbull – Super Virus Man. Ta-ta-ta-TA.' We both laughed louder.

'Striking down the bad guys with a dose of Outer Mongolian,' he was giggling.

'A DEADLY dose,' I emphasised as we both pissed ourselves laughing.

If only I'd known.

16

BIG BALLS, HUGE HEART
1999–2002

'What are you on, Grant?' I'd been watching big Grant Turnbull for a few weeks. He was slipping into a zombie state. Walking as if his feet were weighted, talking shite, repeating himself, forgetting things that had happened just minutes before.

'A'm clean, Paul,' he replied all indignant, almost hurt in that Edinburgh accent of his.

'Aye and I'm the Prime Minister.'

'No seriously,' this was obviously a sore point for Grant, 'I *am* clean – clean as a whistle.' Even as he protested, his words were slurred, his eyes dead and he swayed backwards and forwards on his heels. On his breath I could smell a sweet odour. Not fruit or mint – just sweetness like he'd scoffed a bag of sugar.

'You're not clean,' I looked at him straight. I can't stand bullshitting when it comes to drugs. 'You're stoned out of your box, man.'

'Naaw, A'm naaaw.'

'You're in big shit if you keep this up, Grant,' I hissed. 'You've been high for fucking weeks. I've watched you.'

He slumped his arse down on his bunk and started to roll a cigarette but just spilled tobacco shreds all over his lap. 'Drugs? Want to know about my drugs?' He looked up at me as he licked the gummed paper and wisps of tobacco stuck to his tongue.

'Aye,' I said as I took the roll-up from him and threw it away. In its place, I rolled him one from my own tobacco – at least he should

63

have a smoke if he wanted it. 'Tell me about the smack.'

Now he sat bolt upright, his face serious, eyeballing me. 'Smack is it? Is that what you think?'

I nodded.

He nodded. 'What if I told you I got the drugs from the screws?'

'That wouldn't surprise me.' In every jail in the UK, there are a few wardens who happily augment their earnings via little smuggling rackets. Mobile phones and drugs are their biggest earners. Though, as you'll find out later, some are even willing to go much further.

'Thirty to forty every day,' Grant added.

'What forty hits a day?' I had noticed he was spaced, unsteady, energy-less but forty hits? No way.

'I'm HIV positive, Paul.'

You could have blown me over. Not that Grant was the first HIV positive person I'd met – there's a lot of the virus around these days. But I'd been so bloody insensitive with him.

'Didn't mean to pry, Grant.'

'No problem. I've been HIV for over twenty years – and hopefully for twenty years more.'

Grant Turnbull told me his story. Holed up in Dumfries Prison on a fraud charge around 1983, he had hurt his leg playing football. Suspecting the leg was broken, they took him to the local hospital. It wasn't broken but the ligaments were badly strained. He'd need complete bed rest. As a precaution they kept him in hospital overnight and took blood tests – just routine. The next day, his two warden guards were ushered urgently out of his room. Half an hour later, a posse of spacemen walked in wearing coverall suits, big boots and sealed helmets fitted with an air supply. Grant shit himself big time. Wouldn't you? One of the spacemen told Grant that he had HIV, something people knew little about back then. Grant was going to be dead in months or so they said.

Back in Edinburgh in the early 1970s, the street players there were among the first in Scotland to discover the mass appeal of heroin. To Grant and his friends it was just another hit so they partied and shared needles. Back then, not even the doctors knew they were dicing with death. Later, Grant would be told he'd been positive for some years, probably from around 1973. One of his first hits had infected him.

If the docs and Grant knew little about HIV, the prison service was totally ignorant and didn't give a fuck about their first-ever HIV prisoner. There followed threats of strikes by the screws. Grant was thrown into an old, manky, freezing solitary cell and left to die. His food was thrown at him by some screw in a spaceman suit. He wasn't allowed to shower or shave or see any other prisoner. The screws called him Plague Man and hoped he would die soon.

To speed the process up, the caring bastards let water hoses loose under Grant's cell door, soaking his bedding, his clothing, everything. Then they left him to freeze. Fuck that – Grant never caught as much as a cold and, the next time a screw came near him, he ripped his space helmet off and punched his head in. Well, you would, wouldn't you?

After this treatment had been going on for many months, Scottish doctors had finally gained some real knowledge of HIV. They said Grant should be allowed out of solitary, back to free association with the men and there was no risk of infection unless blood was spilled. It took another two months to convince the screws.

About nine months after Grant had been diagnosed, they started carrying out HIV tests on all the prisoners in Dumfries jail. On the first day alone, nineteen other prisoners were diagnosed HIV positive and, a few months, later he wasn't so much not alone as quite unexceptional.

'Most of my mates are dead now, Paul,' Grant said, having told me his story. 'Every time I think of the old days in the Edinburgh razor gangs and later, with the organised mobs, almost all the people – men and women – all of them I know are dead from AIDS.' I nodded. No wonder at football matches against Hearts or Hibs, all opposition supporters chanted and sang:

You're AIDS-carrying bastards,
Nothing but AIDS-carrying bastards,
AIDS-carrying baaaaastards,
Nothing but AIDS-carrying bastards.

In Scotland's capital there was an epidemic on a scale not matched anywhere else in Europe. In street terms, almost an entire generation of players were wiped out. No wonder so many outsiders now run organised crime in that city.

'But you're not dead, Grant,' I added, stating the obvious.

He nodded, a sad expression suddenly pulling his usually smiling face a hundred degrees south. 'No, not yet,' he said in a manner clearly conveying that he didn't think it would be long before he was. 'My health's not good,' he went on, 'and that's why I'm taking new medication – a lot of medication. That's why . . .'

'I thought you were stoned,' I butted in, feeling really stupid.

It turned out that not only was Grant taking a stack of pills to combat HIV but also the heroin substitute methadone in huge doses, as a painkiller, and several other drugs that would zap the strength from him. It would have been enough to make an elephant weak-kneed.

'Why are you taking all that?' I asked.

'Because they prescribe it,' he replied, not unreasonably.

'Even the methadone and all those uppers and downers?'

He shrugged and looked puzzled, 'Aye, of course.'

'Just because they say so?'

He nodded.

'You used to be a bit handy, eh?'

Now that got a smile.

'Well, you can't let anybody push you around in here – especially not the screws. You know that, Paul.'

'Changed days for you then, eh?'

He looked sad again and nodded, knowing he was putty in their hands.

'Keep taking all their pills and you'll be a shadow of yourself.

You'll probably go downhill fast and they'll be quite happy to see you off in a coffin.'

Grant was nodding faster and faster. 'You think?'

'Yeah.' The power of the prisons is something I detest. I hate seeing a man taken down and owned by the system – any man. Sometimes the obvious needs to be said. Sometimes that's all it takes.

'The fucking bastards.'

Within a week, the sparkle had returned to Grant Turnbull's eyes, the skip was back in his step and his wit was as sharp as ever.

'You're looking great, big man,' I said to him one day.

'Cheers, Paul, I feel much better.'

'So how did you do it?'

'I just said no to the drugs.'

'That'll be a first then,' I smiled.

'Grant Turnbull just said no to drugs,' he laughed at the irony. 'Just Say No.'

And the two of us pissed ourselves laughing at the old anti-drugs slogan.

At the time of writing this book, Grant Turnbull is still alive, thirty-two years after the docs reckoned he contracted HIV. Now there's a strong man.

17

LYNCHING THE QUEEN
1999–2002

'Who is the big guy, Grant?' I asked, nodding in the direction of a prisoner who looked edgy and was pacing the ground, like a terrified beast caught in a trap.

'Just some bloke called Fitzgibbon,' big Grant replied. 'From a family in Liverpool.'

They must have been the exception, I thought, because most of the Scousers I'd met were small and wiry but this guy was huge, well over six-foot tall, and built like a wall of the Liver Building.

'Looks like he's cracking up,' I added, unnecessarily. All the prisoners could see he was about to blow. That's never good in any jail but worse in a closed unit like the one in Frankland. The bloke's fear and tension was likely to spread unless he calmed down or the screws noticed and took him off the wing for a while. 'Any idea what's eating him?'

'He's in for some drugs rap. Word is he cheated some heavy team out of a lot of money.'

'Serves him right then but why the fuck's he so uptight in here? Surely this is one of the safest places he can be?'

'Aye but there's whisper that the team have put out a hit on him. And he's worried about all of us.'

'The screws should get hold of him before he goes truly paranoid,' I added.

'Think they're too late, Paul.'

Within the hour, Grant Turnbull would be proven right. Fitzgibbon jumped the youngest guy on the wing and gave him such a doing that he was hospitalised. Big mistake.

His chosen target, Darren Mulholland, was young, slim, sweet looking, well educated, softly spoken and a member of the Real IRA. Sooner or later Fitzgibbon was going to pay the price. Darren had been part of a Real IRA bomb squad that were arrested at a time there was a campaign in London. If the cops and security services had been a week later, Darren would have exploded a massive charge in a crowded part of that city.

Stupid Fitzgibbon hadn't done his homework and had just chosen the youngest, least threatening-looking guy. All he wanted was the chance to prove himself a troublemaker so he would be flitted out of Frankland pronto – out to safety, he thought. How wrong can you be? You just can't hide from a team like the Real IRA.

A couple of days later, articles ran in newspapers about this desperado ex-paratrooper who had to be shipped out of top-security Frankland because he had beaten a Real IRA man to a pulp. I had to read it twice to realise they were referring to the same Fitzgibbon. The closest he had come to a parachute jump was falling over when he was as high as a kite from some drugs. Not so much paratrooper as paranoider. What crap.

An approach was made to me by one of the politicals in the jail to point out the implications of the article. 'Paul, this is nothing more than British propaganda,' he said in a private corner of the jail. 'You know – brave paratrooper beats up Real IRA animal.'

'I can see your point,' I replied truthfully. Most players, like me, don't give a monkey's about what the press print as long as it's accurate. We might not like it but, if it's true, so what? It's when they get fed rubbish about us that it really gets the blood flowing. I guess we're no different in that from non-combatants except the law doesn't think we have a reputation to defend so we're sitting ducks for whatever the headlines say. It was one of my ambitions to influence that. To have more written words about crime and criminals that were true, real.

'Is there anything you can do to set the record straight, you think?'

'I'll make a phone call.'

'Good man.'

By the Sunday, one of the UK's best-selling tabloids ran the headline: THE WORLD'S MOST STUPID CON. I had simply phoned Reg and let him talk to a few people so that he could make his own mind up about what actually happened and he made sure the truth was reported. However, to do this, I had to break prison rules by talking to a writer about someone in jail. Funny rule that. What are they doing? Trying to hide the truth?

The Fitzgibbon Family was known to me from my time spent around Manchester and Liverpool. They were a big mob and involved in everything and anything – one of those families who seem content to continue the way they've been for generations without moving up or out. Some time afterwards, I discovered that they were hooked into what appeared to be just another scam but it had consequences at the highest political level in the UK. But we'll get to that later.

Young Darren recovered in double-quick time and was back on the wing with his same wide smile and quick wit. Young and intellectual as he was, I still reckon Fitzgibbon would have come off second best if he hadn't jumped Darren from behind.

Back on the wing, Darren was one of the more pleasant people around. Some folk might say that those who plan on bombing crowds can never be pleasant. Would I have wanted me or mine to be at the hot end of one of Darren's bombs? No. Would I have smiled if hundreds of other folks had died in some blast of his making? No. But is he political? Yes. Did he believe there is a war on? Yes. Did he believe he and his people have been subjected to worse for centuries as the rest of us did nothing? Yes. Most of the other prisoners were in jail because of greed. Darren was in jail because of political beliefs. Who do you judge more severely?

Darren always looked as if he was playing some practical joke. But, as is my experience with all Republicans, he had strong principles and you could easily stumble into them by accident and get a verbal roasting in return. He was a clever man with his nose constantly in a book so one day I showed him a piece of writing I was involved in for my first book, *The Ferris Conspiracy*.

'What do you think?' I asked him.

'It reads well,' he replied, much to my relief. 'I like the short chapters ending in a question. Drives you on, wanting to know what happens next.'

Coming from a university graduate who read great literature and philosophy in his cell rather than watching the goggle box like most of us, I was preening myself, valuing his positive appraisal. 'Thanks . . .'

'But tell me,' he interrupted.

'Sure,' my confidence was still high.

'What fucking mainland?'

'What?' He caught me by surprise and, as a man who rarely swore, his use of the word 'fucking' had a huge impact on me. Darren was not a happy chappy.

'Exactly what fucking mainland are you referring to in your book?' The section I had passed to him was about ten thousand words long. I hadn't a clue what he was getting at. He did and rhymed off the sentences exactly. 'That'll be the mainland of some wee island then?'

'Eh, no.'

'Maybe the Isle of Wight? Or would that be Skye? Maybe Arran or the Isle of fucking Man?'

I just blushed.

'No, no. That'll be the mainland of that wee island of Ireland, eh?'

I put up my hands in defeat. 'It was a mistake, Darren. It slipped through.' I knew how strongly many Irish people felt about their own identity and they were quite right to consider themselves significant enough not to be seen as an island off of any other place. Imagine calling continental Europe the mainland of Britain. Then again, maybe that's not so wrong.

'I know it was a mistake, Paul. No worries. But does your writing partner's computer have a delete button?'

He did and it was used.

Reg decided to write to Darren but there was a complication. The envelopes couldn't have Queen Lizzie's picture on them or, if they did, her image had to be upside down. To have done otherwise would have been to insult Darren whose view was, 'She's not my fucking queen.' The sub-post-office manager Reg dealt with was well used to his frequent visits to send thick Special Delivery packages to me and TC Campbell – names he would have recognised for sure. The guy thought he was as wide as the Clyde and believed he knew more than Reg did. Why is it that everyone thinks they know more about street players than everyone else? He would chatter on about this player and that while, for reasons only known to himself, humming the theme tune from the film *The Third Man*. He also had this nasty habit of farting a lot. When Reg asked that the stamps with Queen Lizzie's face be stuck upside down on the envelope, the guy just looked at him strangely and went on humming and farting.

A while later, Reg went to post another package to Darren. By this time, he had become the last man to be repatriated under the Good Friday Agreement and had taken up residence in Portlaoise Prison in Ireland. There had been some coverage of his move in the press at the time. The postmaster eyed the address and the penny dropped. A couple of months later, Reg realised that, since that day, he had never heard *The Third Man* theme tune being hummed and the postie stuck the stamps on all his letters upside down. Unfortunately the farting got worse – much worse.

What the hell did the postmaster think Reg was up to? The Troubles in Ireland have far reaching effects that go beyond those shores, that's for sure.

And practical jokes travel well too – as I was about to discover.

18

THE BEST CRIME BOOK I NEVER READ

Darren Mulholland was a great reader with a huge collection of books – a valuable commodity in jail. Well, usually it is.

One day, Darren loaned me one of his books, *The Brothers Karamazov* by the great Russian writer, Fyodor Dostoevsky. Darren described it as the best crime novel he had ever read – right up my street. For a week, I worked bloody hard at that book but I just couldn't get into it. God it was tough going.

Early in 2000, I was sent up to Barlinnie Prison, Glasgow for accumulated visits. Throughout my whole sentence, I had discouraged my partner, Sandra, from visiting me for good reasons. Glasgow to Durham is a hellish drive – especially with a youngster. All it needed was road works or a crash and she would run the risk of not making it for visiting time. More than once she was turned away because she was five minutes late. Sod that.

Also, every time I had a visit in jail from her or some close family member, it reminded me I was locked up. It just slapped me in the face with what I couldn't do and reminded me too much of the people I loved and how I couldn't help. It took me a week to get over every visit.

The English Prison Service allowed me to go to BarL to have all these unused visits over an intensive period of a few weeks. Because I was still Cat A and high risk, they wouldn't tell me exactly when this move would happen in case I arranged a breakout ambush en route. Early one morning, while the other prisoners slept, I was roughly wakened, told I was heading north and ordered to get a few things together – like right now. Not wanting to give them any excuse to cancel the trip, I hurriedly scooped up some belongings, including Darren's book.

In BarL, because they didn't house Cat-A prisoners, I was put into the Segregation Unit, what the cons call the Wendy House. It meant no free association with other prisoners and twenty-three-hour lock-ups every day but, for once, I didn't mind. After all, most days I would have at least one, probably two, visits. Along the wing from me were other prisoners who were in trouble. I knew some of them, including a young guy called Scott Simpson. As we moved in and out the visiting room or to and from the showers, we would catch short conversations with each other. On earlier occasions in the Wendy House, I would have received a bollocking from the screws for such breaches of the rules but, this time, they were more relaxed and treated inmates with respect. It resulted in a trouble-free zone. Why can't all the prisons learn that?

One day, Scott asked if I had any books to read. It so happened that I'd been handed in a bundle of crime novels including some by my favourite crime writer, James Ellroy. But I wasn't going to give him one of those, was I?

'I've a cracker, Scott. Best crime novel I've ever read,' I told him.
'Brilliant,' he replied.

Later that day I arranged for *The Brothers Karamazov* to be passed to Scott by a prison officer, as you have to do. It's so boring and dull in solitary that everything becomes intensified. A small repeating noise can drive you crazy and a boring book can send you well mental.

Every time we passed each other, I asked Scott how he was getting on with the book.

'Great,' he enthused to start with. Then, later, he said, 'I'm finding it a bit hard going.'

I encouraged him to stick with it because it got easier after a couple of hundred pages and, fair play to him, he persisted.

About ten days after I'd passed *The Brothers Karamazov* to Scott, I was lying out in my bunk one night, totally engrossed in some really good novel. The whole wing was in total silence when 'FERRIS. YOU DIRTY ROTTEN CUNT!' rang out. Scott had reached the page-two-hundred mark and realised it didn't get any easier. By then, he'd totally lost the plot – literally – and sussed I'd been taking the piss.

A short while later, I wrote to Darren and mentioned the wee lark with Scott Simpson and *The Brothers Karamazov*. Then and only then did the bastard admit that he too had struggled with the book. So who had the last laugh?

Last I heard, that book was still circulating in the Scottish prison system, being passed from one con to another with the recommendation, 'It's the best crime novel I've ever read.' Aye, right.

The accumulated visits in BarL were great – a real chance to spend quality time with Sandra and wee Dean as well as Paul Junior and some friends. But even visits can carry sinister undertones as someone was about to find out.

19

WHO'S MENTAL?

'People think he's a bit crazy, Paul.' The comment gave me the jumping heebie-jeebies. Why would anyone want to bring up the state of another's mental health and apologise for it early on before any accusations are made about his lack of sanity? Usually because they really are pure mental. 'He just looks a bit, well, wild, you know.'

It was my pal Lance Gray talking to me in Frankland. Lance was from Middlesbrough and spoke in a gruff broken whisper due to the cancer that was gnawing away at his throat. When I first arrived in Frankland, I struggled to understand most of the staff with their broad north-east England accents. It wasn't a trivial matter when a Geordie screw has just made an announcement over the tannoy and the only word you've caught is your bloody name. So you learn fast. But, with Lance's throat condition, I had to work very hard at catching his every word. 'What's so wild about him then?' I asked.

Lance coughed and broken glass crunched in his gullet. 'He's got some ideas about bent cops and corrupt businessmen.' Now he had my full attention. 'In fact, he's got evidence.'

We were discussing a friend of Lance called Jeremy Earls known as Jez. Thirty-four-years-old, Jez had been handy in his younger day but now he was plagued with a bad stomach condition and, more importantly in his view, a campaign to out what he believed was an unholy alliance between a Nottingham businessman, his associates and several high-ranking Lincolnshire cops.

It had started when Jez was accused of firing a gun at the back of his house – something he denied. That day, he reckoned the cops searched and re-searched his place till magically they found a box of ammo under his bed and shells at the back door. It was a set-up. Jez reckoned the trouble had come from the businessman since he'd had problems with the bouncers at one of the guy's clubs. So he started following the bloke and his associates, catching them playing golf with cops whose lifestyles were well above what their brown wage packets would fund. He dug further and came up with a thick portfolio of incriminating intelligence. Then Jez went to the cops. Big mistake.

Over the next while, Jez found bullets in the footwell of his car. His house was broken into and the only thing stolen was some private porno pics of his young, good-looking, blonde girlfriend. He was followed almost everywhere he went so Jez took off, moving from area to area, house to house. He went to different police forces in England and, almost immediately, he would be followed by faces he recognised from Lincolnshire. Paranoid? Seemed like it but then people would have suggested I was para at one time.

On the advice of Peter Forbes, my lawyer in the 1980s, I had written down everything I did every day and still do so now. This came after Glasgow cops tried to incriminate me in offences that had sod all to do with me. I'd been raided by armed cops, one carrying an unofficial gun. A pal secretly taped a detective saying that I'd come close to being bumped off by them. Jez Earls paranoid? It wasn't for me to say.

With Reg's permission, all I did was put Reg and Jez Earls together and then promptly forgot all about it.

Things were going well for me – as well as they could be when you're stuck in the jail. I'd made good new friends in the pokey – men like Kevin Lane. An ex-boxer, young, sharp, well-off and, women would say, good-looking, Kevin seemed to have everything going for him. Then he got done for a hit job – shooting a businessman while he was out walking his dogs.

There was sod all to connect Kevin with the job apart from a detective with a long-standing grudge against his family. This guy,

Detective Sergeant Chris Spackman, swore to get Kevin on anything and he did. Later, Spackman himself would be jailed for stealing money that had been seized from arrested guys. Corrupt is corrupt and Spackman was as corrupt as they come.

Did they immediately review all of Spackman's cases? Did they hell. So Kevin set off to publicise his appeal through a website and working with the media. For ages, he worked with a journalist from *The Guardian*, with the full knowledge of the prison.

'This writing lark's a lot of hard work, Paul,' he moaned one day, 'and it takes bloody ages.'

'How do you fancy tackling it when you're banned from communicating with the writer?' I asked.

'Nah. No way.'

But that's exactly what had happened to Reg and me.

Martin Clarke, then editor of the *Daily Record*, had bought serialisation rights to *The Ferris Conspiracy*. It was the best-selling paper in Scotland and the deal ensured TV and radio advertising. For me, none of this was about money – it was about getting people to read my true account of cop corruption and the trading in flesh by certain players. Everything seemed to be going ace. Then Clarke left the *Record* and was replaced by a guy called Peter Cox and that's when it went sour.

Clarke had admitted to Reg that publishing extracts from *The Ferris Conspiracy* would lose his troops the cooperation of the cops but, in spite of a lot of grumbling from within the *Record*'s ranks, he was going to go ahead. It was all signed and sealed in a legal contract and then Cox stabbed us in the back. Part of the agreement included an interview with me which was to be published the day before serialisation began. We set it up the only way possible with me phoning Reg's house at an agreed time when their journalist would be there. We just had to hope that the censor screw who would be listening in didn't smell a rat.

The *Record* sent their top writer at the time, Anna Smith, who is now a novelist. I'd been begging, borrowing and bribing to get my mitts on extra phone cards for weeks – it's not cheap to phone from jail. For ninety minutes, I answered each and every one of Anna's questions. We thought it had been a good day's work – till the next morning. To coincide with the serialisation, the piece wasn't meant to be published for a fortnight but there it was within twelve hours of the interview. There were pages of negative shite about me and an editorial asking, 'Who'd buy a second-hand car from Ferris let alone a book about his life?'

It constituted a very public deal-breaker. The publisher immediately sued the *Record*, of course, although I always thought it was Peter Cox they should have gone after – it was his decision to print it, after all. In the meantime, the Home Office wasn't chuffed and, because the interview had so obviously happened at Reg's home, he and I were banned from communicating with each other – a wee bit difficult since we were by then writing another book, a novel called *Deadly Divisions*.

Although the *Record* piece was negative about me, I still couldn't see the difference between that and, say, Kevin Lane working with *The Guardian* and he wasn't banned from having contact with the broadsheet's journalist. Even wild man Charles Bronson had had a whole film crew in the jail making a documentary just a few weeks before. So what the hell was so special about me in the Home Office's eyes?

There's no appeal against such bans – that's the power the system has over you when you're jailed. Reg and I found a way round it, of course, and the book was written.

Round about this time, Reg got a call from Jez Earls saying that, in spite of his efforts at hiding, wearing disguises, only using public call boxes and never declaring himself, he was being followed again. Jez had a feeling of dread and said, 'I think something bad's going to happen.'

Three days later, Jez Earls' body was found in a car on a quiet rural road outside Lincoln. He had been shot and an Uzi lay across his lap. The day before, two young brothers had been found shot dead in their house in Lincoln. Straight non-combatants, there seemed to be no reason for their murder – except that they had swapped houses with one Jez Earls. Within a day, articles appeared in most English papers implying that Jez had killed the brothers and then shot himself. As evidence, his association with serious players was cited. Well, one serious player – me. The articles claimed that Jez had visited this notorious gangster up in Frankland. There was just one problem – it was shite. Jez had visited Lance Gray as the jail records would show. I had never met Jez Earls so why the hell was I getting dragged into this?

Around two years earlier, Jez had been in touch with the journalist who had written those articles in the English press but he soon broke off from him, suspecting that he worked too closely with the cops. Maybe Jez was right.

A couple of months later, a deputation of Lincolnshire and Glasgow plainclothes arrived unexpectedly at Reg's door. In spite of Jez's extreme secrecy, they knew where Reg lived, exactly when they had spoken on the phone and that Reg was the last known person to talk to Jez alive. No surprise to us that they were tapping Reg's phone. The cops were after Reg's files on Jez. He told them to get lost. At the inquest a couple of months later, they dragged out a psychiatrist who had never met Jez but said he was paranoid. His mother told tales of him wearing wigs and brandishing guns and his ex-girlfriend told of his tempers and strange behaviour. All very straightforward, even though a doc said he couldn't rule out murder. But the suicide verdict was sealed when the inquest was told that Jez had been in the habit of visiting a notorious gangster – me.

The authorities had used my reputation to sully Jez Earls' and protect their own. Bastards. The one person that wasn't called to the inquest was Reg, the last person to talk to Jez alive, according to the cops – the one who had promised the cops that, one day, we would write about Jez Earls and do our best to get the truth out there to the public.

As my last months of prison crawled by, I became stronger than ever in my resolve to give up my life of crime but not once did I think of giving up fighting. This whole episode taught me something I already believed – that the pen really is mightier than the sword.

And we were going to have some fun proving it. But first the politics of the world was about to explode. There's no protection in prison from that. Some prisoners were about to discover this the hard way.

20

ALL FALL DOWN

11 September 2001

'Fuck sake!'

'Paul, come here. Quick.'

'What?' I had just left the gym with Brendan and Darren. Brendan was one of the fittest guys I knew and Darren was quick on his feet and gave anyone, me included, a right hard time on the badminton court. All I wanted was a cold drink and shower.

'Come and see this on the telly.'

'Aye, give us a minute.' Just then two cons ran past us. Running isn't allowed inside the jail, punishable big time and these guys knew that fine well. It must be important and they were heading for the TV room. I scampered after them.

'C'mere and watch this,' croaked Lance Gray. 'There's been a big fucking air crash.'

On the large TV screen, an aeroplane seemed to be going in slow motion. Gliding over skyscrapers, one wing gently swaying up, then the other, the pilot struggling to keep it on course – a crazy course that was bound to fail. He was just too close to the buildings. The commentator was hardly saying a word. It was as if he was shocked, stunned into silence. It was the same atmosphere in that room in that jail. Why should it be different for cons?

'He's going to fucking . . .' I started.

'Just watch, man, just watch,' it was big Grant Turnbull watching it for the second time.

There it went slap, bang, crash into the tower. In the room all that could be heard was the low, almost mournful words of the commentator.

'Some fucking accident,' someone said, breaking the silence.

'There must be hundreds dead in there.'

'Thousands – that's one of the highest buildings in the world.'

'Yeah?'

'Poor buggers working away, like just another day, and then that.'

'Fuck sake.'

'And the passengers on the flight just fucking imagine it.'

'Sitting there having a wee drink and reading a book when a big building suddenly appears.'

'Do you think they would've seen it? I mean you're travelling fast on a plane.'

'Christ. Let's hope they didn't. Just lights out, eh? Poor fuckers.'

The room was full of heavy-duty players. Most of these guys had handed out some major punishment in their time without hesitation or remorse. Now here we were stunned by the enormity of all the deaths of those ordinary people – accidental deaths they thought.

I stood quietly, transfixed by the TV screen and thought – thought of me in that prison and Sandra, Dean, my mum, young Paul and my pals outside. How I hated not being able to be there for them. You really don't know the minute you and yours are going to be taken and, a lot of the time, there is sod all you could do about it. Still I'd rather be out there with them and for them. That bloody plane and tower had reawakened all my fears for the people I cared about. Then I saw it.

At first I thought they were showing the plane crash from a different angle. Then I spotted the reeking damage to the other tower and heard the words coming from the TV set.

'WATCH!' I roared at the room, drawing the others away from the excited prattling.

'What?'

'There's another plane.'

'No fucking way?'

'Watch.'

As the second slow-motion crash of the day happened, no one said a bloody word. Most of us stood and watched and, like the rest of the world, tried to comprehend. Attempted to take it all in. We had to understand something before we could begin to make sense of it all. Right there and then, I doubted if there was much sense to be made. It was unreal, mad.

'That was deliberate then,' I said quietly, after what seemed like an age, and it was met with nods from around the room.

'Who would be mad enough?' someone asked.

'Sshh,' someone demanded.

From the TV, a panicky, fearful voice told us that another passenger plane had been reported on its way to the Pentagon. That US fighter jets were tying to intercept it. It wasn't a one-off outrageous incident but an all-out attack. How the hell could the US cope without its centre of operations? Who the fuck had the balls to attack the biggest state in the world? And why?

'They're saying Osama Bin Laden's behind it,' someone said. 'Who the fuck's he?'

I looked around the room. There was Brendan Quinn, bank robber and escape artiste extraordinaire. His family had been wrongly accused of having links to terrorist groups in Ireland. The security forces don't drop these suspicions even if they can't prove them.

'You all right, Brendan?' I asked and, for once, he didn't look well.

'Pheeew,' he sighed, 'I'm fretting for my folks.'

I turned and looked at Darren, the Real IRA bomber, a young man who was fighting a political fight he believed in. His face was as grim as death. Worse even than Brendan's.

'What? About this?' I stuck my thumb in the direction of the TV showing reruns of the planes crashing into the towers.

'Aye, life's not going to be the same ever again,' mumbled Darren. 'We're fucked.'

Suddenly I realised that everyone suspected of links with terrorist organisations was going to be thumped. No one could commit that kind of atrocity against the biggest power the world has ever known and expect to get off with it. First it would be the politicals and next the street players.

There would be no problem now in the cops and security services getting approval to bug phones, carry guns on raids, shoot first and ask questions later. All of that already happened, of course – it would just get easier, more common. Street players were in the shit. And maybe ex-street players too. Maybe me.

A few feet from Brendan, two black guys stood alone hardly talking to each other and not to anyone else. They looked the most shocked of all of us. Maybe they had people in New York was my first naive thought. Then I caught a smattering of some bloke on the TV, '. . . Osama Bin Laden . . . Muslim . . . worldwide terror organisation . . .'

Now I understood. Our two black friends were committed Muslims and political. Trouble was brewing for them.

21

THE HOLY WAR

There was no racial problem in Frankland Prison till 11 September 2001. There were one or two different groups and some had their own ways but everyone tolerated everyone else, gave them space. If 9/11 was going to bring changes all over the globe, overnight it brought hatred and violence to my world of that time. It was true of any prison in the country. Those dungeons are already volatile tinderboxes just looking for an excuse to go off. Now the politicians gave the cons a big hint – a religious war. The jails ran red with blood.

Maybe it was my upbringing in Glasgow with its tense sectarian balance. I'd grown up being friends with and working with people who took their religion more seriously than me. Very seriously – deadly seriously in some cases.

The place I went to secondary school, Royston, had once been called The Garngad. Almost entirely Roman Catholic, it had its bloody street battles with Protestants and its holy day marches celebrating old victories. Lest anyone doubted this was also political, for decades, the first thing you saw entering the area was enormous graffiti declaring, 'YOU ARE NOW ENTERING FREE GARNGAD'. The IRA would have been delighted. Protestant Loyalists were organised just as well – if not more so. Street players I knew were often involved at the highest levels – like The Licensee's brother-in-law, Snadz Adams, who was an honorary colonel of the UDA for years.

He wasn't unusual. Street razor gangs, housing schemes, pubs, clubs and a whole heap more were often identified with one side or another. In Glasgow, you learned to step beyond those divisions or run the chance of becoming bitter. I stepped beyond them. Others in the jail fell into the trap.

'There's a bad smell of shite, isn't there?' one English con asked another who was standing in a corridor of the jail.

'It's really stinking rotten, man,' replied his mate holding his nose and screwing up his face.

'I think it's close by as well.'

'Very close.'

'You haven't shit yourself have you?' He was addressing the con responsible for collecting the rubbish and taking it outside to the garbage dump. A small, quiet man and old for the jail, he was a well-liked character and entirely inoffensive. A good laugh, he was helpful and someone who created no problems. He was also black and a Muslim.

'He's speaking to you, Mustapha,' one of the cons said as he grabbed the small man by the collar.

'No . . . no . . . no shit myself,' the cleaner protested holding up one hand, his head cowering, anticipating a blow.

'Prove it, you black bastard.'

'No . . . no . . . no shit myself,' the terrified man repeated.

'Maybe we should have a look, eh?' And the two much larger, younger cons started tugging at the guy's top, yanking at his trousers, laughing while all the time their victim was squealing.

'Got something to hide, Mustapha?' One grabbed his arms while the other busied himself with roughly tugging at the struggling man's trousers. An insult to anyone, this debagging would mean a huge dishonour to the devout Muslim.

'Just as I thought,' growled one of the attackers, 'what a smell of shite.'

The old man's trousers lay around his ankles and he was sniffling and crying, his arms wrapped round his torso as if comforting himself.

'What the fuck are you two playing at?' I had just chanced upon the scene and asked a stupid question. It was immediately obvious they had been tormenting the old bloke.

'What's it to you? He's nothing but a murdering Muslim bastard,' said the bigger of the pair.

'Just leave him be – that's what it means to me,' I replied, squaring up. I knew the guy in question and he was handy in a battle. Here was me a few months from release yet running the risk of a square-go and getting into trouble with the screws – exactly what I'd been trying to avoid. But bullying I can't stand.

'So what?' the big guy demanded. 'What the fuck are you going to do about it?'

'If you don't stop, I'm going to fucking stop you – my way, you arsehole.' Here we go I thought and I braced myself, looked around for an improvised weapon and grabbed the old boy's long-handled wooden brush – not much but it would have to do. The two guys moved in, I lifted the brush and then I heard a voice.

'Y'all right, Paul?' It was Everton Salmon and a group of the Yardies, making their way to the kitchen to prepare their evening meal.

'Never better,' I replied, keeping my eyes on the two bears. One step closer and I'd have to go for them but I could see fear in their eyes as they clocked the Yardie crew behind me. No one in their right mind would want to tackle that lot.

'A waste of time anyway,' said the bigger of the pair, starting to retreat but slowly.

'Wouldn't dirty my hands with the blood and shit on him,' said the other.

'In fact,' the bigger of the two said, as he grabbed one of the black bags the old bloke had been collecting the rubbish in, 'he's nothing but an Osama.' He dumped the contents of the bag all over the floor. The pair were backing off all the time but facing us.

'Fucking right,' said the other grabbing and emptying another bag. 'Nothing but an Osama Bin Liner.' And they were off, laughing as they strode away.

It was one day after 9/11 and already the trouble had kicked off. The poor old boy got stuck with the nickname Osama Bin Liner from then on in. Even those who didn't blame every Muslim for the tragedy used the name, thinking it was funny – no more than that and no offence intended. Some of his Muslim brothers even started using it. The old boy didn't like it, of course, but that's prison life for you.

A couple of days later in the exercise yard, two hefty Geordies started beating up this black guy. If you have to settle any scores, exercise time is a bloody stupid time to do it since so many screws are watching you. In this case, there was one no more than six feet away.

'Muslim cunt . . .'

'Woman killer . . .'

'Terrorist fucker,' the Geordies grunted as they lathered into him. It didn't last long – most street fights don't – but what a mess they made of him. These were big men. While the violence lasted, the watching screw didn't budge or raise the alarm. When the target lay mangled on the ground and the Geordies panted and puffed over him, only managing the occasional boot into his face and guts, the screw strolled over.

'Have you finished?' he asked and the two turned and slunk away.

The bloke wasn't even a Muslim as it turned out. He was just black though some of his pals were devout. The irony is that he was serving time for the same type of conviction as his attackers – heroin trafficking – and both sets were claiming that they'd been set up by an agent provocateur put in by Customs and Excise. It's the type of common cause that brings prisoners together. But 9/11 and the chest-beating of the warmongers had ruined all of that. Now they were enemies, if not religious then certainly racial. Or was it just politics?

Like the guard who watched the two Geordies hospitalise the black guy, most of the screws joined some of the white cons in a brand-new hatred of all the Muslim prisoners. Life for them would never be the same. Where could they hide? They were locked in, trapped with those who hated them. If the world had got more dangerous on the outside, it had just become more tortuous in the inside. It's a world I wanted no part of – ever again.

Yet life for me was about to change as well – for the better as my release date came ever closer. I was about to embark on a new life, a straight life, where I never wanted to leave my kids and my loved ones ever again – at least not to rot in the pokey.

But would the blue coats let me?

22

FREEDOM DAY

21 January 2002

The big dog stared up at me with cold eyes. Was he looking at a target? Begging me to move too quickly so he could spring and snap? We were moving slowly through Frankland Prison – me, three screws and the big dog tethered on a lead but ready for action at the most trivial excuse. I wanted to get to that gate as soon as possible but no way was I hurrying. The dog's pace would suit me just fine.

It was early in the morning, still night really. The rest of the prison slept on, oblivious to this final procession that would end with my freedom. Why so early? Did they not want the cons to see one of their own getting out? Was it to stop anyone witnessing the screws relinquishing power?

At each gate, the delay was agonising. The lead screw would call ahead, checking that the next stage was ready for us. Then he would take his time before sending the electronic gate slowly swishing open. There was plenty of room to have stepped through when the gate was halfway on its journey – but no, no. As the gate clicked into the fully open position, our weird wee group moved forward, went through and then waited – waited till the gate closed behind us. Modern security or not, there's a golden rule in all jails that's as old as all jails – never have more than one gate open at any time. Open one, step through, close it. Proceed to the next, open that, step through, close it. It all makes sense when you have someone looking at twenty-five years inside ahead of him but this was my freedom

91

day. What was I going to do? Make a break for it?

If I had wanted to do that, it would have been a long time before. Like when I tested positive for drugs. It was no big deal but it makes you feel that the system has you by the balls and won't let go. Ever since the Home Office introduced mandatory drugs tests, prisoners have taken to smack in large numbers. By drinking gallons of water and pissing it out all night you can wash the heroin out of your system in hours whereas with dope it's there for weeks. It's now well established that all British prisons have major heroin problems and much of it is caused by those tests. But I'd have no truck with smack. Good move? In a funny way, it was my downfall.

Prisoners in Frankland would often group together to buy food and cook meals. It meant you had the variety of what everyone was good at and most days your grub was cooked for you as long as you took your turn. One day, this guy was making a huge tureen of curry for about twenty of us. He'd made it up early in the day and was letting it simmer for a few hours like all good curry makers. Most of the time, he'd get on with his other business and, now and then, he'd pop back to the kitchen to check on his pot. Noticing this, some smart alec decided to give us all a wee secret treat and dumped a load of dope in the grub. That night we all had seconds of the curry and congratulated the cook. It was very tasty indeed as you can imagine.

Next day, there was a random drugs test and every one of us came up positive. We all loudly protested our innocence, of course, and, for once, we all meant it. As cons, we were well used to the accuracy of forensic tests. This one was no different. It took us only a few days to find the joker and have him confess – some lark. Certain guys would spend more time in pokey because of his antics. Not good. Me? I now had a black mark against my name. The biggest risk I'd taken with substances was to make a few gallons of jail hooch from time to time. Hooch is powerful stuff but it's booze and not seen as nearly so serious as drugs by the prison system.

Now I had a drugs record so you'd think I'd learn a lesson – no chance. Christmas in the nick is more relaxed all round. The staff and the prisoners try and put tensions aside and have a few days off from the usual rigmarole. It's also a lonely time away from families and no one wants to add grief to that. We stick together, have a laugh and relax.

On Christmas Eve 2000, there had been a particularly mellow atmosphere in Frankland. I passed by a cell where a few friendly faces were sharing a joint.

'Happy Christmas, Paul,' shouted the man with the J.

'And the same to you,' I said, going in to the cell and shaking hands. It was full of the Yardies I'd had the dispute with over the kitchen facilities on my first day. 'I'd give you a drink, lads,' I joked, knowing that none of them touched the stuff, 'but we're saving the next consignment of hooch till tomorrow and the Christmas dinner.'

'Terrible stuff,' said one, meaning it. 'You should stick with this.' The guy blew a fat smoke ring and passed me the joint. It's nice to be nice. I took one drag and passed it on. 'This is for you, Paul,' he said, as he handed me a fuck-off stash of powerful skunk, 'from all of us.'

I could tell it was good gear with my eyes closed – it smelled even before it was cooked up. The skunk was top class and a very generous gift any time, never mind in jail. There were still some rumblings between me and a few of the Yardies and I took the gift as a peace offering and right away resolved never to use their cooker again.

But that skunk was burning a hole in my discipline. I just couldn't resist it and went back to my cell for a blast – just the one and a small one at that. It was Christmas, after all. I'd hardly stubbed out the joint when a patrol came round. Sure enough the sniffer dog sat down at my door. That was me in the shit then.

Next day I got drugs-tested again – positive of course. It's the two-strikes-and-you're-out mentality. That was me with an official drugs problem now. A plateful of curry and one joint and I'm carrying the same status as a junkie or crackhead.

Early parole isn't something guys like me get but I'd applied for it anyway just to prove that point to myself and see what reason the Parole Board would give for refusal. I'd taken every class, every human-growth session, every discussion group they had asked me to do. Yet, of course, I was knocked back for early release. Reason? I had a drug problem apparently.

That curry and the Christmas drag meant I had to take addiction management classes in the jail and, when released, I would be obliged to follow through with similar efforts. If I refused or skipped sessions, my release would be delayed and later I could be recalled to prison. Meantime, major smackheads were serving long sentences without being caught out on one test. They were wrecking their lives, of course, but no one was picking up on their problem. None of it made sense and it had angered me for a long while but, now that I was about to be free, I didn't care. I'd go to any bloody therapy they asked me to – just let me out.

Finally, in Frankland, on my freedom day, our procession reached that gate, the one I thought of as liberty. Stepping through there, I'd enter the reception area, a kind of no-man's-land, leaving the real prison behind me. There I'd shower and shave. Spray on eau de toilette and dress in the full outfit of new clothes from suit right down to boxers and socks that had been delivered to the jail the night before. I was going out of there looking good and feeling good – a damn sight better than how I'd been brought into the place.

At that liberty gate they took the longest of all. No surprise there. I looked down at the big dog and smiled. He didn't smile back. Two feet in front of me, the gate remained firmly shut. The bastards were taking their time, making me sweat out long, unnecessary seconds in that place. I knew they would. That was OK by me. As of that day, I had all the time in the world. I smiled again at the big dog, staring him straight in the eyes, daring him to blink. I swear he did as the gate whished open but we'll call it a draw, Towser, OK?

'There's a fucking mob out there, Paul,' the gruff but friendly reception screw had said after I got cleaned up and changed. 'You'd think somebody important was turning up, eh?' He smiled, warmly.

The mob he was referring to was the media. It wasn't yet seven o'clock and most had been there for hours. I'd find out later that *The Sun* had had two guys posted there all night. And a certain group we won't name to save their blushes had a film man outside Durham Prison – the wrong bloody jail – all night. But most had got it right and were present and correct. I knew that Anna Smith, the *Daily Record* woman who had written that spoiler of a feature that resulted in Reg and me being banned from communicating, would be there. Reg had received an interesting phone call just a few days earlier offering £10,000 for the first pic of me leaving jail. What was the upper limit? £20,000? £30,000? More? For a fucking snapshot of me in a suit?

When Reg reminded Anna there was a dispute between the publisher of *The Ferris Conspiracy* and the *Record*, she consulted Peter Cox, the editor, and agreed a contract in writing, giving editorial approval to us and more money. They even confirmed it by fax. Not that we ever considered making a deal with Cox. On past performance, he was obviously capable of agreeing to everything then putting it in his own words and calling the article 'The Devil Returns' or something. We don't work with people who stab us in the back but we were astounded by the gall of the bastard – and I thought I was meant to be the bad guy.

'That'll be you, Ferris.' It was the gruff-voiced, pleasant reception screw in Frankland again. 'Be sure to be good now and if you can't be good be very fucking careful.'

The three guards and the unsmiling dog walked me to the main gate. Again there was hesitation – just there at the wrong side of the wall from freedom. Finally, the gate was opened and the screws drew back. Here we go.

I stepped into a no-go zone. The screws had kept all the press back beyond a stretch of grass and the short entry road to the jail. 'Prison property. Security reasons,' they'd growled, ordering the journalists and photographers back in the early hours of the morning.

Reg was there somewhere and I scanned the group as I walked straight at them. The night before, the prison staff had said they'd let him park his car on the entry road so we could avoid the scramble but, when it came to it, he was banned too. It was as if the jail wanted to exert their authority one last time.

'Good morning, ladies and gentlemen,' I said, as they gathered round me with their Dictaphones and cameras. 'Thank you for being here. I'm now going home to be with my family and to continue writing more books,' I said, staring to my left where the bold Anna Smith was standing, 'with my co-author, Reg McKay. I'm now going straight and straight back home. Thank you.'

As I headed towards a revving car nearby which had Reg at the wheel, they followed, calling out, 'Paul. Just one photo, Paul.'

'Will you be seeing Billy, Paul?'

'Are there celebrations planned for tonight?'

Ignoring them all, I jumped into the passenger seat and, as soon as I slammed the door, Reg sped off. By the time we reached the first roundabout, some of the media were already on our tail. Reg hadn't been the only one with the engine running.

The press weren't going to leave me in peace but would they be the only ones hounding me?

23

REUNION
January 2002

'I'll drive if you want me to,' I said to Reg several times as we drove from Durham to Glasgow.

'No fucking chance, Paul,' he replied for the umpteenth time. 'We're giving the cops no reason to stop you today.' He was right, of course – they would have loved to do that if only to cause me some grief. Then there would be a phone call to the newspapers and an embarrassing headline the next day. But driving is one of my pleasures, always has been, and a pleasure I missed while I was locked up. Still we breezed gently up the road at a steady seventy miles an hour. 'Besides, Paul, you have the rest of your life ahead of you. What's the rush?'

We were heading to Glasgow city centre and a rendezvous at the Arthouse Hotel on Bath Street. Knowing that some of the media would have got ahead of us, worked out where we were going and could be waiting at any of the main motorway exits, we cut off early and took a wee detour through the east end of the city. It was a meander through my past.

Mount Vernon and Thomas McGraw – The Licensee's mansion with his wife's name over the door. Everyone knew her as 'The Jeweller' because of her fondness for gold but he called her Mags. When he had bought the place, The Licensee had every type of security device imaginable installed. As it happened, BarL Prison was carrying out some security upgrading at the same time and a load of the gear ended up at his place.

Baillieston – where I lived for a while. Happy days before I lost my pals, Bobby and Joe.

Further back, McGraw's pub, The Caravel, razed to the ground one night – not a brick was left – when word was out the cops were going to carry out a forensic search in connection with Bobby and Joe's murders.

Parkhead – the home of my football team, Celtic. In the shadow of the stadium, a guy called Tank McGuinness was beaten to death. Officially, it was a fall-out between him and his pal 'Gypsy' John Winning. I reckoned it was a hit paid for by Arthur Thompson, The Godfather, to clear the way for evidence to get his old pal, Paddy Meehan, out of jail for a murder he didn't commit.

The Cottage Bar – a sad one, where the bodies of my two mates, Bobby Glover and Joe Hanlon, were found dumped in Joe's car.

Off to the right, Blackhill – where I was born and raised. A wild place of street gangs, bombproof cop shop and unmarked meat wagons full of rozzers brutalising the locals.

Just off to the left, the old High Court – where I emerged after fifty-four days on trial for the murder of Fatboy – not guilty on all charges – to stare out at a sea of cheering bodies sweeping down Glasgow Green. The last phase in my life had started that day in 1992. Now I was about to enter another phase. I was going straight.

We had made an agreement with the *News of the World* to give them exclusive coverage of my release. There was no money in this. After the deal with the *Daily Record* had gone belly up, the *News of the Screws* – no prison pun intended – had serialised *The Ferris Conspiracy* and done well with it. What I mean is that they covered the book straight – no stabbing in the back, no breach of agreement and they printed the words just as they were written. To a street player like me, used to newspapers making up any old thing they want about me, that reliability was worth diamonds.

Given that I was released on a Monday and the paper went on sale on the following Sunday, they wanted to hide me for a week so that their exclusive features couldn't be spoiled. My spell in hiding was going to start at the Arthouse Hotel. Walking in there with its modern art deco style, I felt displaced, a bit weird. The feeling wouldn't last long – I knew that from experience – but what else was I to expect when I'd spent years in prisons and had left only a few hours earlier?

Up in the room they'd booked under a different name, I knew I'd meet David Leslie, the journalist, and a couple of photographers. David would chatter and ask all sorts of questions while the snappers would be busy around us. That prospect wasn't fazing me at all. What I was excited about was meeting my older brother Billy for the first time as free adult men.

According to the newspaper headlines, Billy was a murderer and that was true but to simply say that and leave it there does no justice to the situation. Billy had been in jail and he had moved south to England to get himself away from Glasgow and a probable life of crime. Although he had only been out of prison for a few weeks, he robbed a post office and ended up in jail again. While he was in the clink, his wife had had affairs and was pregnant. When he got out, he knew they were finished but he was still hurting, still raw. When he was out for a drink with a couple of pals in Corby, two young blokes across the bar started slagging Billy off and bad-mouthing his estranged wife in loud voices. Billy was all mixed up – well, who wouldn't be? – and he was getting angrier by the minute.

Unable to take their taunts any longer, he crossed the bar and quietly challenged the two guys. They laughed and spoke even louder. That was it – fight on. It was Billy against them – one against two. Billy had been out for a social night, not looking for trouble so he wasn't carrying a chib. They were. It was a long and bloody battle. Eventually, Billy took the knife off one of the men and gave him some of his own medicine back. The blade went an inch too far into the wrong place and the bloke died.

Murder? Of course it was. Crime of passion? Of course it was. Does that excuse it? No. That's not my purpose. It explains it a bit more, that's all.

If Billy had killed in a country like France where crimes of passion are recognised and treated with some understanding, he might have been jailed for four years tops, if that. As it was, in England, murder was simply murder and he got life. He was only a young man at the time but life is exactly what it almost meant for my brother.

Billy Ferris refused to accept the jail. He was forever getting into scrapes and being sent to solitary confinement and, time after time, he had more years added to his sentence for deeds he committed in pokey. One time, during a visit to our old man who was very ill and knew he was dying, Billy escaped – with the help of a wee stash of cash from our da. It was our father's dying gift to his oldest boy – a taste of a bit of freedom. He took full advantage of the opportunity for about a year, living in Blackpool.

Billy's shenanigans and the fact that I – the man they blamed for every crime everywhere – was his brother combined to encourage the authorities to hold him inside for as long as they could. They certainly didn't want two Ferris brothers free at the same time. He could've been out after twelve years, maybe less. In fact, he served twenty-four, almost twenty-five, years. Now we were about to meet for the first time as free adults.

'There he is – the man who'll set Glasgow on fire!' This was accompanied by a big, wicked grin from Billy and a big hug from us both.

'Have you put on a bit of a belly?' I asked, leaning back, taking the piss. Billy looked fit, tanned and healthy.

In spite of just coming from a place where enforced close association with others is one of the punishments, I was a bit embarrassed to be meeting like this in front of strangers. The *News of the Screws* had been given the wrong room – a single one where there was not enough space to swing a short-tailed, earless moggy. It was bloody crowded in there.

'Fucking belly! Fit as a fiddle, man!' he said and, just to prove it, he gave me a bear hug. Strong man is Billy – just as well I love him.

The greeting over, we settled down to a drink. The two photographers got busy and David Leslie, the journalist, just chatted, saying we'd have plenty of time during the rest of the week but maybe a few questions on the brothers getting together for the first time?

'Some say that with you and Billy together at last, you'll now take over organised crime in Scotland?' David asked at one point.

'That's right,' roared Billy, 'Ferris & Ferris.'

I realised Billy had been waiting for me for some time in that room and had been helping himself to a steady supply of booze, courtesy of the *News of the World*. 'There'll be some frightened people in this city tonight,' I offered calmly.

'Fucking right,' added Billy, slapping me on the back.

'But the only ones who need be scared are those corrupt individuals who deal with the police and trade innocent people for convictions just to get themselves a license to commit crime.'

'Do you mean Thomas McGraw, The Licensee?' asked David.

'Oh, I think he'll be sure to be locked up in his house long before dark tonight.' Loud laugh from Billy. 'But I mean them all and I mean to prove that the pen is a scary weapon. I'm going to write books – maybe make films. I'm going straight. But that doesn't mean I've forgotten the corrupt individuals who inhabit this city or the cops who trade with them – far from it.'

As we chatted, Billy reached out every now and then and touched my shoulder, my head, my neck. I turned and caught tears in his eyes. My big brother, the hard man, was crying. Mourning maybe all those years that he lost – that we lost. We were going to have to get to know each other all over again. I prayed we'd be given the time.

But freedom day wasn't over. We had people to collect and places to go – if we could avoid the obstacles.

24

THE GETAWAY DRIVER

When a prisoner is released on licence to live in Scotland, they are supervised for a period by specialist social workers. I was obliged to clock in with mine that day. Reg had agreed to come in with me and drove us the few blocks to the meeting. In the short distance between the car and the office, three people, including a *Big Issue* seller, came up to shake my hand. This was new.

Inside, the only other people in the waiting room were a young couple. Both addressed me by my name and talked about my first book. This was definitely new.

While I was in seeing my social worker, a female member of staff came out and said hello to Reg. He'd been Director of Social Work in Scotland for an organisation called NCH. One of the plans he'd worked on while there was to take over some of the criminal justice services in Glasgow. Now this woman was telling him that it had happened. Many people from his old wage-slavery days think that, because he now writes about true crime, Reg has somehow crossed the line – he has turned traitor and is working for the other side. Not this woman. She was very welcoming indeed.

We left that office two very happy men. This had been a good day and it was about to get better – we had to fetch Sandra. First, we had to stop off back at the hotel. Driving up, we spotted a posse of reporters and photographers at the front door. A quick call to David and it was agreed that one of the *News of the World*'s photographers,

Brian Anderson, would meet us at an agreed place and drive me to get Sandra. Then Reg would breeze back into the hotel, giving the scavenging journalists the impression that I was still there. Meantime, Brian would drive us to another hotel miles away in the country where we were all to stay that night. Sounded like a plan.

Belling ahead to Sandra, we found that, sure enough, a group of reporters had set up camp out front since dawn. No problem. She slipped out the back door, stepped over a low fence, walked a short block and met us there. As Brian drove through the busy city streets and I sat in the back with Sandra, holding her hand, for the first time that day I felt truly relaxed, free.

Brian's car was a VW Golf and, to be blunt, the poor motor was one step away from the scrap yard. 'Sorry about the state of the car,' said Brian as if reading my thoughts.

'This car is perfect,' I told him genuinely. 'The cops and the press will think I'm swanning about in a big limo.'

'Instead, you're in my wee fucked-up Golf,' laughed Brian. 'I hadn't thought of that.'

'Bet we could drive straight past the stupid bastards and they wouldn't spot us.' Just then, I saw a cop car in the distance and watched till it indicated and turned off left. Old habits die hard and that one will be with me till the day I finally sign out.

Brian was just an ordinary street boy like me who happened to take pictures. Obviously he was good at it as well – the *News of the Screws* doesn't hire failures. I liked him instantly.

'Shit, there's another one,' cursed Brian.

'What?'

'That cop car.'

I'd noticed the car but that was me. Why was this photographer keeping an eagle eye out for them?

'Paul, there's something I should've told you.'

I took a deep breath and sighed the words melodramatically, 'Oh, no.'

'Oh, aye. The motor isn't road taxed.'

I laughed – big-time criminal, eh?

'Nor insured.'

Me driving about in an uninsured car? That'll be a first – not.

'And there's a warrant out for my arrest.' He started rambling on about road-traffic charges and scrapes he got into when he took uninvited snaps of big-time stars when they least wanted him to and I could see his face had gone deep red as if he thought he'd really fucked up. 'It's just they'll have this registration number and they'll be looking . . .'

'Brian, it's perfect,' I interrupted.

'Perfect?'

'Here's me in the back, the man the cops would hang if they could. Sandra, who they think is in cahoots with whatever badness I'm up to even though that's always been crap. Then there's you.'

'Aye, me.'

'Straight Joe photographer for one of the country's biggest newspapers – just doing your job. And you're the guy they could arrest.' I was sniggering away to myself but Brian wasn't catching my mood.

'I'm sorry, Paul.'

'Sorry what for? This is exactly the way it should be. I feel right back at home.'

He laughed.

'But I'll tell you something, Brian.'

'What?'

'As a getaway driver, you make a great photographer.'

Good to be home. But I was soon to discover that some things hadn't changed while others had. This wasn't going to be so easy.

25

OLD ENEMIES AND NEW PALS

The *News of the World* was absolutely serious about keeping me away from other media folk. After a couple of nights in that swanky country hotel, my hack minders drove Sandra and me to pick up my boy, Dean, and we headed south. As we drove over the border and into England, it felt as if I was going back the way – towards jail. Spooky.

The next hotel was more child friendly than the first one had been and, believe me, with young Dean, they needed to be very child friendly. He was four years old, bright, energetic and as curious as hell – a handful, in other words, and exactly how my old dear describes me at that same age.

After the child-free routine of jail, looking after Dean was exhausting – delicious but knackering. One night Reg and the *News of the Screws* team gave Sandra and me some time off to have dinner on our own. When we joined them three hours later, they all looked frazzled and worn out – well, that's my boy for you.

Dean and I were going to have to get to know each other but there were other things I'd have to learn that I didn't even know about. Small things, like one-arm bandits, had all changed. The price of booze had certainly swollen – as had the amount of choice. I couldn't believe you got vodka and mixers sold in one bottle in almost every flavour under the sun. It simply didn't make sense to me. So I tried a few and then it made sense – at least it did when I sobered up.

One morning, I woke early. As Sandra slept on, I realised we were running low on cigarettes. A bit hung-over, I decided to go to a garage across the road to get some fresh air and see if Irn-Bru had travelled south of the border yet. While I was at it, I decided to take Sandra's pay-as-you-go mobile phone with me and get the credit topped up – it had been a busy few days on the phones. I was well used to mobile phones before doing jail time – they were, in fact, an important tool of my trade and had been used by the cops to track me on my last charges – but pay-as-you-go? Now that was new to me.

Deciding to take a short-cut, I found myself confronted by a high fence and a six-lane road – not smart but I couldn't be bothered going all the way back. As I struggled over the high fence and dodged the speeding cars, I could see the bored petrol attendant watching me from his kiosk. 'Who the fuck is this madman?' he must have been asking himself. I know the feeling.

'And a top-up for this phone, please,' I asked politely, once I'd gathered together the rest of my goods.

'What network?' he asked.

'Oh, any one will do,' I replied not having a bloody clue what he was going on about.

As he eyed me up, I could see I was confirming his earlier suspicions. 'No, mate,' he sighed, 'you can get Vodafone, Orange . . .' and he reeled of a list of names that might have been a foreign language to me.

I recognised one. 'Vodafone will do,' I instructed him.

He was shaking his head as he said, 'A particular SIM card is tied to a particular service.' There was some hesitation as he watched me carefully. 'Don't you know which it is?'

'Tell you what,' I decided, 'I'll leave it just now. There's some juice left in it yet.'

The big-time gangster who, they said, was going to take over the streets of Glasgow, and I couldn't top up a fucking mobile phone. Thank God that embarrassment had happened in front of an anonymous service station attendant in the north-west of England rather than his equivalent in Glasgow. Up there, one phone call to

106

the tabloids and it would've made a headline. Not cool. But at least I got the Irn-Bru – result!

On the same day of that first week, Reg got two particularly interesting phone calls via our publisher of the time. The first said *The Daily Telegraph* wanted us to write a weekly column.

'What do you think?' I asked him.

'Well, right-wing newspaper but with liberal licence for more creative stuff . . .'

'What?'

'Write what you want, in other words. Bang up our street.'

'Great,' I replied, knowing we could have a lot of laughs.

'Good on crime as well,' he added.

'Really? Even better.'

The second call wasn't so easy.

'This is a hard one, Paul,' Reg said with a smirk.

What the fuck was he coming out with now? 'Go on.'

'Richard and Judy want you on their show.'

I just laughed and so did he. 'Reg . . .'

'I know, I know,' he butted in, 'but they have big viewing figures just now and, if we manage it right . . .'

'We could give them both barrels.'

'To more people in one half-hour sitting than any book that was in the best-seller list for years.'

He knew I meant exposing bent cops and flesh-trading gangsters. 'And now you're free to name names,' he said.

'We'll do it. Right?'

'Abso-fucking-lutely.'

Even as I agreed, I blushed red hot inside. Guys like Brendan, Darren and my Yardie pals back at Frankland would slaughter me for appearing on something like the *Richard and Judy* show – unless, of course, I had my say. But it's not so easy to do that when you're working with these media types. I knew from past experience how they promised you one thing and then just delivered what they wanted to. I didn't have to fret for long.

In Scotland, the publisher had enthusiastically told the press about both approaches. Next day, the newspaper headlines were full of what a disgrace it was that a gangster like me was being given airtime. *Richard and Judy* grabbed the headlines rather than the *Telegraph* – well, papers weren't going to write about another newspaper, were they? The bloody outcry ran on for days and had the expected result. *Richard and Judy* and the *Telegraph* both pulled out.

'No loss there,' I said to Reg later. 'We don't want to work with anyone who lacks the balls to let us do it our way.'

He nodded quietly. 'True,' he said with another nod and then he added, 'but those fucking interfering bastards, Paul – who do they fucking think they are? The pricks . . .' and he was off on one.

But he was dead right about the media – if you let them run all over you, they will. You can't tackle them by doing nothing or ignoring them. You have to engage with them, meet with them or, better still, become part of them but on your own terms.

The media isn't the only form of communication though. Shortly after my release, I travelled down to Dumfries with a pal. He was supplying stewards to work on the doors of pubs and clubs and this owner had asked for his help with a wee problem. It was the usual – a few big guys coming in drunk and starting off in the club – and it was bad for business. I'd just gone along for the ride and a night out but, of course, did the bad boys not just turn up that night? As we were sitting having a drink, minding our own business, the worried owner came over to us and said the gang was at the door and his bouncers couldn't hold them back – would we have a word? Fuck it, we'd have a word all right.

My pal is my height if not smaller – we were wee, in other words. The team must have been farmers' sons because they were fucking huge and brick shithouses didn't come close. The way to deal with this scene is quietly and politely but assertively. The idea is to use diplomacy and lots of eye contact to diffuse the situation. So that's what we did although we had to crane our necks back to look up into their mugs. The idea of two small guys coming to have words with them spooked most of the guys and they started to back off but one of them was too pissed and was well up for some aggro. As his mates pulled him back, I just kept walking towards him, smiling and talking calmly. Eventually, he must have thought I was going to chib him or something – the Glasgow accent has that effect – and, all of a sudden, he was terrified.

'Touch me and you're in big trouble, pal,' he bawled.

'How's that?' I asked.

'I'm a mate of Paul Ferris.'

'That's good,' I replied trying to keep a straight face. 'Give him my regards when you next see him.'

'And who the fuck are you, like?' he growled, regaining some confidence as I just kept on smiling.

'Oh, you stupid cunt,' his minder mate groaned, suddenly recognising me. He grabbed his mate and slapped him hard. 'You stupid fucking prick,' he said.

As he hurriedly pulled the bloke away, we could hear him protest, 'What? What the fuck have I done now?'

If I had a fiver for every mate I'm alleged to have, retirement would have been on the cards years ago.

A couple of weeks later, the local press reported that I was taking over all the pubs and clubs in Dumfries – not good in their view. But I had only been there for a drink and to see a pal. That kind of thing happens to me all the time and it was something I didn't miss in jail. Even innocent visits like that result in media coverage stirring things up by saying that I'm going to take over the world. It might sell papers and I respect that but they could at least keep it real.

It was definitely on my agenda to try and change that for the better. That was for the long term but, back when I was only weeks out of jail, some newspapers had been drumming up hysteria about how I was going to take over Glasgow and settle old scores while I was at it. Of course, the journalists who wrote this stuff didn't talk to me – they just believed every drunk wanting a wee brown envelope for that night's gargle.

The real trouble was that certain other parties were swallowing the headlines – one in particular. And he wanted me in a coffin.

26

THE INVITATION

'We've agreed to clip you, Paul.' He didn't mean trimming my hair or giving me a short back and sides but a bullet in the brain.

'Hope it's going to be worth your while,' I replied straight-faced.

'Aye but we had to negotiate.' The man laughed.

There were two men, both major faces in a team from Glasgow's north side – very handy indeed. If you wanted somebody hit, they would be the very ones to approach – if you could afford them. I had only been free a matter of two months and already life was interesting. Any re-adjusting I had to do to feel free again was all worked out in that first week of freedom.

Thomas McGraw, The Licensee, was a very worried man. Here was a bloke worth at least £30 million, living in a house surrounded by CCTV and sensors, who hired a group of assassins as minders and used them every minute of the day. In spite of that, from the day I walked out of jail, he was rarely seen in public and was always tucked up inside long before sunset. Maybe he had a Dracula complex in reverse? Always a paranoid man, those who did spot McGraw out and about said he was looking drawn, tired. Apparently he wasn't sleeping much. Yet his house dripped with electronic gadgets so sophisticated he could tell when a dog farted two blocks away and had the wherewithal to film it too.

At that time, McGraw had a particular habit and it is one he still has. Every night about 11 p.m., he'd make sure he got the first edition of the next day's tabloids. He reads every single word in them, keeping a special lookout for a mention of anyone he knows and an extra keen eye for a mention of his favourite person – himself. All those headlines talking about me wreaking revenge, settling old scores and taking over all organised crime might have been tosh but, for The Licensee, they meant only one thing – his neck on the block. Very soon after my freedom day, he had decided to act.

'He offered us £50K to clip you to start with, Paul,' said the north Glasgow face as we sat in The Corinthian, a swanky champagne bar with a high, ornate ceiling, in Glasgow's city centre – nice but not my cup of tea. The only good thing about us drinking there was that it used to be a courthouse and all three of us had appeared there on more formal business in the past.

'Is that all I'm worth?' I laughed and they joined in.

'We negotiated him up to £100K,' the other face smiled.

'Tempted?' I asked, with a smirk.

'Not without a deposit,' one of the team said. 'Well, you know what the fucker's like for not parting with his money.'

'Too true,' I agreed. I'd always reckoned McGraw loved his cash more than his wife. And he worshipped his wife, Mags, The Jeweller.

'So, he grumbled and complained a bit,' said one face.

'Asked us if his handshake wasn't good enough,' said the other, smirking fit to burst. We were all enjoying this.

'What did you say?' I asked, laughing.

'No.' And the bloke managed to say it with that deadpan, dead-eyed expression – exactly the one I knew he'd wear. The one I'd seen so often before.

'So, it's like this,' the other guy was digging into his side pocket, 'he gave us ten grand.' He dumped the notes on the table, not giving a monkey's for the middle-class luvvie types who tended to use that bar.

'Nice,' I said.

'Aye, nice for pocket money.'

Was I worried at any time? Was I what? McGraw had only gone and asked top players who happened to be close friends of mine for over twenty years – and not only were they close, they were also old-fashioned like me. They weren't going to take out a mate for any amount of dough. Besides, they didn't need the money.

Hit men don't come and tell you that they've accepted a contract on you. They just pop you one night when you're walking to your car. It's not what you know that should frighten you on the street – it's what you don't know. I've had something like five so-called hit men come and tell me that they've accepted contracts on me. Most often, the customers were Arthur Thompson, The Godfather, or his son, Fatboy. They tell you so there's no ill will then they fuck off out of town to spend whatever loot they've managed to wangle. But the two facing me now weren't going to skip town for anyone and certainly not for The Licensee. What were they going to do?

'We're going to have party,' the bigger of the two smiled, fanning his face with the dosh. 'This should pay for it.'

'Pay for a great party,' I said, smiling too.

'It'll do for starters.'

'So who's invited?' I asked, beginning to warm to the idea.

'A small select group, I think,' the big guy said in his poshest accent before rhyming off the names of a dozen Glasgow faces, all friends of mine and their team. 'Yourself, of course,' he added, 'and anyone else you might want to invite.' It was men only so he didn't mean me to take Sandra.

'How about a guest of honour,' I suggested.

The penny dropped quickly and the big man said, 'It would be fucking rude of us not to invite the guy footing the bill for the shindig wouldn't it?'

'Absolutely.'

That's how Thomas McGraw, The Licensee, came to be invited to a wild champagne night in one of Glasgow's most up-market bars. On the list of invitees the bogus hit man had rattled off, there were at least half a dozen sworn enemies of McGraw. All of them agreed to come along, of course, and, just in case McGraw hadn't cottoned on to the ploy and actually turned up, some of them planned a wee surprise for him.

THE INVITATION

The venue was close to George Square, the impressive centre of Glasgow which is always crowded with folk out for a good time, especially late at night. Close to the square, they parked a van holding certain equipment. The buggers were going to tar and feather The Licensee and leave him chained to one of the statues in George Square.

'That's what happened to collaborators after the Second World War after all,' one of the plotters said to me and I couldn't disagree. It was appropriate punishment.

Of course, the ultra-cautious McGraw smelled a rat and didn't come near. Besides, it was after dark and way past his bedtime. But it was a laugh and a superb night out. It's always great to have a good time with The Licensee picking up the bill. However, if anyone thought he was going to leave it at that, they were very much mistaken. He had more deadly games in mind.

27

GOLF CLUBS AT DAWN

Summer 2002

'I think she needs some medicine,' said Tommy Campbell, fretting over his little daughter, Shannon.

'Och, Tommy, you're too worried. It's just one of those kids' things,' his wife Karen said and with good reason.

Tommy, better known as TC, had just been freed from Shotts Prison weeks before me. He wasn't free for life, only pending his appeal against conviction for murder. He and Joe Steele had been found guilty of murdering six members of the Doyle Family in 1984. In the middle of the night, someone had torched a cupboard (Glaswegians call them cellars) next to a tenement flat's front door. But that cellar was full of old tyres and oil cans and the house went up in seconds, killing six members of the family, including a baby. It was a hellish murder that the cops said was another incident in the ongoing 'Ice-Cream Wars'. The Ice-Cream Wars involved rival teams fighting for control of lucrative territories where they could sell drugs. That was going on for sure but there were other things to consider.

In the early 1980s, no garage in Glasgow was allowed to sell cans of petrol because torching doors was so common. It was the type of threatener that players would use in any set of circumstances, only this time it had gone badly wrong. But Tommy Campbell wouldn't torch a door – that's not his style. If he had an issue with anyone, he'd tackle them face to face. There's no denying that Tommy was a hard man and there were a lot of people, the cops included, out there who would've gladly seen him locked up – whether he was guilty or not.

Tommy and Joe had led a campaign from their dungeons proclaiming their innocence. Joe engineered audacious escapes from jail and, one time, he chained himself to the gates of Buckingham Palace. Tommy went on hunger strike, surviving 100 days without food. They were innocent all right and now they were free and awaiting appeal.

'OK, I've been away for a long time, Karen, but I know flu when I see it,' said Tommy to his wife. 'That hasn't changed since I've been in the jail.' If it was difficult for me to come to terms with the changes that had gone on while I'd been away, it was even worse for Tommy. Far more had changed in the world since he was jailed – a great deal more.

'OK, Tommy, you know best.'

Tommy kissed his daughter Shannon bye-bye, threw on a jacket and headed out to the street. He was only going to a chemist shop, a short distance up the road. As it happened, he made this trek at the same time almost every day. Usually wee Shannon went to nursery school and, since his release, Tommy had been in the habit of going to collect her. The chemist shop and the nursery gates both looked on to a public car park and, as he approached, he noticed a big jeep – one he hadn't seen before. Tommy was no fool. He knew that some people would see his appeal as a possible threat – people like the real murderers. That's not what it was about for him. All he wanted to do was prove his innocence not prove who was guilty. But the real murderers wouldn't see it that way so he kept his eyes skinned for a possible attack at all times.

'I've got a message for you, you big prick.' Walking across the car park towards Tommy was a bloke called Billy McPhee. A big man, younger than Tommy, McPhee was known to be The Licensee's equaliser and it was no secret that he carried a knife in each hand.

'Well, you'd better give it to me then,' said Tommy, quickly slipping his jacket off and wrapping it round one arm to fend off the blades. Then he squared up and waited for the attack.

'STOP CALLING THE BOSS A GRASS!' roared McPhee as he rushed at Tommy, slashing out first with one knife then the other. But neither landed where it mattered. This was going to be a long battle and not the easy hit McPhee had envisaged.

Ten minutes later, an exhausted McPhee ran back to the jeep. He'd had his knives taken from him and was battered bodily like he hadn't been battered in a long time. He had forgotten one thing – TC Campbell was one of the hardest street fighters Glasgow has ever seen. And the bold Tommy had forgotten nothing.

If a hit isn't over in seconds, usually it's abandoned. That's what Tommy assumed was happening when the jeep flew out of the car park. While he sat on the ground catching his breath and licking his wounds, mothers, grannies and young kids were gathering around him as the nursery and nearby primary school finished for the day. Then the jeep came back at speed and that's when Tommy saw him – Thomas McGraw, The Licensee, at the wheel. McPhee was out in a flash and running at Tommy again, knives back in his mitts. Kids were wailing in fear. Mothers were howling. There was panic everywhere but no one was leaving.

This time was harder for Tommy. 'Who the fuck are you anyway, son?' he demanded of McPhee as they grappled skull to skull.

'I'm The Iceman,' growled McPhee up close, as he tried to shove a long blade into Tommy's stomach.

'No you're no',' puffed Tommy. 'That was Frank McPhie and you're a fucking pussy compared to him.'

Frank McPhie was a well-known Glasgow drug trafficker and hit man. He was called 'The Iceman' because he was cold about his work and would take out his granny for the right price. He'd been shot and killed by a sniper at his own front door in Maryhill a short time before. His murder remains unsolved.

'You and your fucking books,' snarled McPhee. 'Stop calling the boss a grass.'

Tommy had written a book, *Indictment*, about how he came to be convicted of the Doyle murders. In the book, McGraw was given his colours and none of them were pretty.

'You tell your boss to do his own dirty work cos you're no' up to it.'

By now Tommy had prised one of McPhee's knives from his fist and stuck it into his guts except the damn thing just bounced off. So he stuck him in the kidneys – same result. It was then he sussed that McPhee was wearing a bulletproof vest. No problem – he just stuck him in the skull. McPhee let go and started howling like a banshee. The blade had bounced off the hard bone but sliced under the skin and was stuck there, dangling. Out of the jeep came his boss, The Licensee, brandishing, of all things, a golf club. McPhee and McGraw stood at either side of Tommy, one trying to chib him the other trying to smash his brains in.

'Leave Mr Campbell alone.' The order came from a tiny old woman who had stepped out of the terrified crowd of onlookers. 'I know who you are, McGraw,' she screamed. 'I've phoned the polis and told them – now leave him alone.' One brave wee soul and so typical of Glasgow dames – you mix with them at your peril.

The struggle had lasted an hour. As piggy in the middle, Tommy was taking golf club blows and knife stabs to his arms, his shoulders and his back. Towards the end, even he was tiring.

WHACK. The golf club had caught him on the side of the nut – right on that soft, vulnerable triangle above the ear. Pain seared through his whole body, he went blind and he was staggering all over the place. 'Stay on your feet. Stay on your feet,' he told himself. 'Try to sense where they are. Listen. Just fucking listen.'

McGraw and McPhee closed in and tried to finish him off but Tommy's street-fighting skills saw him through as he punched out one way and kicked the other. Deafened by the beating of his own chest and napper, Tommy stood and waited for that fatal blow.

'It's OK, Mr Campbell. It's OK now.' He felt a gentle hand on his arm. 'They bastards have gone. Come on now and sit down here. It's OK.' It was the game wee old woman taking care of him and now she had company as other women fussed around Tommy. Some state he was in. Practically stripped in the melee, he had lost his jumper, his shirt, his shoes and his socks. His face and naked torso

117

were streaked in blood – his own and Billy McPhee's. At the side of his head, the shape of the head of the golf club and a large imprint reading 'No. 9' were visible.

Ten minutes after the end of the fight, a cop car arrived. According to onlookers, they had been phoned several times about an hour before.

'I told them it was you and who was trying to kill you,' said one. 'We all did.'

Some emergency response, eh?

But, this time, with all those witnesses in broad daylight, surely McGraw, The Licensee, and his muscle McPhee were in big trouble? Or were they?

28

BAD NEWS

Even the dogs on the street knew that McGraw and McPhee had attacked TC Campbell but not everyone let on – some for very good reasons.

When the cops asked, Tommy Campbell told them he didn't recognise his attackers. That was his way – the way of the code of the street. Don't believe middle-class writers when they say that doesn't exist. Aye, it does – it's just that there's less and less of us living by the code these days. Tommy Campbell does.

Be in no doubt, it was a hit intended to kill Tommy. Why not use a gun? It's not the traditional Glasgow way. Up close and personal is how many street players are still taken out in my city. Stick the knife in low into the genitals and the lower guts to avoid any bulletproof vest – close enough to feel his fear and for him to smell your breath and hear your curses. Even as he sticks the blade in, the hit man is likely to have a gun in the waistband of his trousers. He could just shoot his target but that's not the point, not the point at all.

Tommy's skull was fractured and he was hospitalised for a few days. The shape and the number of the golf club remained visible for weeks and he suffered blinding headaches but his sight was back and he was alive. In broad daylight, The Licensee and his top muscle had tried to kill Tommy Campbell. They knew he would be there at that time since he always picked Shannon up from the nursery. If the wee girl hadn't been unwell, she would have been there with her da when the bastards struck.

But McGraw and McPhee had been seen and fingered by about thirty women. Nearby shops had CCTV cameras trained on the car park where the hit took place. McGraw's golf club had shattered when he smacked Tommy's napper and lay there on the ground. McPhee's numerous knives lay on the ground. There was blood on those weapons and on Tommy's ripped clothes. Some blood was Tommy's but some was his attackers'. The place dripped with forensic evidence. So it looked like McGraw and McPhee were finally in big trouble. But were they?

When cops interviewed Tommy after he was released from hospital, he still refused to tell them anything but they then told him that McGraw and McPhee had been fingered by the crowd.

'If that's the case,' Tommy said to the young, fresh-faced copper, 'you might as well rip up your notes.'

'Why?' the cop asked, genuinely perplexed.

'Because, son, your bosses will make sure that McGraw never goes to jail. He's too valuable to them in other ways – whoever he tries to kill.'

The young cop didn't believe Tommy. The young cop thought there was a cast-iron case what with all the evidence. The young cop was sure there would be a successful prosecution because a terrible crime had been committed. The young cop was wrong.

We didn't know it at the time but the CCTV cameras at the shops had been turned off that day. We never found out what happened to all the forensics and the witnesses but eventually it would emerge that neither McGraw nor McPhee would be charged. We didn't know that at the time but we all knew that's what would happen. Why? It had happened time after time before.

I hadn't met Tommy till I came out of jail. In fact, he had been very friendly with my old man, Willie, as a kind of younger, honorary member of my dad's generation. But I had long since been convinced that Tommy Campbell was innocent and, in my own way, supported his campaign. Tommy and I had got into correspondence, jail to jail.

When we were both free, I went to visit him early doors. The man I met was a gentle, humorous, intelligent guy much more likely to break into some song – sometimes one that he'd written – than to get violent.

It might seem strange to call a guy who'd led a street razor gang, been an armed robber and was convicted of torching six people 'gentle' but that's what he'd become. Of course, he hadn't forgotten a thing about street skills as McGraw and McPhee found out to their cost. You can't undo your life and nor should you try.

I also discovered that Tommy's wife, Karen, was a cousin of mine. Small world. His wee one Shannon was just a bit older than Dean and the same bright, curious, creative kid. So, did I become close to Tommy Campbell? Bloody right I did.

When McGraw and McPhee tried to kill Tommy, I was furious. He'd been jailed eighteen years before for something he didn't do. At first, the world hated him so much, they beat up his friends and relatives and one man tried to blind his five-year-old son, Brian, by throwing lime in his eyes. In the prison, they'd beaten Tommy to a pulp, breaking his back, his arms and his legs and, one time, he was actually declared dead – all for something he didn't do. Now he was out yet they let some lowlifes try to kill him in broad daylight and did sod all.

Angry? You bet I was fucking angry.

Hands up. In the old days, I would've got tooled up and paid a couple of visits. And I don't mean social calls. Tempted though I was, the old days were over. The new Ferris went public, condemning the cowardly pair in whatever way I could. My cards were truly on the table – not that McGraw would ever expect me to take his side. I was angry and said it and that would make him nervous.

Next thing, I got a call at home early one morning asking if I'd read the *Daily Record* yet. There was a front-page piece alleging that McGraw and I had had a set-to – with me trying to chib him and him smashing at me with yet another golf club. It didn't happen. A few phone calls later, I found out the truth. McGraw had been severely embarrassed by this guy who had taken him on after a chance meeting. But for his bulletproof vest, The Licensee would have been no more. McGraw's minders had sat in his motor, too scared to come out. Apparently, they were a couple of Bosnian ex-troopers he'd hired at that time. It seems a bloody civil war is one thing but a Glasgow hard man with a chib . . . now that's something else. The hapless guys were soon to be jobless.

The other man involved was strictly low key. McGraw wouldn't have liked it to get around that he'd been shown up by this guy. So somehow the press got told that it had been me. I wonder who passed that wee lie to the media . . .

To help get the truth out, I gave Reg a hand in meeting up with some people – guys who would normally run a mile from a writer. The story grew legs and it ran and ran. Every newspaper in the country was phoning Reg every day, putting questions to him, and articles were appearing day after day. One journalist in particular, the pocket-sized Andrew Walker, who was the chief crime guy for the *Daily Record*, phoned Reg at least five times a day, every day. He'd tell Reg what he'd been *told* had happened and Reg would tell him what he *knew* had happened. But, next day, the paper would print what Walker had been told had happened rather than what Reg was telling him.

Like the politicals would say, it was pure propaganda and I was the target. A year later, Andrew Walker would move on to be chief media relations officer for Central Police. A strange move for a top tabloid journalist? Not in this case, obviously.

This press feeding frenzy rolled on for so long that it became tedious. But then I got a call from Paolo, the senior social worker who supervised my release licence from jail. He said he wanted me to come in early the next day. We met weekly and, as we had just had a meeting, I insisted he told me what was up.

Eventually he relented and said, 'Your licence has been revoked, Paul.' He let that sink in as I stood holding my phone in stunned silence. 'I'm sorry but you're going back to jail.'

Back to prison? We'd see about that.

29

LOST IN THE DARK

May 2002

'Are we sure they've got the right motors?'

'Well, it's what he was last known to drive and the other ones belong to his close associates.'

'But we know for sure it's no' his, right?'

'The guys watching his house say that one hasn't shifted.'

'But how the fuck do we know he's no' sitting in his house having a wee lager and watching the telly?'

'We just know that's all. They don't tell us fuck all except they know he's heading our way.'

'Looking for five different motors on this busy road. Fucking useless, man.'

'Think we've got it bad?'

'Aye.'

'Fucking think of the boys who were all geared up to hit his house.'

'Ha, right ye are.'

'Thirty cops in body armour. Armed response vehicles. Even the chopper pilot was in for the briefing.'

'All ready to play at SAS, eh?'

'Then they get word that the chicken has flown the nest.'

'Chicken? Fucking slippery eel more like.'

'Eyes up. Is that no' a Beamer?'

'Yep. Right colour too.'

'Wait for it. Wait for it. Fuck! Wrong reg number.'

'Aye, a-fucking-gain.'

The A74 turns into the M74, heads south from Glasgow and stretches for many miles within the Strathclyde Police boundary area. All along the motorway, cop cars were on the alert, looking for me. I'd been reported as a fugitive from justice – so they thought. When I was told that I was being forced back to prison, my first thought *was* to run. I knew I had done no wrong. So what game was this? Run away and then, when I'm safe, clear my name – that's what I thought. Then I thought again.

If I'd gone on the hop, the Strathclyde mob – or at least the Serious Crime Squad along with the Scottish Crime Squad – would have got tooled up and come after me. For years, the ones I have feared most are the cops – not that they might arrest me but that they would shoot me one night. I have one polis on tape saying just that. What was I going to do – give them the excuse? No chance.

After I got that call from Paolo, I made two phone calls only. The first was to Reg to talk through my options. We agreed that I should hand myself in but not to Strathclyde since they'd put me in the Scottish jail system. Both of us knew that the cops had to have interviewed or charged me before my liberty licence could be revoked. They had done neither. So why the hell had the Home Office agreed to recall me to jail? It must be based on what Strathclyde had told them. But what? So we agreed that the safest bet was to head south and hand myself in in Durham. Not only was it a close location in the north of England but it was also where Frankland Prison was – the jail I'd been released from. I'd get treated better down there and at least I'd be safe.

But I wasn't to go alone. Who better to accompany me and ensure that the cops didn't get up to nasty tricks or that a wee accident didn't happen than the press. Reg made a call to David Leslie at the *News of the World* and, within the hour, he was at my place, team-handed with photographer Brian, the failed getaway driver of my freedom day, and a hired people carrier.

Later, we'd find out that, at the nearby London Road cop shop, a major team was being briefed on hitting my house that night. Yet I had been asked to hand myself in the next day. They wanted to be sure that I was sitting at home when they called mob-handed and, no doubt, accompanied by legions of the press. We were also to discover that they knew I was heading south. I had spoken to two people by phone, Reg and David, both on mobiles. Reg had spoken to no one else – it's as simple as that. David had met with his editor face to face and also in person with Brian – it was in the paper's interest to keep it hush-hush. So how the hell had the cops found out?

They had to be tapping my mobile phone. That's been possible for a few years but it's not easy or cheap. As I understand it, at that time, they would have had to allocate officers to tail me round the clock and deploy scanner-type technology. It's the kind of gear they used on IRA bomb squads. Did they think I could create as much damage as them? Did they have a warrant to bug my phone? Who knows? And I'll probably never find out. The rules around an individual's rights to this information, even many years later, are so damn secretive. Then again, the legal bods don't know about unsanctioned phone tapping now, do they? Or do they?

In the car, David and Brian chatted as we sped along. 'They honestly haven't given you any idea why, Paul?'

'Not one. What I do know is that Paolo the social worker was pressured into revoking my licence but he told them there was no reason.'

'Good man, eh?'

'He's got balls all right, saying no to the cops. But, David, you know I never want to go back to another jail in all my life.'

'Aye.'

'So I cooperated with Paolo in every way – even went to extra meetings.'

'It must be the cops then.'

'That's certain. But they haven't been near me. And talking of who . . .'

A cop car came speeding up behind us. We pulled over to let it pass and I looked away at the countryside, showing them the back of my skull. 'How many's that?'

'At least four,' replied David.

'In what? Forty minutes?'

He nodded. 'I drive this road all the time, Paul. I've never seen as many police cars.'

'Wonder why it's so busy tonight then?' I replied with a grin.

'Don't think we need three guesses, eh?'

As we drove across the Scotland–England border, I sighed with some sense of relief. Strathclyde Police might well have persuaded other Scottish forces covering the rest of the M74 to hunt for me. My bet was that they'd have less luck with the English cops. That was my theory at least.

Driving into Durham late at night, I now felt safe. There was no happiness or satisfaction in this, of course. Who would be happy turning themselves in for jail time? Then we hit a snag. Where the hell was the cop shop?

Though I'd spent a few years of my life in Durham, I'd not exactly been allowed to tour the town. David, though a Geordie, worked in Scotland and knew it like the back of his hand. But Durham, just a few miles up the road from where he was raised? Clueless.

With the help of an *A–Z* and by stopping and asking a few pedestrians for directions, we eventually found the place. It was a massive building, with a long wooded driveway and a big sign saying it was the cops' HQ. No local station for us. Out in the sticks, it would take them hours to suss out what to do with me and I couldn't be bothered with that hassle. Just let's get it over with.

As I breezed through the front door, Brian whizzed away with his camera. One deep breath of freedom and in I went followed by David and Brian. I've been a wanted man once or twice before and I fully expected to be jumped on and shackled as soon as they knew who had arrived. Instead, I found . . . no one. The front reception was deserted. We waited and shuffled and coughed loudly till, finally, David called out, 'HELLO!' Nothing.

'Funny fucking cop shop,' I thought. 'Sleepy valley more like.'

The wait was getting on my nerves so off I went through the main swing doors in search of a uniform to hand myself in to. We moved through big rooms and offices and down long corridors. Totally bloody deserted. Eventually, we found ourselves in a big, oak-panelled room with a long, highly polished banquet table and on the wall behind were paintings of Queen Lizzie and old Dukie Philip, flanked by a massive Union Jack. They themselves were surrounded by rows of pictures of high-brass coppers. This had to be the right place.

We then moved beyond that into another room and still there was nobody about. It was getting so bizarre, I was thinking of going home. Then, rounding a corner, we bumped into a sole policeman who almost jumped out of his skin. I got as big a fright as the Jobsworth.

It took a few goes at explaining who I was and why I was there.

'You're here to do what?' he asked for the third time.

'Hand myself in to Frankland Prison.'

He shook his head in disbelief.

'And you're Paul Ferris?' he asked, as if the name didn't match my actions. At last, he got on his radio. As he was being briefed from the other end, he pressed his earpiece further into his ear and turned and looked at me with an expression of horror. I think he'd finally got the message.

'Mr Ferris,' he said loudly, having received instructions, 'you'll have to step outside, please.'

'No problem – but why?' I asked. Having handed myself in to a cop shop, this was the first time I'd been told to leave one – ever. The cop escorted me outside the building to the centre of an empty car park.

'If you could just wait here, please. Someone will come for you shortly.'

I had no idea what all this palaver was about. Did they think I was wired up with a bomb? I didn't have to wait long.

Two cop cars came speeding up with lights flashing and sirens blaring. You'd think they were on their way to deal with a bank robbery, not some wee guy standing in the half light of a car park who was there to hand himself in.

A suit jumped out of one of the cars, followed by his blue serge mates.

127

'Paul Ferris?' asked the suit – as if anyone else would be daft enough to hang around there.

'Yeah.'

'I'm the police liaison officer from Frankland Prison and I've come to arrest you.' And he did – handcuffs and all.

As they bundled me into the back of a car, the bold Brian kept snapping away. When we did finally arrive at a proper cop shop in Durham, up ahead, gathered on the pavement, was a clutch of journalists and photographers – all from Scotland, it transpired. Now, who could have told them I was going to be there? And told them early enough to beat us to the police station?

Inside, they were waiting for me. The Strathclyde mob had already been on the line with another agenda. They wanted me shipped back to Glasgow pronto. Though I suspected they'd try that one, my faith in the English system proved to be right. They took the view that the Home Office issued the revocation order and, since my original sentence had been south of the border, south of the border I'd stay. Result.

The Durham cops also treated me very well. Rather than coop me up all the time, they allowed me to stretch my legs in this bigger security cage. Smoking was banned in the cells so, in the cage, they gave me some of my cigs to smoke while I walked. Like I said, they treated me decently.

One young cop took a particular interest in me and came to chat. 'How did you get in again?' he asked, referring to my visit to their HQ.

'Like I said, through the front door,' I replied.

'And it wasn't locked?' His tone had a worried, disbelieving edge to it.

'No, no. I just pushed it open.' What did he think? That I'd broken into a polis station to hand myself in?

'And what rooms did you get into?' The bloke was looking a wee bit peaky and white about the gills.

'I've told you,' I said, getting a bit pissed off, 'the front reception through the swing doors, up the stairs, into what looked like a banqueting hall . . .'

'You were in there?'

'Yeah.'

'Oh, fuck.'

'Then we were in that office at the back of it . . .'

'Oh, no. Oh, fuck, fuck, fuck.'

'What? Is there something special about that room?'

The young cop didn't answer but just bolted from the room. Two minutes later, two suits came in and asked me the same questions.

'Wha'd'ye mean ye got intae the banqueting hall?' The most senior looking one almost bawled at me. Like the young uniform before them, the two suits bolted from the room without explanation. I'd obviously upset them but why?

It turned out that the cop shop I'd visited first was supposed to be a really high-security police HQ – one of the most secure buildings in the country. Or so they thought. Not only were the big operations planned there but it also had a special anti-terrorist role. The place dripped with posters warning people to be on the lookout for anything dodgy. The very type of place some group might have fancied planting a big bomb and I'd just breezed in there and wandered through the place. I guess a few cop arses got severely kicked that night.

After a night at the police station, I was expecting to be shipped to Frankland – to be in a jail and among people I knew very well. That would make my next task – appealing against my recall to jail – a damn sight easier. Then the English bizzies let me down.

'We'll take you now, Paul.'

'Right,' I said, glad that the craziness that had kicked off the day before was coming to some sort of end.

'It's only a short drive to Durham.'

'What?' We were in Durham so what the hell did they mean?

'Durham Prison. We've to take you to Durham Prison.'

I had never been there but knew all about it by repute. It was BarL with toilets, a hellhole dump of a place with big thuggish screws who like to beat on the prisoners. What game were they pulling now?

30

ONE BLEAK DUNGEON

'Ret, son, you're for the seg.' The Geordie screw was twice my size and that was the standard issue in Durham Prison.

'Solitary? What for?' That was punishment and here was me still clueless as to why I had been returned to jail. Not only that, it would be weeks before I got a chance to appeal my case.

'It's share a cell or that's where you've got to go, lad,' the screw replied, unhelpfully.

'But I've done nothing wrong,' I protested again and I'd been sweetness itself since I'd handed myself in. 'And I'm sharing no stinking cell in this dump. If I'm a Cat-A risk, treat me like a Cat-A risk in all respects.'

'Look, lad, we don't have a Cat-A secure unit here so you have to go to the seg.'

Of course, I should have realised. I had been released as Cat-A security risk now I'd returned to be a Cat-A security risk. Trouble is, in the meantime, I'd done sod all against the law. This wasn't ironic – this was a bloody disgrace.

'So, why send me here?' I asked, not unreasonably, I thought. 'Frankland is just down the road.'

The big screw shrugged his shoulders, 'Fucked if I know. And I dinny care, like.' He took hold of my arm and led me in the direction he wanted to go. I shook his hand off and walked on my own. There was no point in creating any more fuss. The seg would be better than sharing some overcrowded hovel with an arsehole I'd never met. Besides, I'd lose any argument with the jail and I wanted this to be one brief, trouble-free stay and to get the hell out of there as quickly as possible.

Durham Prison wasn't a place I wanted to be in. Even compared with any other prisons, it was old, decrepit and, for generations, the staff had ruled with fists and boots. From the screws I'd met so far, nothing had changed. Probably grieving over the good old days. Good old bad days.

In recent times, Durham had been home to the most evil men of our times: Ian Brady, known as the mad Moors Murderer which was just a way of saying child killer; Denis Nilsen who killed his gay lovers so he wouldn't be alone (Nilsen, originally from Fraserburgh in the north-east of Scotland, showed a practical touch by keeping the rotten corpses around for months); Peter Sutcliffe, the Yorkshire Ripper who liked to smash working girls' skulls in with a hammer; and a whole heap of their type. Not great company.

The serial killers had been kept in a special hall separate from the rest of the prison. That approach had long since been abandoned and the thrill killers were now spread out over many jails or psych institutions. But some people still think that Durham is loaded with those mental types and, from what I could see, some of the screws thought that as well. I just hoped that the seg unit wasn't in what used to house those beasts. It had been a bad enough day as it was.

'Look, Paul,' said this younger screw who was also escorting me to the solitary, 'we don't have a Cat-A unit here so we have no choice.'

I gave him a sour look as a reply.

'But we've got a Scottish lad in here, from Glasgow.'

'Aye?' Now he had my attention.

'He's got his cell well set up TV and all that.'

Now he really had my attention. I quickly scanned my memory to see if I could think of any Glasgow bloke who might be in that jail, paying special attention to guys associated with players back home who may bear a grudge against me. I drew a blank.

'You could share a cell with him if you like,' offered the prison warder.

'Yeah,' I said slowly, not wanting to come across too keen, 'yeah, OK.' The TV swung it, in truth. A luxury? Maybe but, in my circumstances, I wasn't going to be given a job or allowed much free movement so I'd be left kicking my heels most of the day, every day, in a cell. The telly would help blot out the mind-rotting boredom.

As we approached the door of what was to be my cell, I asked if I could have something to read and maybe some paper and a pen.

'We can sort that out tomorrow,' said the screw, probably because he couldn't be arsed. It was OK for him – he wasn't going to lie alone and sleepless in that dump.

And I didn't sleep – not a wink. All that night, I just lay and ruminated over the past few months. To make it worse, I was on the bottom bunk and my cellmate farted vociferously and repeatedly all night. As far as I was concerned, things on the outside had been going well right up to that bloody phone call. I hadn't been involved in any crimes. Who better to know that than me? But, of course, I wouldn't be given my say until I'd been in jail for weeks, maybe even months.

One thing I knew which might have pissed the cops off was some of the company I'd kept. When first released, I welcomed everyone I had been friendly with back into my life. Some were still active in crime but it wasn't for me to judge them. How could I, given the life I'd led so far? It was a bit awkward in certain company. We'd be sitting there having a quiet drink when some party would start to go on about some job and I'd have to get up on my feet, put hands up and say, 'I can't be hearing this.'

'You what?' they'd mutter in disbelief.

Of course, it wasn't their fault – all my adult life, I'd been keen to hear about everything that was going down. I'd been thinking of changing my ways for some time but these guys were just getting used to the idea. It would take them some time.

Because some of these guys were active, no doubt some were being tailed by the cops. In spite of me very publicly declaring that though I was going straight I wouldn't turn my back on my old pals, the cops would see it differently. The bizzies' approach to many things is black and white. If you associate with crooks, they reckon you must be a crook. It's simplistic crap. But no doubt my name, telephone number and picture had turned up on one or two surveillance files. Just being there – surely that wasn't enough to get me sent back to jail?

Then there was that matter of national significance. Some wise guy had gone to the papers with a tale about me bidding for a house against the Scottish football team boss of the time, Berti Vogts. Seems that's somebody spotted my brother, Billy, near the house, put two and two together and came up with the crock of shit that I was going to buy his house. The Scottish team were in the doldrums and, by all accounts, Berti needed his home comforts to see him through. Crap national team or not, we Scots still take our football seriously. Maybe it was worth sending me to jail for upsetting the coach. Aye, right you are then.

All night, I mulled over crap like that as I listened to and whiffed my cellmate's wind – not the best of starts. It could only get better. But would it?

31

STABBED IN THE BACK

First impressions can be so misleading. Just because a guy farts all night doesn't mean he's going to raise a stink.

I had scored lucky with my cellmate. He was a young guy from the huge and decidedly mental Pollok housing scheme in Glasgow's south side. Much of that area was run by a mob led by Stewart 'Specky' Boyd. Like me, Specky was small and – surprise, surprise – wore glasses. He didn't look like a mobster but was one of the most dangerous men in Glasgow.

Specky and I didn't agree on a few things but we weren't exactly enemies either. Some of his team, on the other hand, were desperadoes who would have happily taken a pop at me just to collect a scalp – aye, they'd hope. My cellmate knew all of them, of course, but he wasn't part of that scene. Good man.

The young guy's nickname was Eatso which went some way to explain his constant capacity for flatulence. I've never met anyone else who passed wind so loudly, so frequently and so effortlessly. Thank God. Eatso was serving seven years having been caught on a drugs run to Holland. He was adamant that he'd been set up and, given the company he'd been keeping, I wouldn't be surprised. But he didn't let that do his head in. He'd done the crime and would do the time. What had to be settled regarding the fit-up could wait – a very mature head on the young bloke.

Something he wasn't mature about – being a Rangers supporter. I mean a mad, daft Rangers supporter who just wouldn't shut up about it. Eatso already knew I was a Celtic man but it's not something that occupies much of my daily thinking – at least it wasn't till I met Eatso. The pair of us would jibe at each other all day, every day, about football, the best way to make tea, some article in the news, two flies crawling up the cell wall and football. We'd wind each other up about anything and everything. Eatso kept me on my toes, made sure my mind was alert and took my aching noggin off the serious matter of why the hell I was back in jail. Young Eatso I owe a big thank you to – a real diamond in a fuck-off, hellhole, dump of a jail.

A week or so after being locked up again, Eatso was out working and I was locked in the cell as usual. Every day, he bought in the *Daily Record* as most Scottish prisoners do down south. I reckon that paper must owe a small but significant share of its sales figures to cons in the nick. Lying back on my bunk, reading Eatso's *Daily Record*, I caught sight of an article written by their pint-sized crime reporter, Andrew Walker, who'd soon work for the cops – officially. It was front-page stuff and there was a huge colour picture of a lock knife with the blade drawn. This was the knife that McGraw had used to stab me twice, according to paper. Now this was too bloody much. The article claimed that I had demanded £2 million compensation from McGraw, blaming him for my last prison sentence. The money was apparently to compensate me for the loss of several legitimate businesses after I was sentenced.

According to the drivel, McGraw came off worst but I was stabbed twice – in the shoulder and in the side. So here I was, sitting in a jail for reasons unknown to me and a major daily was writing, as 'fact', that I'd been involved in a knife fight. That was the type of propaganda that the powers that be would use to keep me inside. Worse, a newspaper with such evidence would normally photograph it and then hand it straight to the cops but this time, it seemed they had lost the bloody knife. I wonder if their then editor, backstabbing Peter Cox, got grief for that? Somebody was up to seriously bad tricks and I was the target. I had to do something about it and so I rang the buzzer.

'You have a major security problem,' I said to the screw in charge who came to my door. 'Get the fucking door open – now.'

'I can't do that!' he roared.

'You'd fucking better, pal, or you'll have to take responsibility for what's going down.' I heard grumbling and moaning coming from the other side of the metal door and then I heard the screw's boot studs crunch sharply down the hall. A couple of minutes later, there was the scraping of a key in my door. When it swung open, the governor was standing there along with a few screws and the ever-present big Alsatian.

'What's the problem, Ferris?' demanded the governor, obviously well pissed off at being dragged away from his paper pushing.

'This is the problem,' I said, handing him the newspaper.

As he began to read it, I started to strip off.

'What're you doing, sonny?' demanded one big security screw who looked, sounded and acted ex-army. He could have played Mr Mackay, the uptight screw in TV comedy series *Porridge* starring Ronnie Barker. Come to think of it, Eatso and I behaved much like Barker and his younger cellmate, Richard Beckinsale – except this wasn't funny, not funny at all.

'What's it look like?' I demanded, now riled up. 'I'm taking my clothes off and I'm not your sonny, you prick.'

Howls of disapproval continued from the screws but not one took a step towards me as I knew they wouldn't. I was Cat A. What were they going to do, provoke an escalation?

It was the quickest I'd ever taken off my clothes – not counting for pleasure, of course. I stood there bollock naked in front of them and slowly twirled. Then, lifting my hands above my head, I twirled again. 'Can anyone see any signs of wounds on my body?' Another slow twirl. 'Or scars or stitches or recent damage?'

The disapproving howls had gone silent. The governor's expression had changed from irritation to calm. He had read the newspaper article and now understood.

'I have to advise you that I intend calling you all as witnesses as I've not been stabbed nor am I wounded. What's more, I demand to see a doctor urgently. Not a fucking quack orderly but the prison doctor.'

As I turned and started to put my clothes on, the governor mumbled something and the group moved off. The security screw reached in, took hold of my door and scowled at me, hatred all over his face. He was fizzing.

BANG – he took his temper out on the door. As if I gave a fuck.

My ploy had worked as far as I was concerned. It was even better that they came team-handed under the rules of dealing with a Cat-A prisoner. Now they'd all have to lie if they wanted to put me in the shit so I began to think I had a chance of hooking them in on my side – whether they wanted to or not. They would be rattled though. Very angry indeed – especially that security screw. So, I reckoned they'd get some payback. It came with an outcome and a speed that caught me napping.

'All right, Ferris,' a big hand roughly shook me by the shoulder one day as I sat on my bunk after I'd had my visit from the governor and co.

'What the fuck?' I sat bolt upright, wondering what they were up to now.

'Come on, get your gear together,' said the gruff voice.

'Why?'

'You're going on a wee trip, bonny lad.'

Three screws and a big dog walked me out of Durham jail. I was in serious danger of getting used to this rigmarole and believing that I actually *was* some big public enemy. Half an hour after being told to pack my stuff, I was perched in the back of an armoured truck being driven through the prison gates. Thank fuck I was leaving that hellhole. But I was being shanghaied and taken to another prison.

Eatso was at work when they came for me. That had undoubtedly been part of their plan so that I had no chance to say goodbye or anything. It's part of the dehumanising impact of jail. But I had time to leave him a wee message – a set of rosary beads under his pillow. I could just imagine the Rangers-daft Protestant getting comfy in bed that night and putting his hand under the pillow. Wonder if he had nightmares?

The question going round my head was which prison they were taking me to. The screws would tell me nothing. It's against the rule with Cat As in case we somehow used the info to orchestrate an escape. From the back of armoured truck surrounded by uniforms? Like how?

'Aha, Mr Ferris, I'd like to say it's good to see you again,' said a friendly face, 'but under the circumstances . . .' It was the reception screw who had treated me with some respect, some dignity, the last time I passed through his terrain in the opposite direction. That was when I was leaving. Now I had returned to Frankland Prison and it was back to the familiar routines in the jail I knew – face to face with screws who treated me well and nose to nose with prisoners I knew and who knew me.

Good. I had some people to sort out.

32

NO HOME FROM HOME

'You've upset a lot of people, you know, Paul.' My Yardie pals and Ando and Tabbo, a couple of the Salford Team, had just finished commiserating with me over the reality of my position – being back in jail.

'Seems to be,' I replied, as if I didn't care. 'But good of them to put me up again,' I said, motioning to my all too familiar surroundings.

'Aye,' one of them nodded and then added, 'but no.'

'No, right enough.'

'OK, some bastards have stuck you inside,' the guy continued, 'but there's some in here been lipping it big time.'

'Right?'

'We'd heard you'd been put back in jail the very next day, you know.'

'Aye, through the newspapers.'

'Before that,' he went on, 'from the screws.' The cons in Frankland would have got their newspapers early the day after me being slung into Durham Prison. The jungle drums must have been beating fast among the uniforms.

'Ach, they'll know screws who work in Durham,' I tried as some obvious explanation.

'Sure but it was more than that,' the speaker looked uncertain, searching for the right word. 'Like they were passing on a message. You know?'

I knew all right. And, once I'd learned what had been going on at Frankland since I'd left, I understood a lot more clearly.

Fat bitch, Jason Vella, from Essex had started mouthing the minute I'd walked through the gates to freedom. From a number of sources in the jail, I was given the same reports. Vella claimed he had made phone calls to have me seen to. That he knew where I lived. The stupid bastard had even bribed a few prisoners with tenner bags of smack to get my phone number. Out in the big bad world, I was going to be given a very bad time or so Vella claimed. In spite of being scared to go at me when I was there with him in the jail, he promised he would get me as soon as I was on the other side of the walls. Even when he had heard that I'd been dumped in Durham Prison, he had boasted that he knew people there who were going to sort me out. Brave, eh? But with good reason.

Certain screws in Frankland had been saying that I was in big trouble – that I'd been extremely active since my release and I wasn't just going to be held for the rest of my sentence for gunrunning but would go to trial on other dirty deeds. It was news to me and all crap. The screws added that no way would I be going back to Frankland. It would be Belmarsh maybe or Full Sutton – anywhere but not Frankland. And, because Jason Vella believed every word and thought he'd never see me again, he reverted to his normal bullying, boasting type, sexually abusing the younger prisoners and running amok as he wanted.

'Good morning.'

'What the fuck?'

I was in the prison gym and Vella almost dropped the weights he was pumping on his throat. That would've been fun to watch. He was lying on his back doing bench presses, huffing and puffing with the strain. I'd seen my old dear lift heavier bags of shopping and not break sweat.

'At least it would be . . .' I paused, standing over him as he lay back on the bench, the iron quaking madly above his head, 'if I wasn't in this dump with arsewipes like you.'

I was dressed in the gym gear, holding some clothes in my hand –

all borrowed of course. Well hidden from the view of any screw was a long football sock and inside it were three small but hefty weights. I'd decided that if Vella or his apes started on me they were going down.

One of Vella's mates approached him cagily, keeping his eyes fixed on me. Standing over him, he lifted the barbell and weights out of the fat man's hands and carefully placed them on the stand. If Vella was going to have a go, now was his time.

'Got nothing to say now loudmouth?' I asked, holding my ground as he sat slumped on the bench wiping his face with a towel.

'What about?' he said and looked up, acting calm.

'The crap you were saying about me when I wasn't around?'

'Don't know what y'are talking about.'

'Think you're that frightening, you prick? So frightening that people don't tell me what you've been up to?'

'I'm just doing my time . . .'

'Aye, doing that and the young boys you find cute and the guys who you think can smuggle in some smack and any other poor cunt that you set your bears on.'

'What's it got to do with you?'

What? Did the stupid fucker think he could have a go? Or had his thick skull finally worked out that there was just me against him and his two knuckle scrapers?

'Everything,' I replied, letting the weighted sock swing from one hand and dangle a foot from his skull.

He went white. Even Vella knew that it was game on if he wanted it to be.

'I'm back,' I announced after a long minute of silence. 'Now shut the fuck up. OK?'

Nothing.

'OK?'

He nodded his head a fraction.

'Can't fucking hear you,' I spat.

His two apes hedged nervously from foot to foot.

'OK,' he said.

'What?'

'OK.'

I turned and left the gym relieved that nothing had gone down. Why would I want to lose more jail time over a closet gay, smackhead bully? But I knew Vella's type – I'd met them all over the country and in every jail I'd been in. If you think yourself above their shenanigans and ignore them, they take it as sign of weakness and escalate their nastiness. They need to be confronted face to face and, if necessary, given a good slap.

Point made. I wouldn't be getting any more trouble from Essex boy – or so I thought.

Meantime other folk had had troubles, inside and out of jail. Plans were afoot to kill a pal of mine.

33

A LOT OF KILLING

Vella wasn't the only one who'd been bitching while I was away from Frankland. Why do so many people do that?

Lance Gray, the gruff-voiced bloke from Middlesbrough, had set up a legitimate enterprise with me on my release. It was nothing exciting but it was a decent earner and, as the guy on the outside, I'd be doing most of the work. Lance had been reading the Scottish papers while I was at liberty and predicting gloom and doom. I'd been in touch with some guys at the jail and told them that the headlines weren't true but Lance believed the papers rather than me and his approach totally ruined the business. He and I had strong words.

Basil – Grant Turnbull – had been embarrassed. Some guy had written a true-crime book and alleged that Grant had given information to the cops which resulted in a couple of guys going down. Now this was a serious state of affairs. Grant was adamant that he had never been an informant. Knowing the guy, I tended to believe him but that wasn't the point. It was up to him to prove to his world – me and the other players – that the allegations were crap. He had to do it alone and do it in a manner that convinced everyone. Till then, there could be no communication between us. Does that seem hard? Too bad – that's how important it is. I had been in that position a couple of times with other faces trying to ruin my reputation, the worst one being that bogus Crown Office letter circulated by Arthur Thompson, The Godfather.

Thompson had it drawn up and circulated at the time I was standing trial for the murder of his son, Fatboy. The idea was to put all my witnesses off giving evidence on my behalf. Serious consequences? If it had worked, I was looking at twenty-five years inside. To clear up that libel, we got hold of the alleged author, a Mr A Vannet who did work at the Crown Office. He duly gave evidence that the letter was entirely bogus and, in fact, a poor forgery. Vannet's testimony helped with my defence but a stink always hangs around.

For years, I worked hard at tracking down people who were putting that letter about. Old Thompson had used his special relationship with gangland torturer Mad Frankie Fraser to have it circulated in London. I swanned into a pub there, the Tin Pan Alley which was run by Frankie's nephew, and told him, in no uncertain terms, that the letter was shite and to stop putting it about. Mind you, it helped that I was flanked by some well-known faces associated with the Adams Family. Later, I'd even go to Spain to pull up some arsehole who was putting the letter about. Gary Dennis's old man, Ginger, was a well-known London face and well respected but his boy wasn't a chip off the old block. The Dennises were well in with Thompson but, that night, Gary Dennis learned that being Thompson's pal wasn't good enough any more. Did I hurt him? No need. I frightened him so much he broke down in tears.

Later, when a journalist wrote about that letter as if it hadn't been proven to be bogus in court, I took advice from a QC about suing. Of course, he advised it would be a waste of time. It cost me several thousand pounds to be told I'd no reputation to defend. That's shorthand for them being free to write lies about me. But that's the type of effort guys like me have to put in to save our reputation – the one that's worth something on the street. Big Grant would have to do the same if necessary.

Eventually he came up with the dates and revealed he couldn't have been in that cop shop that night for a very good reason – he was in jail, miles away. But that book will still stay in circulation, will be read by the public and used by researchers. Grant's problem isn't going to disappear that quickly.

Life also goes on outside. Word reached me that an old mate, Jaimba McLean, had been blasted in the stomach with a shotgun. Jaimba had been one of the fiercest players in Glasgow till he became mentally ill. The wire was buzzing from Glasgow. Some said that Jaimba hadn't taken his medication and wasn't himself – maybe he had stumbled into serious trouble? But most of the lines claimed that Billy McPhee, Thomas McGraw's sidekick, had gone out looking for Jaimba and that McPhee had decided to get him while I was locked up out of the way.

Whether he's ill or not, you are wise not to get up close and personal with Jaimba McLean. McPhee would have known that and, after his near miss with Tommy Campbell, he chose the shotgun as safer than the knives that were his usual weapons of choice.

Most folk would have lain down and died after being blasted in the chest. Not Jaimba. He was going to live and, no doubt, he would equalise the matter of that shooting in his own way.

But he would have to get on sorting that one out himself. I had more pressing problems to deal with – like getting myself out of jail.

I was about to find out that loose tongues can be really dangerous. They can get you locked up.

34

NOT WORTH THE PAPER

'What the hell are you doing?'

It was obvious enough – I was stripping and I didn't stop till I stood bollock naked in front of him.

'You'd better explain yourself,' said the Frankland quack.

No problem. 'I'm in here because my licence has been revoked.'

He nodded and listened.

'This journalist claims that, just a short while ago, I was involved in a knife fight and was wounded twice.' I handed him my copy of the front page of the newspaper.

He read it quickly. 'I see.'

'And you understand that, if the Home Office believe this report, I could be kept in here for a long time.'

Another nod.

'If I'd been stabbed as the report claims, would you say there would be evidence of the wounds?'

'Oh, yes. Without doubt.'

'Right, I'm formally requesting that you give me a full medical to see if there's any trace of such wounds.'

I've known a few prison doctors in my time and some of them have been right cruel bastards who take pleasure in not giving a con the treatment they need for some painful condition. I'd been victim of that several times as they let my psoriasis rage on till my skin was raw and bleeding. This might be one of the evil ones.

'OK,' he said simply, switching an angle-poise light on and training the strong white beam on my body. My luck was in – he was one of the good guys.

An hour later, I emerged with full medical clearance stating there was no sign of any recent scars or healing wounds anywhere on my body. The beauty was that the examining medic wasn't my own GP or some private quack I'd hired but one appointed by the Home Office. What were they going to do? Dismiss their own doctor's professional assessment?

A copy of that medical would be put in my file. I knew that, of course, but I made sure I had a copy and got one to my lawyer, Lisa French. Lisa worked for Goldkorns, a top London legal firm. I'd gone there on the recommendation of Dessie Cunningham back in Belmarsh in 1997. Dessie had been full of praise for their senior partner, Paul Robinson, but it was Lisa who did most of my work. Normally, I would've been totally pissed off to be given somebody more junior than a legal firm's top person but not this time. Lisa was small, energetic, feisty, beautiful and a bloody great lawyer. She'd do just fine.

When a licence is revoked and you're returned to jail, it's because a court, the social worker or the cops – often all three – have written a report to the Home Office recommending your recall. I hadn't been to court and the social workers were on my side so it had to be the bizzies alone. No surprise there. Once recalled to jail, you're allowed to appeal directly to the Home Office. That meant I'd get access to the damning report that dumped me inside and so would Lisa.

'I can hardly credit it, Paul,' Lisa breathed to me down the phone one day. She has that kind of strong, husky voice that's as sexy as hell – not good for a man locked away from the world.

'Go on.'

Lisa was a very experienced lawyer so it had to be something special to shock her.

'I've got Strathclyde Police's report in front of me.'

'At last.' I had been stuck in jail for weeks and made repeated requests to be told why. At best, the screws just gave me the general patter that I was in breach of my licence. But I wanted detail.

'I've had to read it twice, slowly,' Lisa continued, 'to be sure I hadn't missed something.'

'Is it long?' I asked, anxious to get to the point.

'Not as long as they usually are,' replied Lisa, ' and . . .'

'What?'

'It's lacking in detail.'

This didn't sound good. 'Lisa, can you just tell me the main points?' These would be crucial in giving me a sense of the appeal and how we had to fight it. There was an unusual and long silence down the line. 'Lisa?'

She gave a big sigh, 'Rumours, gossip and hearsay.'

'You're fucking joking.'

'I'm fucking not.'

'There has to be more to it than that.' Even I didn't think the system was that corrupt, that biased towards police forces that bore grudges.

'Paul, there isn't. It quotes newspaper headlines about you and Thomas McGraw fighting with knives.'

'Bastards.'

'Were you interviewed by the cops on that?' She was asking a question we had already covered since my return to Frankland but now she was being thorough.

'Lisa, not only was I not interviewed, the incident didn't happen.'

'Right.'

'What else?'

There was another uncharacteristic silence and then she said, 'Not much.'

'There has to be.'

'Something about them carrying out surveillance on some guys they suspected of drug trafficking.'

Here we go. Associating with known criminals – the line I thought they'd pursue. Lisa rattled off a few names and, yes, I knew the men involved. Then the car I was meant to be driving in. I'd never been in such a car ever. Then me being with a blonde with long hair. That would be my partner, Sandra, they were getting at. Sandra who had never met the guys in question and who I always kept back from those still active in the world of crime.

'Lisa, it's pure crap.'

'I know.'

'Mean, I wasn't there at that time in that motor with those guys and any blonde. Full stop.'

'Even if you had been,' she was now fired up, 'there's nothing against the law.'

'But I wasn't.' I couldn't get beyond a feeling of anger that they had jailed me for what newspapers wrote and being in a place that I hadn't been in. I'd lost a month of my life so far over this rubbish – so far.

'Paul, they have to charge you or prove that you're part of a criminal investigation before they can recall you. This says neither.'

'And it didn't happen. Not the knife fight or that bloody meeting.' There was an angry man on one end of the phone and an outraged lawyer on the other.

'It's a clear breach of the law. We'll roast the bastards,' Lisa almost shouted, at last getting more personal than legal.

'One thing – who signed the report?'

I heard shuffling of papers at Lisa's end then she said, 'Eh . . . Graeme Pearson, Assistant Chief Constable.'

'Ah, the top brass then.'

Pearson was the senior Glasgow cop who was increasingly in the media representing the force. Part of his remit was to tackle organised crime. That'll be me then or so he must have thought. Or was it just personal? Strathclyde, as with most police forces, have long bitter memories. They were quite blatant in chasing me for something – anything – because I'd had the nerve to be found not guilty a number of times and this had made them look stupid. But did Pearson have any other agenda?

At the time, I was oblivious to Pearson's wider role. In a short while, he'd be promoted to head up the Scottish Drugs Enforcement Agency and, as this book goes to press, he is about to head up the Scottish Organised Crime Agency, a new Scotland-wide unit made up of the top cops and Customs officers – a Scottish FBI. Soon he'll be one of the most powerful polis in Europe. But there was more to it than that.

In his early cop career, Pearson met with difficulties when he was posted out to the sticks on one occasion. Somehow he had fought his way back up the career ladder. Ability? No doubt. Determination? Must have. But he was also one of the handlers of Thomas McGraw, The Licensee, registered informant.

McGraw had been a grass for years and, in return, was allowed to get on with his own crimes unheeded – thus the title of The Licensee. He had started by dealing with local bobbies and grassing up small-time crooks. Then he had graduated to the big-time stuff.

John 'Goldfinger' Palmer had been found not guilty of handling £25 million from the Brink's Mat robbery in the 1980s. Goldfinger was good friends with the likes of Kenny Noye and an accountant for the big London firms, Hatton Garden jeweller Solly Nahome. The cops were none too chuffed when they failed to catch him on the bullion rap. Goldfinger took the hint and got out of town to Tenerife but not on holiday. On that island, where it's sunny every day, Palmer set up the biggest timeshare fraud in history. He surrounded himself with what he called his dream team, hand-picked men he trusted men. Shame he didn't choose his pals better.

McGraw had bought a house on Tenerife and, inevitably, the two guys were introduced. When Palmer was arrested and sentenced to eight years, those in the know didn't look to good detective work or betrayal from the inside – they looked to his pal, McGraw. As rich as the Queen, Goldfinger was one big scalp for the cops and he is just one example of how important McGraw was to the blue serge mob – important enough to protect.

Who was most worried by my freedom? Mr Paranoid himself – The Licensee.

One trouble with the Home Office is that the power is entirely with them. They not only decided if I was in or out of jail but also when they would hold the appeal. All right, it was personal but I think there's something unjust about the pen-pushers taking their time to hear an appeal against being in jail. For folk like TC Campbell, Robert Brown, Paddy Hill and Paul Blackburn, it took decades for their appeals to be heard.

None of them had succeeded with their first efforts. Would I?

35

NO WAITING ROOM

On the day of my appeal, I wasn't even there. Lisa was down in London in some anonymous office pleading my case. Mind you, I read her 'letter'. That's what it was supposed to be but it was longer than most newspapers. And did she rip into the cops.

Apart from referring to rumours, hearsay and gossip, there was one other point she was going to raise hell on. A Strathclyde cop had been in touch with the officials to provide some background to their case against me and had offered to do so again at any time. This was a luxury that Lisa was denied and quite right too. The committee who hear these appeals are meant to be impartial and independent. So why were they having cosy chats with the cops? It was such a clear breach of my rights that, if they didn't concede the point, Lisa would get them their jotters – their arses would be out on the cold pavement. I really wish I could have been there to see her in action.

On other days when decisions were made about my innocence or guilt, freedom or detention, I would be marched into court by the cops and would have to sit there like a condemned man. That's what I was used to and I could cope with it. Kicking my heels around the jail, pretending it was just another day? Now that *was* difficult.

Lisa had warned me that the appeal might be adjourned till a later date if the officials wanted more information or the like. I've always subscribed to thinking the worst and expecting no breaks.

That way, if that's what you get, you aren't disappointed. On the other hand, if you get a result, then you can celebrate big time.

'Ferris!' It was a screw who had a habit of shouting at people from a distance away rather than getting them up close. I couldn't decide if he had a power complex or was just a lazy bastard.

'What?'

'Governor wants to see you.'

'In his office?'

'Naw, he's coming to you so don't budge.' That was a bit weird.

When the suit appeared with two screws flanking him, I decided I was in trouble. It couldn't be anything to with my appeal as it was only mid morning. The committee kicked their day off at 10 a.m. and had a number of cases to hear. No, I must be in some shit. Had Vella gone and made some false claim, hoping I'd get solitary so that he could go back to his evil games. I braced myself.

'Good news, Paul, you're free to go,' the suit said without a trace of warmth.

So don't be happy for me, eh? I nodded calmly and just said, 'And so I should be free.' No way was I going to celebrate this – not in front of the system. I shouldn't have been in jail at all. There's no celebration in getting what's rightly yours.

'The men'll go with you to clear your cell.'

There's an old lags' rule that you hand out whatever property you have to other prisoners and all you take from jail is the personal. I'd got so used to being wakened at night and quietly walked out of the prison in secret that it was strange walking round handing stuff on and saying cheerio to people.

'I'll need to make a phone call,' I said to the screws, 'to arrange a lift.'

I was hundreds of miles from home and no one was expecting my release. The standard arrangement was for the departing prisoner to make that call and for the prison to let him stay in reception in comfort with a cup of tea to wait for their lift. This wasn't just a courtesy, it was also to make sure that the con was driven away from the jail and not tempted to cause grief nearby.

'Sorry, Paul, you can't wait here,' said the senior screw.

'What?'

'Orders are that you are to leave the prison immediately.'

'But how am I going to get back to Glasgow?'

'You can make one call, then meet them outside. Sorry, man.'

'Can't I wait at reception?' I asked, thinking they had just been rattled by the timing of my departure. The whole prison was well awake and cons were gathering together from all over the building to see me off. Some fondly, others glad to see the back of me.

'No. You've just to get changed, collect your possessions and money and leave.'

'But . . .'

'Paul,' he said as he stopped, turned and looked at me square in the face – close up so that no one else could hear. 'There's no use arguing,' he shrugged. 'I'm powerless in this. Orders come directly from the Home Office.' He kept looking at me straight on. 'The Home Office,' he repeated for emphasis.

That would be the same Home Office that agreed to have me locked up again on the back of that garbage report of fairytales from Strathclyde cops. They'd forced me into jail and now they were throwing me out without ceremony or decency. I didn't have a clue what the fuck was going on except that I was leaving but I'd settle for that.

The two screws had been joined by a big dog and his handler for that procession to the gate.

'There's nothing like a bit of line dancing, eh?' I said to no one in particular.

This ceremony was becoming too ludicrous for words but it was their show so off we started on that familiar route. But would I make it out without any trouble?

36

GROUNDHOG DAY II
13 June 2002

The big dog stared up at me with cold eyes. Was he looking at a target? Begging me to move too quickly so he could spring and snap? Or was it familiarity? Was he saying hello? I'd met that dog before.

We were moving slowly through Frankland Prison – me, three screws and the big dog tethered on a lead but ready for action at the most trivial excuse. I wanted to get to that gate as soon as possible but no way was I hurrying. The dog's pace would suit me just fine.

The slow trawl through the jail had attracted onlookers from every corner, wondering if I was in big trouble and being taken away to the seg. When they realised that I was being let out, they followed behind the procession, giving me a farewell send-off. Since this rigmarole is usually carried out when it's still dark, it's not often the cons get the chance to say cheerio to one of their own. But not everyone watching was a well wisher. Jason Vella and his two heavies hovered at the edge of the group. I saw him watching, making sure I left the premises no doubt so he could return to his evil ways.

Why the security? I was a Category-A prisoner and so I was deemed to be an escape risk and a threat to the community – even when locked up. Why the procession? I was being released but, until the exact moment I stepped through the gate to freedom, they would still treat me as a public enemy – some said Public Enemy Number One. Then again, maybe they knew about something at the other side of that gate that I didn't? Fat chance.

155

The screw with me looked a tad nervous. What was up? Was it that they expected the other prisoners to go stir crazy once I'd walked to freedom?

On death row, they carry out a similar ceremony, deliberately walking the prisoner past other condemned men. I thought of Scot Kenny Richey, an innocent on Ohio's death row for most of his adult life, watching other men walk that walk. The night after an execution, the screws batten down the hatches, knowing fine well they have provoked hell in the minds of the other cons. Maybe the Frankland screws suspected something similar would be caused by my daylight departure.

Me? I didn't give a fuck – I was off home.

They were going to set me free from Frankland for the second time in six months and, apart from the timing, nothing much had changed. We edged, step by slow step, towards the big gate that would allow me through to reception for a shower and a shave. Then, dressed in my civvies again, I would be ready to step out into the free world. But that's how they were going – step by slow step.

I knew their game. Well, call me a quick learner, eh? Three screws and a dog taking me through one of the most secure jails in the country – bombproof, tank-proof and impervious from attack from the air. Why? It was that last demonstration of power. One final show that said I left only when they let me leave – no matter what the Home Office had ordered. I knew their game. I wasn't about to grumble, complain or suddenly go mental. Why should I when, within a few hours, I would be home, drinking a glass of wine, holding my woman's hand and playing with my youngest boy? I knew their game and I was enjoying it.

As the gate loomed closer, the sense of déjà vu became stronger and stronger. It didn't spook me at all. Why should it? This was no dream or distortion. I had been here before.

I looked down at the big dog and smiled. He didn't smile back. Two feet in front of me, the gate remained firmly shut. The bastards were taking their time, making me sweat out long, unnecessary seconds in that place. I knew they would. I smiled again at the big dog, staring him straight in the eyes, daring him to blink.

The gate began to open slowly and that's when I got jumped. The bastard grabbed me round the neck from the back and was scratching at my face – so much for the three screws and the big dog. Who were they there to protect? Not me, for sure. The next I knew, two of the screws jumped on me and pinned me down. Everything inside me screamed defence and the best form of defence is attack.

Just then I caught sight of my attacker for the first time – the fat bitch, Jason Vella, was running away through the jail. Adrenalin pumped through my body, my teeth gritted and fists formed. My whole being was ready to kill the fucker.

'YOU BACK-STABBING COWARDLY BASTARD,' I screamed as I was held helpless by the two hefty screws. If they had just loosened their grip for a second, I'd have been up and after him in a flash but something, somewhere inside me, said, 'No.' Maybe it was that gate I was about to step through. Maybe it was a glimpse of my wee boy Dean's smile as I arrived home that night. Maybe it was just instinct.

Vella had broken one of prison's universal rules – don't do anything in front of the screws. But he'd done so for good reasons of his own and he'd chosen the perfect time for a coward. If I had smashed his face in, I would have ended up on a charge and got more jail time and, if I'd decided to kill him with my bare hands, there were plenty of screws around to stop me. Just minutes from freedom, I would have paid a huge price for exacting revenge. Yet, if I'd done anything, the screws would have stopped me taking him all the way. It was the perfect scenario for the coward that he is.

The very public attack would result in him being put on a charge right enough but he probably thought that it would make him look good – a few days in solitary for attacking Paul Ferris. Plus it was in front of most of the Cat-A prisoners. The stupid bastard probably thought they'd be impressed but they knew a lot better than that.

Even as I stepped through that last gate, I remembered the time in the gym with the weights in the sock. Maybe I should have taken my chance then and just lathered him senseless. I would've in the old days. Was I going soft? Or had I changed?

Suited, booted and wearing a medley of scratches and bruises on one side of my face, a short while later I stepped through the gates of Frankland Prison. This time though, it was to no crowd of waiting media, no Reg with his car engine running, no secret rendezvous in a Glasgow hotel – it was just me and the fresh air of freedom. It smelled good.

My lift wouldn't arrive for another hour or two. What was I going to do? Hang around outside the gates? Fuck that. I'd done enough jail time for two lifetimes and this would be the last. So I was off into Durham to see the town. Why not? I was a free man. But would they let me be free for long? If so, would they leave me in peace?

No chance.

37

DEMOLITION MAN
March–September 2002

'You busy the night, Trevor?'

'Eh, no, Tam, nothing special.'

It was 1992 and Thomas McGraw, The Licensee, and an associate of his, Trevor Lawson, were having a chat in the back room of McGraw's pub, The Caravel, in Glasgow's east end.

'A've a wee bit of business for you,' said McGraw, lighting another fag. He was smoking heavily, almost chain-smoking.

'Good, good, can always do with more work.' Among other things, Lawson was a builder who had carried out a number of jobs for McGraw and others.

'Urgent job, like,' said McGraw, drawing hard on his cigarette.

'Och, aren't they always?' replied Lawson, thinking of the big building jobs that were his legit earners. A punter might hum and haw over a building job for months, years sometimes, but, as soon as the decision was made to do it, it needed doing now. Every job was the same.

'This one needs sorting tonight,' McGraw continued. 'After dark.'

Trevor Lawson thought he had heard it all before but this was a new one on him. 'Fuck sake, it's a bit hard to build after dark, Tam.'

'A can imagine,' said McGraw, 'but that's no' what A'm telling ye.'

'Whit?' Lawson wondered if it was just straight tobacco McGraw was puffing so ferociously.

159

'No' build.' The Licensee went silent for a bit. 'Knock down.'

Trevor Lawson didn't like the sound of this one bit. 'Whit?'

'Ye're standing in it,' replied McGraw.

'Whit? The back room?' Trevor Lawson looked round the store-room. It had crates of bottles, barrels of beer, cases of spirits and cartons of cigarettes. Where would the bar staff keep these things if they had no back room?

'Naw, no' the fucking room,' McGraw drew deeply on his cigarette, 'the pub.'

'The whole place?' What was he getting at? The Caravel was a good earner. Why knock it down? 'Ye're joking?'

'Naw, A'm no' fucking joking.' This was too serious for him to crack funnies about. Too serious by half.

'How?' What Lawson meant was 'why' and it was a serious question. Deadly serious. He was as tuned in as anyone to the recent events. Arthur Thompson's son, Fatboy, shot dead, me jailed accused of his murder, my mates, Bobby Glover and Joe Hanlon shot and dumped on the route of Fatboy's funeral on the morning of the funeral itself. Of course he had heard all about that. It was all everyone and the media were talking about. Trevor Lawson had also heard the rumours that The Licensee had been involved in Bobby and Joe's murders.

'A need the place demolished in a hurry, Trevor, simple as that. So get the fuck oan wi' it.' McGraw was getting irritated now. Hadn't he put a lot of work Lawson's way? Wasn't he due some loyalty?

'Aw right, Tam, aw right. Keep your shirt on.'

'Look, Trevor . . .' McGraw rubbed his face hard. He hadn't had much sleep lately and it showed. 'All ye need to know is that The Caravel can't exist tomorrow. Not one fucking brick, right?'

'Whit, you want . . .'

'Every fucking bit removed. By light tomorrow, this pub will not exist, will have never existed. Just a flat piece of land. A'll make it worth your while,' promised The Licensee. 'Very worth your while.'

'A'll have to get the bulldozer brought here. And two lorries with drivers . . .'

'Well, get on the blower the fuck 'n' fix it.'

By next morning, nothing existed of The Caravel. The act itself was illegal since you need planning approval to demolish a building. Yet no action was ever taken against Thomas McGraw or his wife, Margaret, the official owner whose name was above the door. What did she think about her man knocking down her pub? Did she know why?

Trevor Lawson didn't know it but, the night he agreed to demolish The Caravel, he charted out the rest of his life. And he had just bought himself an early and bloody end.

38

ONE DOWN

Isn't it funny how one single act can change almost everything about a person's life? This was never truer for anyone else than it was for the Demolition Man.

Trevor Lawson was widely felt to be an OK guy, at the start. He was from travelling folk and had taken to doing building work, starting off with laying tarmac driveways and moving on to bigger jobs. Then he met someone who was to change his life – Gordon Ross, The Licensee's second-in-command. Ross got on well with Lawson who soon signed up with The Licensee as his transportation man. When he was told to, he'd secure vehicles and see to it that certain items – most often guns – were moved from A to B.

For years, McGraw had been trading in weapons to the cops in return for favours such as charges being dropped against some of his people. In one case, Chic Glackin, an old pal of Gordon Ross, had been caught with thousands of Es and gone runaway to Spain. A few shooters to the cops and Glackin was allowed to come home under a false name for one uninterrupted Christmas with his family. In early January, Glackin was meant to hand himself in but, instead, he shot off to Canada where he was eventually lifted. In spite of that, when he went to trial, he was found not guilty. Trading in arms was important all right and Lawson was up to his neck in it.

With that came expectations. At the time of the chat in the back room of The Caravel, McGraw was ordering Lawson to do a demolition job on the pub. Without needing to spell it out, he was also threatening Lawson that, if he didn't do as told, his lucrative connections with the team would be severed. Some people would have just walked away – not Lawson.

If Trevor Lawson had been in any doubt as to why he carried out that night duty demolition, within a week, the reasons became plain and public. Since Bobby Glover and Joe Hanlon were killed, information circulated Glasgow that their bodies had been taken to The Caravel and laid out where a deputation from Arthur Thompson's team came to see the proof for themselves. Pressure was on the cops to act. Eventually, a forensic team was briefed and poised to hit The Caravel – except it wasn't there to be searched any more. Officially, Strathclyde Police responded in outrage. It had been a top-secret forensic team, most sensitive information, with only those and such as those being informed. But somebody had given the nod to The Licensee and it could only have been a cop.

It wasn't just street players who were suspicious of the cops' role in Bobby and Joe's deaths. The night they were killed, they were meant to be under twenty-four-hour surveillance but somehow the polis 'lost' them. And nobody was being interviewed, nobody was pulled in and nobody was grilled about their murders. The dogs on the street knew that the cops were quite happy about the deaths of Bobby and Joe – almost as happy as they would be if I ended up on a slab.

A couple of years later, more proof came into my hands in the form of a letter from Leslie Sharp, Chief Constable of Strathclyde Police. Dated 15 January 1992, the letter was passed to me by an anonymous well-wisher. It is marked 'IN CONFIDENCE – FOR THE PERSONAL ATTENTION OF THE EDITOR' and it is addressed to the Glasgow office of *The Sun*. After the usual formalities, the Chief Constable revealed that he was seeking the editor's cooperation in restricting information in connection with a major criminal enquiry. The day before the letter was written, there had been a police raid on a house in the north of Glasgow which had resulted in the arrest of a man and woman, both aged sixty, in connection with possession of a number of firearms in their home. The letter continued:

The following information is supplied to you on a not for publication basis. There would appear to be prima facie evidence that one of the firearms recovered is the weapon which was used in the murder of Joseph Hanlon and Robert Glover whose bodies were found in a car in the east end of the city on 18 September 1991. Clearly this is a major breakthrough in the murder enquiry . . .

Major? If the cops get the gun, they usually get the killer. Why do you think hit men are so careful about disposing of their weapons? And that doesn't include leaving them with two ordinary citizens.

The letter goes on to say, 'Obviously, the criminal element will know of the arrest of the two sixty-year-old people and our recovery of the firearms.' Yes we did. The house was in the Blackhill scheme, the territory of my upbringing and a stone's throw away from The Ponderosa, the house of Arthur Thompson, The Godfather. 'However,' it continued, 'what they will not know is the result of our ballistics examinations.' He was bloody right – we didn't. Neither did the public and nor would they be told. It then reads:

Even a chance reference could therefore seriously hinder our ongoing enquiries. I therefore seek your co-operation in not reporting the two accused's appearance in court today or, if you deem this impossible, I ask that no reference be made in any reports connecting yesterday's operation and court appearance with any reporting of the Hanlon/ Glover enquiry.

It's typical awkward cop-speak but the meaning is plain – keep your traps shut and they did. The letter went to all the newspaper editors in Scotland and they all kept quiet. Responsible journalism? Maybe but some questions remain.

Did the cops not realise there were more street players hunting the murderers of Bobby and Joe than there were celebrating my pals' deaths? The hit man was sloppy in leaving his gun in that house. Maybe he was sloppy in other ways. If he knew the gun had been found, would he have panicked? Broken cover? There was more than one killer involved, for sure. One man, even one with a gun, couldn't take my pals out. If the hit squad knew the cops had a vital clue, would they have started grassing on each other?

If there were several guns, including that murder weapon, how come the old couple were never convicted? I know these people and they tell me it was all crap about any of the guns having anything to do with Bobby and Joe. What? Weren't they asked about that? Weren't they interrogated? Seems not.

Was the letter even genuine? Or was it some ploy to throw up rotten scent? I think it's the real deal.

Then the most serious questions of all. With the bodies, the car the bodies were found in and the gun, why did the cops not solve Bobby and Joe's murders? Why haven't they solved them yet? Have they even tried? Do they still have the gun? Probably not because they soon got rid of the death car – it ended up back on the street as a taxi. So why wouldn't they have the gun melted down? After all, it's only vital forensic evidence in a double murder – a double murder of street players. Did the cops want to solve Bobby and Joe's murders? Do they ever?

The night Trevor Lawson demolished The Caravel, he moved to number three in The Licensee's mob. He knew that, that night, he had destroyed evidence and lived with the responsibility with no qualms. Many people saw him as being just as guilty of killing Bobby and Joe as whoever pulled the trigger.

For once, the miser McGraw was true to his word and paid Lawson well and repeatedly. Within months, the Demolition Man had moved to a luxury house surrounded by large grounds in the country. Now that he had compromised himself once, he would be compromised again and again. Lawson became a key member of The Licensee's cartel, a group of legit people as well as mobsters who came together and ran businesses. As a legal face, Lawson fronted many of McGraw's building projects. Beware, if you live in Glasgow, Ireland, Berlin or Spain, there's a fair chance your property was constructed by The Licensed One. Pubs, clubs, taxi firms, mobile phone shops and tanning studios were all run that way – funded by McGraw's crime loot.

Over a period of a decade, Trevor Lawson got rich on the back of the cartel. Then I was released from prison. If McGraw was paranoid at my release, Lawson was terrified. He was convinced all those newspaper headlines were true and I was going to take over Glasgow again and exact revenge for all the ills that had befallen the city in my absence – and number one on my list was the killing of Bobby and Joe.

Many people wanted to avenge Bobby and Joe's deaths. Some decided that Trevor Lawson was the weak link who had crucial information. Word was sent to him through the travelling folk and he got the message loud and clear. These people had no intention of harming Lawson. They knew he wasn't directly responsible for Bobby and Joe's murders. The plan was for him to talk then walk but that's not what others – those in McGraw's team – made him believe. They told him that he was to be killed and that he shouldn't go near the guys. But Lawson had learned a lot about the street since the night he knocked The Caravel down. He knew that he didn't need to go near them – these blokes could come and get him anytime they wanted. It was a recipe for terror.

In March 2002, two months after my release, Lawson was in a pub when a bit of trouble broke out. According to people there, he took it into his head that it was a set-up to cover a hit on him. Terrified, he fled screaming from the pub and scampered across a busy road. He never made it to the other side.

Some might say that at least Lawson had a conscience. I don't think so. What he had was guilt and fear. Others might say there's some justice in Trevor Lawson meeting his end under the wheels of a motor. After all, the night he chose sides, his weapons were a bulldozer and lorries not a gun.

Me? I don't care. I'm neither sad that he died nor glad either. On the rare occasion I think of him, it's Bobby and Joe I see lying dead at that pub – the pub he destroyed.

I feel nothing about Trevor Lawson but someone did. Thomas

ONE DOWN

McGraw, The Licensee had just lost a top man. But would it be his last loss?

39

GONE BAD

'Paul, this is Gordon.'

'How you doing?'

'No' bad, Paul. Yourself?'

'Fine. Fancy a drink?'

It was an innocuous everyday introduction in a bar. I liked the look of Gordon Ross, most folk did. He was big, well built, with the type of looks some women found handsome but I couldn't say that I agreed. It's a shame that I didn't realise then that looks can be so deceptive.

My pal Bobby Glover introduced us in his pub, The Cottage Bar. Ross was working as roofer with a guy well known to us, Chic Glackin. Bobby was good mates with Ross to start with. Obviously, he didn't realise that looks were so deceptive either.

Ross and Glackin had a wee sideline working as runners for Tam Bagan. Bagan and I had been teamed up as young guys working for Arthur Thompson. We were bagmen, collecting the debts and money owed to Thompson all over the city. We were never stuck for work. Bagan and I were good at that work – too good some thought, including Thompson himself. When Fatboy Thompson went down for drug dealing and Bagan was blamed by the old man, Tam decided to walk away.

I already had my doubts about Thompson. When on the run from a load of attempted murder allegations and hiding out in

Thompson's flat on the island of Rothesay, the cops raided the place and claimed to have found heroin in my pocket. In court, I proved the polis planted the smack but one thing continued to bother me – how did they know I was in Rothesay? Apart from me and Anne Marie, my partner at that time, only two people knew we were there – Arthur and Fatboy Thompson.

Bagan and I left Thompson around the same time. The Godfather very publicly called it 'the revolt of the mice' and had a good laugh about it. He should have called it 'the beginning of the end' – for him, that is.

When I was in jail charged with the murder of Fatboy in 1991, Gordon Ross was in prison on another matter. Barlinnie – that's where we both were when Bobby and Joe were killed. At that time, the streets were in chaos. The old order was coming to an end and some people were sizing up which way to play it and what alliances to make. Bobby had been a friend of Gordon Ross for some years and had put a great deal of street work and money his way. Ross was just an individual but a trusted one and his allegiance was in no doubt, particularly given his closeness to Bobby, and I too liked Gordon Ross back then.

At my 1992 trial for Fatboy's murder, kneecappings and so on, I cited Gordon Ross as a witness. A few days into the trial, I scanned the packed public gallery. There was Ross sitting in the crowd as bold as you like. He knew that seeing some of the trial automatically debarred him from being called as a witness later. As it turned out, we had no intention of calling him anyway. My QC, Donald Findlay, put him on my witness list at my suggestion as someone who just might be useful. But Ross, along with a few others, had been cited as witnesses by me to test them out, to see what they would do. As it happened, most played it by the rules – which was great to see – but, right then, Gordon Ross gave me my first inkling of suspicion about him.

By the end of my trial and not guilty all round, on the steps of the High Court, I realised I faced a greater threat than prison. There, in the crowd, were two women – Paul Junior's mother, Anne Marie

McCafferty, and Karen Owens, my girlfriend. There was going to be fireworks and, when it involves those two, you wouldn't want to be caught in the crossfire.

Next, I spotted Stevie Wilkie, a journalist with *The Sun*. In return for a speedy car away from the place and the women, I promised and delivered a series of exclusive articles to the bold Stevie. As part of this, I asked Gordon Ross to meet me at *The Sun*'s Glasgow offices. While we were there, I decided to question him about certain things I'd picked up on the wire. 'Are you working for that snake McGraw?' I asked him directly.

'Eh, aye, Paul,' he said. He looked shamefaced, blushed and hung his head – as well he might.

'You know that he knew about Bobby's death even before the cops had ID'd him?'

'Aye, A've heard the rumour,' Ross replied.

'It's not a rumour,' I said, getting angry. 'He told Bobby's wife Eileen. Do you think she's making it up?'

'Naw, naw,' he said, looking down at his knees again. Ross knew Eileen well and a more honest, straightforward, trustworthy person you'll never meet. After McGraw had told her about Bobby being dead, she had rushed to The Cottage Bar where he and Joe lay dead in Joe's car. When she demanded to go through the cordon to see her man, identifying him by name, the cops pulled her in, questioning her for hours on how she knew Bobby was a victim before they did. The one person they didn't pull in was Thomas McGraw, The Licensee – the very person who had told her.

'You've just joined forces with the most poisonous snake in the grass,' I told Gordon Ross. 'One day that snake is going to bite you bad.'

Ross was a good man but, like so many other good men, his head was turned by the prospect of big and easy money. Also, he thought he'd be protected by McGraw's deal with the cops trading info for no charges. Aye, right.

Ross and McGraw's cohorts set about taking over taxi businesses throughout the city – all for McGraw, of course. They would muscle in, torch the control centres, beat up drivers and threaten and cajole the women on the phones and the owners. McGraw also saw to it that some of the local cops were given hefty brown envelopes for sitting on their thumbs and doing hee-haw. It was typical bully-boy tactics and, because of his involvement, Ross went further down in my estimation. But Ross brought more than muscle to McGraw's camp. Earlier, he had been caught at Dover in a car whose panels were stuffed with dope. It was a line he'd worked for a while. He had made good contacts in Spain and also with top Manchester faces, through his time in the English prison system. Ross's Spanish contacts brought McGraw international connections and a nice wee smuggling racket that resulted in him and most of his team going on trial in 1998. The Manchester faces brought him some street cred. The Licensed One had earned neither. But soon Gordon Ross was firmly established as McGraw's second-in-command and close to him was Billy McPhee – the heavy McGraw went on to use in the attempted hit on Tommy Campbell.

Then came a big change – Arthur Thompson, The Godfather, died. The power balance on the Glasgow streets was in chaos. Arthur Thompson hadn't just been the lead player in the city, he was also a police informant and he worked for the security service giving them the inside lowdown on Loyalists paramilitaries and the big London firms. Not only did the cops need a big player who wanted to rule the city, they also needed a major informant. There was only one choice for the blue serge mob – the biggest snake in the grass, Thomas McGraw.

McGraw's mob celebrated the week Arthur Thompson died but some should have been mourning – not for Thompson but for themselves.

40

BIG ZOLTAN AND OTHER DOGS

McGraw and his cohorts attended Arthur Thompson's funeral. When I heard of that, I thought of the old Mafia tradition of enemies going to each other's burials just to make sure they were really dead. As Thompson was laid in the ground, the cops chose McGraw to take over Glasgow and so Gordon Ross suddenly found himself the lieutenant of the most ambitious, most protected, most power-crazy team in the city.

But it wasn't all sweetness and light for Ross, not even then. One time, around 1994, he searched me out. 'I'm fed up, Paul,' he started.

'Surprised to see you,' I countered telling him a truth we both already knew.

'It's no good working with McGraw,' he went on. 'The prick just wants you to do all the dirty work and he takes all the money and the credit.'

'I did warn you.'

'So you did. But it's like his fucking wife is always sticking her neb in and he's shit scared of her.' I just laughed and he continued, 'And that fucking dog of his. Did you hear about it?'

'Big Zoltan,' I said the words dramatically in a singsong voice. 'No.'

'You know how he spoiled it stupid?'

'Oh, aye.' Zoltan was right up there alongside McGraw's other loves – The Jeweller, his wife, and money.

172

'Well, the big bastarding hound didn't like me, right? Always slavering and growling at me. One time, I got up to leave McGraw's place and the fucking dog took a mouthful out of my arse.'

Me? I'm saying nothing – just pissing myself laughing, thinking there was some natural justice in the world after all.

To be fair to big Ross, he was smiling too. 'So I planned my revenge, OK? Slipped the big bastard a load of paste. Well, it'd eat anything.' (For the innocents, paste is pure speed and it's powerful stuff.)

'The poor fucking dog must have gone out of his mind,' I said, all my sympathy lying with the dog – after all, it wasn't his fault he lived with The Licensed One.

'Aye, well,' Ross continued, as he rubbed his face in an embarrassed sort of way, 'it started to go mental. Then it just keeled over. Fucker died of a heart attack.'

I'm sorry about the dog – I really am. I like dogs, even angry ones, but the whole scene was just so farcical that I was pissing myself laughing.

'McGraw's face has been like fizz ever since,' Ross reported and, at that, he suddenly looked serious and a bit sad. The prick – who did he think he was fooling?

The meeting with Ross ended with him asking me if he could move back to my team. I said no – politely but firmly. As much as I had enjoyed his tales about the poor dog, it was a fly-fishing expedition for his boss, The Licensee. Fuck that.

While I was in jail on the gunrunning convictions in 1998, I got some good news. The Licensee and most of his cronies had been lifted and charged with massive dope smuggling from Spain. Now there's justice. For years, Ross and others had been into taking cars across and packing special spaces in the bodywork and panels full of cannabis. This was an exceptionally lucrative ploy. In the 1990s, you could buy a kilo of top grade Moroccan dope for around £300. In the UK it could be sold on for between £1,850 and £2,200 – some mark-up. And one car could take up to fifty kilos. With a couple of motors coming in a week – nothing too greedy or obvious – there was a healthy profit being made and the drivers got a wee bit of sun as well. But, of course, The Licensed One had to get greedy.

Their mob had minibuses converted which meant they could up the loads massively. The east end of Glasgow, where The Licensee and his bitches are based, is one of the poorest areas in Europe but it's also a breeding ground for some of the best football talent Scotland produces. So, that kind man McGraw offered the buses and his team as drivers and escorts to take boys' football clubs abroad for tournaments. That, of course, wasn't enough either and, before long, it was youth clubs, school groups, Sunday Schools – any excuse and all good cover for drug traffickers. Then they got too greedy and were caught.

Most of the squad, including McGraw, Ross, McPhee and McGraw's brother-in-law John Healy, were held in the pokey pending the trial. McGraw was held with the other crew in Barlinnie. As soon as I heard that, I wrote to one of his co-accused, Manny McDonnell, an Irish bloke I respected, and I warned him well. Manny was an ex-top IRA man who had had a wee fall-out with them over some funds. That's how he came to be working with McGraw, a well-known Loyalist supporter. That's street life in Glasgow for you.

McGraw, along with TC Campbell and a stack of others, had originally been lifted for being involved in the Ice-Cream Wars murders. In prison, all the accused chatted together and shared information. Being accused of a terrible offence you didn't commit binds people together and makes them close and trusting of each other. Big mistake.

McGraw had more to explain than most. He had been near the Doyle Family's house, asking people to torch their door the night they were killed and there were people willing to testify to that effect. In spite of that, he was suddenly released by the Procurator Fiscal and all charges against him were dropped. It seems he had only been in the jail to glean as much info as possible on the bold TC and then pass it to the cops. Manny was warned by me and several others that McGraw would play that Judas game again and not care who he had to sacrifice.

In 1998, while he was in jail accused of the drug trafficking offences, the Licensed One had many visitors and he was allowed to see some of them in private. One day, a young prisoner thought he recognised the bloke sitting gabbing to the snake. When the visitor spotted the young guy, he put his thumb to his nose and stuck out his tongue and that's when he blew his cover. Some time earlier, the young guy had been arrested on a robbery charge, grilled for hours and then stuck on an ID parade. He wasn't fingered by the witness so the cops had to release him. As the young boy reached the cop shop door and freedom, he turned to one polis jabbed his thumb against his nose, stuck his tongue out and roared, 'GET IT UP YEZ!' and then took to his heels. Here was that very same cop returning the compliment. The young guy made sure all of McGraw's co-accused knew their boss was meeting cosy-like with the cops and they weren't happy about it at all.

A couple of days later, McGraw was overheard on the payphone to his wife bleating, 'They're all calling me a grass, Mags.' As if that was news to her. A short while later, he had to be moved to the seg unit for his own protection.

The trial was eventually held in the High Court in Edinburgh, not Glasgow, so all the accused were moved to Saughton Prison. McGraw was still under protection and so he was given a cell in the wing with the nonces and ponces. While on remand waiting that trial, The Licensee was paranoid that he was going to be taken out or that someone was poisoning his nosh. He just stopped sleeping and eating and, by the time he appeared in court, he looked like someone in the advance stages of some terminal disease. Wishful thinking.

Everyone who knew how McGraw worked with the cops was convinced he'd walk free and he did – along with Ross, McPhee and other close team members but John Healy went down big time. McGraw had saved his crew by squealing to the cops on a whole heap of cases but he hadn't seen fit to save Healy. One dangerous player, Healy would come back to haunt McGraw but not for a good few years.

The snitch and his bitches now thought they were untouchable and it showed. But just how touchable they actually were they were about to discover.

41

WORSE THAN MURDER

'Ho, it's that wee fucking tart,' Gordon Ross said as he leaned against the bar and grinned.

'Ha, so it is. You still doing it for free, hen?' Billy McPhee asked. Standing over the three people sitting at the table, McPhee held the floor.

They were in the Shettleston Juniors' Social Club in Glasgow's east end and with them was McPhee's cousin, George 'Crater Face' McCormack – not a pretty sight. Crater Face was a runner and fetcher for that mob although, officially, he was the taxi driver. In the east end, it's the commonly held view that he drove McGraw into Bankend Street, where the Doyle Family lived, on the night they were torched and killed in the so-called Ice-Cream Wars.

'Is that your ma, hen? Jesus Christ, A hope so cos ye'll no' know yer da, eh?'

The three thugs were tormenting a young woman, her boyfriend and her mother who were sitting having a quiet drink on a Saturday night. The reason? Gordon Ross's son, Gordon Junior, had gone out with the girl at one point but she had thrown him over for another young man. It was just kids' stuff really.

After walking free from the 1998 drugs trial, Ross, McPhee and McCormack had formed an alliance from hell. They would get tanked up on Charlie and hit the pubs. Whoever got in their way got it. Slashings, beatings, stabbings, old men, young women, kids, lonely guys out for a quiet drink – they hurt whoever they wanted to hurt and, because they were doing it in their own backyards, their own people were often the ones who came off worst.

'Do you still take it up the arse, ye cunt?'

The shaming continued but it had gone too far. 'Gonnae just put a fucking sock in it?' the girl's boyfriend said, more by way of threat than a request, as he felt obliged to defend her honour.

'No, leave it,' she pled in a fearful panicky voice, grabbing her man's arm. She knew what the evil threesome was capable of. 'Let's just go.'

Too late.

'Whit's that ye're saying? Whit's that?' Gordon Ross was over and the knife blade was ripping down the young man's face in an instant. As he doubled up and groaned, the chib struck again. The two women were on their feet crying and pleading, trying to protect the bloke. For their pains, they too were slashed and battered by Ross, McPhee and Crater Face.

It was just another incident on an ordinary night when the three devils were on the loose. One young guy, just an ordinary bloke, holding down a decent job, was crossing the road to go and meet his pals when he was grabbed from behind. A razor was slid down his face on both cheeks, again and again. What for? No one knows.

An old bloke, sitting playing dominoes with his chums, was battered and stabbed for sitting on a seat one of the three bullies wanted. Night after night, similar attacks went on. Local people were becoming sickened and angry. Then it got worse.

'I want to report a rape.' The young woman's face was ashen, her hands were shaking and her voice was breaking, a sign of the tears she'd already shed and a warning of the weeping yet to come. 'I was raped.'

'Are you OK, pet?' The police sergeant at the Shettleston cop shop was older, experienced and concerned for the young woman who was just a teenager.

'Aye . . . no. I mean I'll be OK.' She turned to her friend, standing beside her for reassurance.

'Just take a wee seat then please, madam,' said the cop. 'I'll not be long. Just need to organise a room.'

Ten long minutes later, the same policeman ushered the woman into an interview room along with a female cop. After he took her name, address and other essential details, he asked, 'When did the incident take place?'

'Last night,' she muttered into a sodden paper tissue she clutched to her face.

Other questions, like where, what time and so on followed. The woman described a violent, vicious, protracted sexual assault by a gang – rape, by any other name – in a flat in the east end. It was difficult for her – very difficult – but she struggled on and gave the cops the information they needed.

Then one cop asked the crucial question – 'Who was involved?'

There were more tears and sniffles from the young woman.

'Take your time, hen,' said the sergeant, gently.

'It was yon . . .' her friend started to say but she was halted by the cop's hand going into air, palm to the front.

'We have to hear it from her – from the victim You understand?'

The girl nodded and sat silently and grim faced.

'There were a few,' the young woman began, having regained her composure. And she reeled off a few names none of which meant much to the cops. 'But there was one who was . . . who did most . . .' she hesitated before blurting out, 'Gordon Ross.'

The sergeant looked up, startled, and put his pen down on the table.

'*The* Gordon Ross?' he asked, quietly.

The young woman nodded and explained, 'The young one – Gordon Junior.'

'It was definitely him?'

'A've known him for years,' she replied, her voice tinged with indignation.

'Are you sure you want to go through with this complaint, hen?' the cop asked.

'Whaaat?' she said, unable to believe her ears after all the pain she had gone through already in just telling them about the attack – never mind all the pain and humiliation she had suffered the night before.

'These are dangerous people, you know,' answered the cop. 'You're likely to get your house torched . . . maybe worse.'

'We're no' scared of no cunt,' said the young woman's pal. 'Look what they've fucking done tae her. They deserve punished right fucking bad.'

The cop nodded at the woman but turned and addressed the victim, 'It's you that has to decide, hen. Do you want to report the crime?'

'Fucking right I do,' she spat. There were no more tears now – just white fury.

She hadn't believed the stories about The Licensee and his team being immune from prosecution for most of their dirty deeds. At worst, she thought they would cover up the scams and the drug dealing but not something like sexual assault. Could they even rape a woman and walk away scot-free? Not if she could help it.

'I want them charged. I want Gordon Ross arrested – he's the bastard that did the worst to me.'

The cop shrugged, 'Fair enough – it's your life.'

A short while before, a slightly older woman had reported an assault by Gordon Ross Junior and his mob and she had also been warned against pursuing charges because of the likelihood of bloody repercussions. Is that what we call law and order? No wonder there's street justice. Too often it's the only justice there is.

However, despite warnings from the cops, both women went on to pursue charges, going through the indignity of medical checks, other interviews, clothes being taken for forensics and swabs from the most intimate parts of their bodies. They suffered but they had done their duty. Now it was up to the police to get the rapists.

News of the attacks seeped through the east end of Glasgow like a poisonous gas. Nobody but nobody tolerates a rapist. Certain parties let it be known they were going to take the law into their own hands – the way they do when they want to administer street justice. The least Gordon Ross Junior was going to get was a severe beating but, more likely, he could expect a sharp razor drawn across his knob. That would stop him raping again. While sympathetic to their motives, I was of the view that this wasn't up to them – Gordon Ross Senior was the one who should be sorting it out. He knew the rules as well as anyone. Though his oldest son, Gordon, was a bit of a tearaway, the old man could handle him in his sleep. To me, it was up to Gordon Ross Senior to administer street justice and that was the view that prevailed. We sat back, waiting to see what Ross Senior would do. We weren't disappointed. Not half but totally.

The old Gordon Ross I knew as a mate of Bobby Glover would have had the matter sorted out in a jiffy and made sure the streets knew. He would have punished his kid big time, maybe even let him go to jail as well, and he would probably have ex-communicated the rapist from his family forever – that's how seriously we take rape. The old Ross would also have compensated the women and kept compensating them for a long time. It isn't that money can remove the pain of the rape – nothing can do that – but, in my world where so many people struggle to get by, some decent money takes one problem away. And, believe me, Ross had a lot of dosh.

Instead, Gordon Ross Senior sent a team after the young women and the two were left in no doubt as to what would happen if they proceeded with the charges – but that didn't work. Then, they offered the old father of one of the raped women £10,000 to encourage his daughter to withdraw charges – but that didn't work either. So the threats started again and, this time, the heat was turned up. The young woman and her old man must have begun to feel nervous. These were serious players they were upsetting.

Then the money deal was re-iterated. Eventually, the fear got too much for daughter and father and she agreed to drop the charges if the cash was forthcoming. Well, if she had to concede, she might as well gain something from it – she was just a citizen, after all. The trouble was she was too late – the charges had proceeded too far. Now the cops – the same ones who warned her against making a complaint in the first place – wouldn't let her drop the charges. She was in deep shit. Her father just wanted to give the money back and get on with the rape allegations. But there was a wee problem with that solution – she had spent some of it. What could she do?

The young woman left the city one night and has never been seen again since. I really hope she's happy and has found someone to help her heal the wounds of the rape.

Ross Senior still had a problem. The charges against his son might well proceed. Then he was saved by a wee accident, an administrative error, the kind that happens all the time – not. The cops lost Gordon Ross Junior's DNA sample which they had taken as part of the rape investigation and that wasn't all – some of the forensics taken from the young woman were no longer to be found either. Even if they managed to track her down and dragged her to court, it would be her word against that of Ross Junior and he was sure to be backed up by some of his lowlife mates who were there that night – and, no doubt, some who weren't.

So the rape case was dropped – full stop. The other assault victim was also too terrified to go ahead and withdrew her complaint. Accept it? No chance. If the cops wouldn't fix it, the street would. Gordon Ross Junior has had to be on his toes ever since. One of these days, someone will catch him and justice will be delivered.

As for Gordon Ross Senior, he had shown the streets that he had gone as low as you can get. Isn't it amazing how one bad deed brings out new information? It turned out that Ross Senior had himself been involved in sexual assaults and rapes some years back. Like father like son, eh? And it got worse when it was revealed that his son had already hospitalised two other young women after similar attacks. Even then, Ross Junior didn't stop. For a while, he took to driving around the city streets late at night in a Transit van, looking for women to pick up, and he wasn't too bothered if they were willing or not. There was more grief for more women coming from him and his old man knew that fine well.

Gordon Ross Senior had just lost his last ounce of respect on the streets of Glasgow. Now he'd have to live with the dogs he called his team mates, McGraw's bitches.

Ross Senior had totally converted to McGraw's side. In 1999, while young John Simpson slept on the couch in his aunt and uncle's house in Pollok, Ross crept in on him and blasted him three times in the skull. Why? Simpson had slashed McGraw's brother on the cheek in a fight. Against all the odds, Simpson survived – well, he wasn't south-side ruler Specky Boyd's equaliser for nothing. But Simpson fell out with his own team and, a few months later, he was gunned down and killed in his own patch in Pollok.

So Gordon Ross had become one of McGraw's bitches, for sure. There was just one problem – one of them was about to bite him big time.

'Let's go outside and sort this out,' is what Gordon Ross would have said if he was challenged in a pub – one his locals, like The Shieling Bar on Glasgow's Shettleston Road where he was one night in October 2002. Ross had been drinking there, no doubt, but then he did drop by for a drink most nights. No one saw him leave – of course – but leave he did. To settle a dispute? To meet someone? By arrangement? Whoever knows isn't saying. But what is certain is that, out in the black night of a Scottish autumn, Gordon Ross was knifed and hit the deck. He lay there in the rain bleeding to death as passers-by ignored him and boozers from the pub stepped over his body as they hurried on their way. Ross was paying the price for tormenting innocent citizens and protecting his son from rape charges. He lay there on the rain-soaked pavement for almost an hour before a passing cop car stopped and found him dead.

But many people knew about his troubles much earlier that night. Across from the pub, there's a service station. Parked in the shadows back from the pumps, away from the lights of the forecourt, was a jeep. As Ross lay on the ground bleeding, two men jumped out and quickly crossed the road. Unknown to them, nearby, the young team watched. They knew who was on the deck and they had left him lying there. Ross had created too many problems for them and their families – so why should they help him now? But they stayed there and watched the two men from the jeep.

Both the men knew exactly where they were going. One stood on either side of Gordon Ross and looked down at him as he lay there like a stuck pig in the black night, leaking black blood on to the pavement. For five, ten, fifteen long seconds, they stood and looked down on the man. Then they turned on their heels and headed quickly back to their motor. As they did so, they crossed the beam of a street lamp and the young team caught their faces. They knew who the two men were and they weren't surprised, not surprised at all.

All the way up Shettleston Road, the jeep driver laughed and sang a favourite song. He fancied himself as a bit of a crooner. It was a good night for Ross's best friend, Billy McPhee. He had just been promoted to number two for The Licensee who was sitting by his side. But for how long?

42

WITH FRIENDS LIKE THESE

'Check that cupboard in the back.'

'He widnae have a stash underneath a fitted carpet would he, boss?'

'Fuck knows. Lift it anyway.'

The Licensee and his team were paying a house call but it was business not social. Even as their partner Gordon Ross lay in his own blood on the wet street, they ransacked his home.

Ross's young girlfriend was in the house, terrified by the thugs she had considered friends till they barged in that night. They cajoled and bullied her, telling her that Ross owed them a lot of money. They demanded to know where he kept his stash and, more importantly, the legal papers for the shops and properties he owned.

Gordon Ross hadn't been stupid. Knowing how The Licensee pulled strings around Glasgow, Ross had gone south and hired a lawyer in Manchester.

One time, I had been fond of Ross. One time. When I heard of his murder in October 2002, I had been out of jail for the second time in a year for only a few months – just weeks really – and I had other things on my mind. Before jail time, I'd been doing really well and mostly on a legitimate basis. One of my best legit businesses before jail had been Premier Security. The company had gone from nothing to being a UK-wide business in less than a year. If I had just stuck to that profession, I would have been OK.

Even before I left prison, I'd been contacted by a number of blue-chip companies, asking if I would advise them on the security issues. By that time, I knew the politicians were circling the security sector, trying to shake out people with criminal convictions. So no way was I going to go down that road again just to be kicked publicly. But others had approached me, asking me to set up a security firm again. Instead of that, I encouraged certain parties to get together – people I knew who had a lot to offer – and set up their own company. Thus Frontline Security was formed.

The trouble was that the media wouldn't leave me alone. I had deliberately established myself as an independent security consultant but they insisted that I owned Frontline. Numerous times they were invited into Frontline's offices to check their registration, their books, their contracts but they always declined. You don't want the facts to ruin a good story, do you?

All I wanted to do was earn a decent, honest living for me and my kids while I was working on long-term creative projects. Every time there was a headline slating Frontline, my name was attached as 'gunrunner', 'gangster' and so on. They say newspapers are to-morrow's chip wrappings. Maybe but they almost cost me my living.

So, I was struggling to stay ahead of that rat pack. It was the number one priority for me and mine. In the old days, something like Ross's murder would have had a significant impact on my life. But the old days were done. All I thought of Gordon Ross was that he was seduced by a lust for power and money and he'd become corrupt – a good man gone bad.

The night Gordon Ross died, the mob he thought were his pals broke into his safe looking for money and papers of ownership of businesses. Ross had got rich on the back of McGraw – or so McGraw thought – and now McGraw was reclaiming what was rightfully his with extras.

Gordon Ross was a millionaire and no doubt. The family didn't exactly try and hide it. His own father would buy rounds of drinks in pubs and blether on about how rich his boy was. Money is McGraw's god and he wanted all of it whether it belonged to Gordon

Ross or not. Before long, properties that were known to belong to Gordon Ross, like a row of shops at Hallhill Road, would pass to McGraw. Not bad for one night's work.

They didn't stop at searching the house but moved on to offices, garages and warehouses that big Ross had access to. There was also the small matter of a bit of dodgy business he had carried out on their behalf and £100,000 he'd collected just that day. Where had he hidden it? The thieves got a lot that night but still weren't satisfied they had it all – they hadn't got the £100K for sure. So they took to the streets searching for a car and not just any car – a black BMW driven by Gordon Ross Junior. They never liked the son – few folk did – and would now take pleasure in making him tell them the hard way where his father kept his loot.

They didn't mess about with politeness in pursuing black BMWs. A young female driver found herself being chased at speed by three motors. One passed her then pulled in front, slamming the brakes on. Another car parked at her offside while the last blocked the rear. She was trapped. Men with baseball bats jumped from the cars and yanked open her car doors. Terrified, she thought she was going to be beaten and robbed, maybe worse. It was a case of obvious mistaken identity and the men drove off. But she knew who they were though they didn't recognise her. She was a female relative of TC Campbell, the very man they had tried but failed to kill.

Gordon Ross had moved to work with The Licensee, lured by money and power. Though he got both, he also got greedy and started working on his own on the side. There's no rule against that. Gang members are always free to do their own thing, as long as it doesn't compete with the team. But Ross was getting too big, too powerful, and The Licensee didn't like that one bit. Then there was the question of Ross's back-stabbing pal, Billy McPhee.

'Paul?'

'Who's this?' It was 1993 and I was in my house at Jaegar Gardens, Baillieston, listening to some male voice I didn't recognise at the other end of the phone line.

'Billy,' he croaked, 'Billy McPhee.' I didn't know McPhee well enough for him to make a social phone call to me. He was always around the scene and I knew he was friends with a good mate of mine, Stevie Moffat.

'How you doing?'

'A'm in bad way, Paul. Need a bit of help.' McPhee had already said too much over the phone and I wasn't about to ask for more info. He was friend of a friend so I'd help him. That was one of the basics of the code. Plain and simple.

'What the fuck's happened to you?' I asked later as he slipped into my car at the arranged meeting place. It was an obvious question since McPhee was soaked in blood.

McPhee explained to me that he had been in the city centre at Victoria's nightclub, known locally as Viccie's. Well, that was one of the more polite names. It was the top club and a haunt for footballers and street players alike. The bold boy, Frank McAvennie of Celtic, West Ham and St Mirren, spent more on champagne there in a month than most folk earn in a year. Butter-wouldn't-melt-in-his-mouth Ally McCoist was another high-flying customer.

One typical Viccie's story concerned a certain Rangers player who, one night at the club, slapped the arse of a really cute young woman in front of him – well, footballers were kings in Viccie's or so they thought. The trouble was she was the daughter of Frankie 'Donuts' Donaldson, a street player of some repute and not one given to forgiving. Next day Donuts was parked outside the Rangers stadium, Ibrox, waiting for the player – and he was there the day after and the day after that and . . . you get the picture. Having been warned who he had insulted, the footballer bought a brand-new, trendy car, had it filled full of flowers and delivered to the young woman in question with a fat cheque – nice try but it didn't work. Donuts didn't need valuables – what he demanded was respect. A short while later, the footballer left Rangers for another club. Some say it was Donuts who made him seek a transfer.

Drugs, particularly high quality coke and Es, swamped Viccie's. Billy McPhee explained to me that he was in the toilet 'seeing to some business' and there was a disagreement with another party. A fight broke out, knives were pulled and the other guy came off second best.

'I stuck him, Paul,' he said in the car as I drove. 'A right good one.'

It was the way of our world. I took McPhee to a safe house, got him patched up, washed and a clean set of clothing. It was what any decent street player would do for the pal of a pal but it was one of the worst calls I ever made. McPhee did the bloke so proper that he died. That night it was no longer a straightener but a murder investigation.

McPhee had told me that my mate, Stevie Moffat, had been in the club toilets at the time of the knifing but I knew Stevie would be safe from any accusations of the killing. Stevie was a martial arts expert and more deadly with his bare hands than most blokes tooled up with a machine gun and he took entirely justified pride in this. Then he was betrayed. Another bloke had been in those toilets that night – Billy Fullerton whose father had been leader of the legendary Billy Boys razor gang. Stevie Moffat was charged with the killing yet Billy Fullerton could have saved him by giving evidence. Fullerton refused and Stevie was found guilty and he was going down big time.

A short while later, Billy McPhee was facing charges of possessing Charlie and skunk. Who popped up as his witness? Billy Fullerton. All of this is more intriguing since, not long before that, there had been an incident between Fullerton and Ross. Ross was giving Fullerton the evil eye at some party and, later, as Fullerton was leaving, he was confronted by Ross with a gun in his mitt.

'Oh, aye,' said Fullerton, cocky like, 'what you going to do with that? Shoot me?'

'Aye,' said Ross and promptly pumped a slug into Fullerton's leg.

Despite this, Fullerton still sang like a canary to get the heat lifted off Ross's pal McPhee but ran a mile from helping the innocent Stevie Moffat. The Licensee's mark was all over it. He'd pull strings to get his men out of the fire but wouldn't lift a finger to help those not allied to him – even if they were innocent. But street justice was to prevail. About a year later, in 1994, Billy Fullerton was found slumped over the steering wheel of his car in Bridgeton. Stabbed and bleeding badly, he died a short time later in the city's Royal Infirmary.

Billy McPhee had started out as a football casual, following Rangers. I don't pretend to understand guys who chase violence for the sake of it but even they have their standards. According to the top boys of that time, McPhee was a second-rater who specialised in slashing those already fallen and were helpless rather than leading the charge. That summed him up. Hurting people remained his speciality. When he tied in with McGraw, The Licensee, originally it was as muscle. When he had gone out to kill TC Campbell that day, he was ambushing a man who had spent years in prison, who had suffered great pain and strife, who he thought was an easy touch. That's the odds McPhee liked – though with TC he'd got them all wrong.

Billy McPhee was about to make another mistake – the biggest wrong judgement of his life.

43

DEAD MAN WALKING
March 2003

'What you looking at, you cunt?' Billy McPhee staggered more than stood in the middle of the bar at Shettleston Juniors' Club, waving a knife in the air. As per usual, he'd been running amok. Elsewhere that night, he'd chibbed two young guys for no greater sin than being in the wrong place at the wrong time. McPhee wasn't finished for the night. 'Ye're aw fucking shitebags,' he roared, glowering at the bowed, terrified heads around him. 'Fucking waste of time.'

McPhee slipped the long-bladed knife into the back of his waistband making sure the handle didn't get caught in the bulletproof vest he was never without. Standing at the bar, he lifted his pint and continued gabbing to his cousin, Crater Face McCormack. He didn't notice the door swing open at speed.

'McPHEE!' someone shouted.

'Who the fuck wants to know?' asked McPhee, turning from the bar in the direction of the voice.

'This is for you, you bastard.' The man lifted his pistol and shot Billy McPhee in the face at point blank range.

Chaos broke out in the pub, with customers diving under tables, running for the toilets, heading to the fire doors. They thought they were all going to die but the gunman took to his heels and fled the building. It was only McPhee he was after. Billy McPhee lay on his back, blood flowing from his mouth and a hole in the side of his face. Surely he was a goner? Then someone leaned over him to check his state and heard a gurgling and the sound of breathing. He was alive.

The hit on Billy McPhee would have worked if the gun had been of any half decent calibre but it was a gas gun nicknamed The Rat Catcher for obvious reasons. Powerful enough to kill small, furry rodents, it was just too weak to take out the larger variety. To make matters worse, the bullet hit McPhee in the mouth slightly off centre. Instead of smashing through the back of his mouth and into the soft tissue of his brain, it crumpled some teeth and ripped off a section of his throat. He'd live but he'd never be much of singer again.

It was December 2002, Gordon Ross had been dead just a couple of months and now The Licensee's brand-new lieutenant almost copped his lot. Me? I didn't care and wouldn't have shed a tear if he had died. But there was some street justice in the damage to McPhee's voice box.

'That's that wee cunt Ferris back in jail again.' It was a stranger, an unknown man, talking to Billy McPhee in Glasgow's Barrachnie Inn on the night I had been recalled to prison in 2002. The two men shook hands and laughed. McPhee took him to the bar and ordered drinks. The pair were being watched by curious local eyes.

The stranger turned out to be a cop. No surprise there – McPhee had gone the same way as his boss, The Licensee. That night, Billy McPhee threw a party to celebrate my return to jail. It's great to be popular.

McGraw isn't known for his socialising after dark. Unless he feels absolutely safe, he'll not venture anywhere with shadows. Mr Paranoia must have felt safe that night with me locked up because he actually turned up to join in the celebrations. With the drinks flowing and everyone in a happy mood, the singing started. McPhee fancied himself as a singer and took to the floor. It was his party after all. Then he went over and kneeled at his boss's feet. Bad enough? There's worse. Staring into McGraw's cracked phizog, he belted out a version of 'He Ain't Heavy, He's My Brother'. There wasn't a dry eye in the house. But you could hear the dry boaking all the way through the east end.

McPhee might well have been pissed but he had paid his homage to the snake in the most sentimental way imaginable. The story of that song spread fast. Billy McPhee might have felt a wee bit of embarrassment with his hangover the next morning but that wasn't the half of his problems. That song had angered a hell of a lot of people.

In early March 2003, five months after his slaying, the cops had finally cleared Gordon Ross's body for burial. The funeral must have seen the biggest collection of east-end rogues in a long time. Gordon Ross Junior was there, of course, and his younger brother, Stephen. Jim Toner, who was done for a large consignment of cannabis in Ireland in 2000, returned to Scotland on bail but the case never went to trial which allowed him to act as one of the coffin bearers.

Tall blonde Caroline Dott cried a lot. She'd been caught with two players, Willie Hassard and John Lyons, in a carload of dope in Spain. One of Ross's girlfriends, he didn't take care of her – for starters, the mule motor was actually registered in her name.

Then there were Willie McConnachie and Alan Cross. Willie was a runner for McGraw between Scotland and Spain and Alan found Bobby Glover and Joe Hanlon's bodies outside The Cottage Bar. Cross was later nabbed with a consignment of smack in Amsterdam.

Jim Steele turned up. A player himself, he was also the brother of Joe Steele who was wrongly convicted of the Ice-Cream Wars murders along with TC Campbell. Big Drew Drummond, a long-time face for McGraw, was there. One time, he threw himself from my car when travelling at speed down the M74 – he couldn't have liked my driving.

George 'Crater Face' McCormack, McPhee's cousin, attended. He helped McPhee and Gordon Ross wreak fear and havoc on the innocent of the east end. And James 'Mudsie' Mullen, a front for McGraw when required was also there. Mudsie's brother Paddy and Craig 'Hairy Hands' Devlin had gone to city's Easterhouse scheme a couple of years earlier to sort out a minor matter. Mullen got shot in the leg, Devlin had a machete stuck in his arm and his new Merc wrecked. Minor? Aye, right. Another pal of Billy McPhee, Willie Quinn, put in an appearance too.

And The Licensed One was there, of course – he had to be. To do anything else would be to lose face. With him were his boy Winkie, now well over a serious heroin problem, and his wife Margaret, as usual dripping with gold. But McGraw stood aside from the family, plotting with his cohorts, talking out the side of his mouth, eyes peeled for eavesdroppers – funeral or not, it was just another business day for McGraw. But what sort of business was he planning?

A photographer was hiding in the bushes and that brave guy caught the lot on film.

Outside the church, away from the throng, a man walked on his own – a tall man and handsome, some might say, but not today. Yet his face wasn't grim through grief – Billy McPhee had just been told that he was next for the coffin.

Gordon Ross's funeral was the first time McPhee had ventured out since being blasted in the coupon. Since leaving hospital months before, he'd holed up in one of his houses, a loaded gun close by his side and an ear cocked for cars outside. Being shot in the face can give you a hell of a fright. But McPhee couldn't stay away from Ross's funeral. That would make him look guilty of Ross's early end. Besides, he would've calculated that he was safe. A golden rule of the street is that, at funerals, all battles are postponed to another day.

In spite of the whispered warning of impending doom, McPhee decided it was time he got back to his normal life. A few days later, he ventured out to a Rangers football match. One of McGraw's mob was there to drive him about. After the game they were intending to go to a pub in the Barras where McPhee had arranged to meet some people. At the last minute, McPhee changed his mind and ordered the driver to take him the Springcroft Tavern in Baillieston. Suspicious of the world, McPhee probably cancelled the meeting thinking there was a good chance word had been leaked that he was due to be at that place at that time. He reckoned he was playing safe. Little did he know.

The Springcroft Tavern was a regular haunt for McPhee. It was part of the Brewers Fayre chain of pubs, a nice place where you could take your kids and expect no trouble. The pub was thronged with families having lunch and watching a Scotland versus Wales rugby match on the telly. A big sports fan, McPhee had some lunch, a pint and settled down to watch the match.

It would have been a totally relaxed afternoon but for the hefty bulletproof vest he wore. His companion saw his unease and suggested he was safe enough to take it off. McPhee agreed – most unlike him. A few minutes later, his pal went to the toilet and McPhee was too interested in the rugby to notice that he was taking his time. Nor did he hear the pub door swing open and fast feet come running towards him across the carpeted floor.

The first stroke of the knife caught him in the throat. McPhee struggled and struck out but the chib kept coming at him again and again and again. Twenty-seven deep wounds later, the hit man clutched the plastic hood he wore on his head and sprinted out of the pub. There was blood everywhere. Children were screaming, grown men weeping, someone was sick and another emptied their bladder where they stood. Two women stooped and tried to save Billy McPhee. They failed.

When the police team hit the Springcroft Tavern, they found the CCTV tape was blank. Funny that. That's what usually happens when a hit takes place. Yet the pub was packed with witnesses, just ordinary families, and all were willing to help identify the killer. None could.

Blood was smeared all over the inside of the bar door – some McPhee's, some belonging to another person. The hit man? Probably but the forensics didn't throw up a known match. Outside the Springcroft Tavern, hidden in the bushes surrounding the large car park, the cops found killing knives, sharp hatchets, heavy hammers, all planted by Billy McPhee in case of an emergency. Good planning, wrong places.

In due course, the cops would arrest and charge someone for McPhee's murder. But that would produce twists and turns of its own as we'll find out.

Immediately after McPhee's demise, someone felt a cold draft – Thomas McGraw, The Licensee. A year before, he had three close henchmen who thought they were invincible in the city. Now he had none. Power and money – would they still be enough to tempt new recruits to his camp? Shrouds don't have pockets after all.

Did McGraw have any power left at all now his muscle had gone? Would he leave the country? Lock himself inside his fortified house and never be seen again? Would he retire?

There is a public version and a real version to what happened next with McGraw. We'll give you the reality later in the book.

With the death of the last of McGraw's team, a journalist came to me and said it was peculiar that all three deaths had occurred since my release from prison. 'A sinister link or just a coincidence?' he asked. That answer will also have to wait till later.

Me? I had a life to lead and I was about to do battle with what the politicians and the cops try to convince us is the evil of modern times – drugs.

44

THE FOURTH EMERGENCY SERVICE

January 2003

'MOBSTERS' £10M DRUG PLOT'. It was a typical tabloid headline and had made the front page, as you might expect. The trouble was it was about me and I knew sweet fuck all about it.

This wasn't just alleging a deal of £10m, serious enough as that was, but an organisation that would sell £10m of smack and coke on Scottish streets every single month. That's not dealing – that's an empire.

The story appeared in the *Daily Record* and I could smell its then editor Peter Cox's touch all over it. He'd been the same bloke who reneged on the serialisation deal with *The Ferris Conspiracy*, whose actions got a Home Office ban on me speaking with Reg, who had printed police propaganda about me and McGraw battling it out and whose headlines were actually referred to in the police report that got me wrongly sent back to jail.

Was it personal? It felt like it.

The article read like crime fiction – the kind of crime fiction I don't read because it simply isn't real. Two other blokes, called David Santini and Ian 'Blink' McDonald, and I were supposed to have set up a factory to cut and wrap the gear just outside Glasgow. You'd certainly need a factory and a workforce to cut £10m of smack and coke every month. That's one big haul especially since we were supposed to be buying direct from Turkey and Afghanistan where quality is high and prices rock bottom.

Once the drugs were landed in the UK, we apparently planned to move them north in vehicles that were deliberately tampered with so they'd break down. Clever sods that we are, we'd fix the cars so they couldn't be repaired roadside then call the AA or RAC breakdown service. They would then have to transport the cars and vehicles the final leg of the journey. The cops would never suspect broken-down motors to be used to move large-scale drug deals, would they? Like I said, crime fiction with a plot thicker than my old mum's custard.

But it's not funny. One of the things that really gets my goat is the effect such controversial nonsense has on my ma, Jenny. Believe it or not, she's of the old school and thinks everything she reads in the papers must be true – even when it's about her own son and I'm trying to tell her it's not true. She takes some convincing and worries like hell I've fallen back into my bad old ways. Not funny.

But, on the same day that story broke, there *was* one humorous incident. A pal of mine – we'll call him Stevie – specialises in personal security, bodyguards, armoured cars, that type of thing. Stevie had gone down south to pick up a new motor – a big bulletproof job with blacked-out windows. The bloody thing broke down on the way up north and he called AA. He phoned me from the back of the pick-up truck towing his car to explain what had happened and that he'd be late for a meeting with me later that day.

'What the fuck are you laughing at?' he growled, unhappy that I thought there was some humour in his predicament.

'Where are you, Stevie?' I asked.

'Near Manchester. Why?'

'When you get near Carlisle, get the driver to stop at a service station and buy the *Record*.'

'What the fuck for?'

'When you read it you'll see what's so funny.' As it happened the paper was a sell-out that day and he'd reached Ayrshire before he could get his hands on a copy.

'Fucking hell,' he said on the phone, 'if I'd found out by Carlisle, I'd have bought a hoodie or a skip cap for coming into Scotland.'

'In case you got mistaken for my first consignment?' I laughed. Believe me, if someone had spotted a pal of mine in the back of an AA truck, on that day of all days, it would have been front-page news the next morning.

There was a stack of stuff about the story that just didn't stand up. Like the so-called warehouse-based factory. Why wasn't there a picture of it? What was worse was my alleged partnership with Blink McDonald and David Santini. I'd been pals with Ian 'Blink' McDonald and his brother 'Alco' since we were kids in Blackhill. Blink had been involved in the bank robbery in Torquay with Mick Healy that had resulted in the trial where the Judas, William 'Tootsie' Lobban, had appeared as some totally un-mysterious Witness X. After the robbery, Blink had gone on the run and was known to be tooled up. That made him dangerous in the cops' eyes.

Blink's weakness was always the ladies and one in particular – his wife at the time, Sheila. He couldn't stay away from her for long. Obviously the cops would be watching Sheila and their home. So the lovers arranged to meet some place public, some place safe, or so they thought.

After giving Sheila detailed instructions on how to lose the bizzies' tail, the two met in a Chinese restaurant in Glasgow's city centre. The place was crowded with couples and groups. Eventually Sheila and Blink relaxed and had their wanton soup, sweet and sour or whatever and a few glasses of wine. That's when every customer in the place jumped up, shoved guns in their faces and arrested them. They were all cops apart from the restaurant staff. In fact, the manager almost ended up getting arrested himself, such was the fuss he made over who was going to pay the bill.

Blink didn't even think about drawing his gun. He was surrounded by shooters pointing at him and his woman – he couldn't take risks with her. So it was off to jail for Blink and, sadly, jail ended Blink and Sheila's marriage – a right shame but not unusual. They were still good friends and Sheila spoke openly about the man she was living with, a millionaire businessman called Pat Sweeney. No problem to Blink but it was a problem for someone else.

A few months before Blink was due to be released, Sheila and Sweeney split up. The next thing you know, the millionaire is all over the newspapers talking about how that mad gangster Blink McDonald is sending heavies with sawn-off shotguns after him because of his relationship with Sheila. It was crap but dangerous crap. Blink could well have been held in jail for months or even years longer if they thought he was up to those games. Sweeney *was* having heavies round at his house and his offices but it was for another reason entirely and one that had zilch to do with Blink.

His sentence served, Blink was released and did this showy thing about getting a big white limo to pick him up at the gates – with a journalist and photographer there to record it all, of course. A set-up, in other words, for money. Showy isn't for me but there was no harm in Blink's antics. I just laughed and hoped he'd made a right bundle out of the deal. But he'd obviously not made enough. A wee while later, Blink appeared in the newspapers again. It was a series of features about what a desperado he was. Aye, desperate for cash.

Blink claimed all sorts of heroics, most of it made up. One of the worst was him talking about the Torquay robbery, being inside the bank and the cops arriving when the money was just three feet away from him at the other side of some bars. Blink McDonald was never near that bank. His job was getaway driver and he was parked half a mile away from the scene and he even blew that by hitting the gas as soon as he smelled trouble. So that was me and Blink finished – long before the headlines about the drug trafficking partnership.

David Santini was another kettle of fish. The first time I met him was through my mate Joe Hanlon. The two had done some business over a car sale and fallen out. Neither would give any quarter and what had started as a minor matter was turning ugly. Joe was all for going to the Santini house to sort it out once and for all. I tagged along with him, hoping to keep a lid on things. Joe was one of the best street fighters Glasgow has ever produced and he could go off on one big time if he thought someone was taking the piss. I just wanted the business sorted peacefully and my mate a happy man. But David and his brothers were well up for a battle. There we were in their house and me thinking it was all going to go off big time. The Santinis weren't exactly seven-stone weaklings either. Just as I resolved there was going to be a scrap, a voice came from the next room, 'Is that Willie Ferris's boy there?' Christ was I pleased to hear my old man's name being called out. The shouter was David Watson, David Santini's stepfather. He and my father were fond of each other and I sat with David Watson, having a good blether about my old man's antics in his younger day. Battle off, thank fuck.

A couple of years later David Santini did me a big favour. I was just setting up in the security business with Premier Security when a great old boy I knew, Archie Rollo from Bridgeton, died. David arranged for some of Archie's security contracts to be passed to me – around £10,000 of work, as I recall, and very nice too.

The next time I met David Santini it had to do with sex. Well, that's what the club was selling. David had bought the old casino in Royal Terrace, Edinburgh, which by then had been made into The Fantasy Bar. The place specialised in lap dancing, pole dancing, strippers, that sort of thing, and was very successful. But no one will go to a sex club if it's full of aggressive drunks and conmen so David wanted to be sure the door security was absolutely watertight. There was a nightclub upstairs that also needed cover. It was run by a very funny geezer by the name of Gordon Wilson except he was always called 'Bond, James Bond' – I'll let you imagine the reasons for this. David reckoned that giving the door contracts to local firms would encourage a lot of slack – stewards letting their mates in, drug dealers paying a wee bit of commission for entry and the like. So Premier Security ran the doors at The Fantasy Bar and there was no bloody slack.

That was the last time I ever saw David Santini. He got nabbed a wee while later with something like £1 million of heroin. The story the cops gave to the media was that, when they busted through his door, he had been cutting the gear. There was so much of it around that everything was covered in fine layer of powder. Apparently David looked more like a baker than a drug dealer. It's a funny story but I don't believe it – that kind of carelessness just doesn't seem to be David Santini's style. Still, he was sent down for eleven years and was released in December 2002, just a few months after my release from my recall.

That's how they invented the threads of that story – Santini the big drug dealer, Blink McDonald the gunman and my childhood pal and, of course, me. I suppose I was meant to be the organised, frightening part of the partnership. Well, that's what they wrote in the papers so it must be true, eh? Crap. I had broken off with Blink and the last time I had seen David Santini was in The Fantasy Bar years before. In fact, even as I write this almost three years later, I've still not met David Santini again – some big crime partnership, eh?

That drugs factory had nothing to with me. In fact, it had nothing to do with anyone for the simple reason that it did not and never has existed. It was the very kind of tale that could have resulted in me being sent back to jail again. Thank God the Home Office saw it for what it was – pure keech.

I had nothing to do with any plot to sell drugs but drugs, on the other hand, have had a lot to with me. As I thought of the ridiculous story about the drugs factory, I couldn't help think back to another time when drugs almost ruined my life – completely.

45

WEE RAB

'Eh? Fifty-fucking-grand worth of guns?' The bloke clearly couldn't decide if it was Christmas or a set-up – celebration or paranoia time.

'Aye,' replied Rab Carruthers, in a matter of fact voice.

'What are you after then?' the illegal armourer asked.

'Whatever you have,' replied Rab, curtly. A small man, he carried the authority of a lion with toothache wherever he went.

'You starting a war?' asked the gun dealer, not unreasonably given the firepower fifty thousand pounds would buy.

'You want this deal or not?' barked Rab.

'Fuck, yeah, Rab.' Of course the dealer wanted the business – there was a tidy profit in it for him.

'Well, don't ask so many fucking questions then.'

That's how it went with Rab and shooters – cash, phone call, guns, done. He had the biggest collection of arms I have ever seen. It was like he had a fascination with them all and wanted to possess the latest and the most lethal. Gun dealers soon cottoned on to his reputation and searched him out. Sometimes some guy would arrive from France or some place abroad, get to Rab's house and stick a video in the machine. There would be a promo film of some latest firepower. Inevitably, the trips were successful with Rab placing big orders. In any other walk of life, with any other goods, Rab would be called a collector. But Rab's guns weren't all for show, not by a long stretch.

Rab was from the Cadder area of Glasgow and about fifteen years older than me. As a boy, he was the leader of the Cadder Young Team during the violent days of the street gangs and soon got himself a fierce reputation. In the early 1970s, some guy was murdered in a battle and Rab could see his name getting stuck in the hat for the killing. Sod that. So he and a few close mates moved to Manchester. Manchester has always had a guns and drugs culture and Rab took to it all like a fish to water. Within a very short time, he had carved out respect from all the big crime families and young teams around Manchester. No easy feat for an outsider, believe me.

Wee Rab Carruthers was one hard man and bright with it. Soon he had a fair empire built up and was happy to stay down in Manchester. Yet, he was so powerful and still connected to the Glasgow scene that some thought he would take over from Arthur Thompson, The Godfather. Rab was close mates with a guy called Bobby Dempster, a big player from Possil and the only man in Glasgow that Thompson was scared shitless of. Carruthers and Dempster, either one of them on their own could have taken Thompson out any time they wanted but that was just it – neither of them wanted.

My first contact with the Carruthers Family was when I met Rab's brother Jim while I was serving a three-year spell in Shotts Prison back in 1988. It was an interesting time inside because the prisoners went on an all-out riot, controlled the prison and took one warden hostage. I was involved in making sure the screw was OK and getting him to write a letter seeking a peaceful end to the authorities. I also backed that up with wee insurances like taking secret pictures of the do and getting live radio involved. It was a lark and no doubt and at least none of the cons got seven shades of shit kicked out of them later as usually happens. It was the most expensive prison riot in Scottish history at that time and it was all caused by the screws treating the inmates like dogs they didn't like. One of the better things to emerge from it was my friendship with Jim Carruthers. We discovered that our fathers had known each other well – always a good reason to bind together – and our views of the street and how to behave matched spot on.

After my 1992 trial, when I was accused of the murder of Fatboy Thompson and all the rest, I was looking to broaden my horizons. Glasgow just seemed too small and, at that time, filled with too many bad memories of the murders of my pals, Bobby and Joe. I had connections in London that were fine but I really fancied making more contacts up north and thought Manchester would suit me dandy. Before long, I was being welcomed with open arms by Rab Carruthers at his house in Liverpool Road, Eccles. We became close immediately but, strangely, someone spread a rumour to the press at that time, claiming Rab had raided a house I was in and hacked chunks out of one of my legs with a machete – it couldn't have been further from the truth. A pal of mine, Jaimba McLean, was wanted on two charges of shooting people and went on the run. Without hesitation, Rab took Jaimba under his wing and looked after him handsomely. In my world, we call that being a real gent.

However, by the time I'd met Rab, he'd suffered a major crisis in his life. His only son had died tragically and young. Rab's heart was broken and, for the first time ever, he took refuge in drugs. There were no half measures for Carruthers – he did heroin and cocaine all day, every day. Being a guest without giving something back is not my style so, one time when Rab had a debt to collect, I offered to tag along. As usual, he'd been hitting the gear and, also as usual, he was tooled up with some of his shooting machines. I drove so that we'd be sure to arrive without crashing. It was as simple as that. In the passenger seat, Rab slumped back and relaxed. You'd think he was going for a Sunday drive in the country – not to confront some heavy about a load of dough.

First off, we went to an address he had. We went up to the door together and Rab rattled the woodwork. A woman eventually answered and Rab asked for his target – wrong address it seemed. Rab wasn't for taking her word and insisted in going in and looking around – sure enough, no sign. Then we drove by two other addresses with Rab reassuring me that he'd recognise the guy's car. As we sat outside one, Rab blasted away on his coke pipe for the umpteenth time that day. He just didn't care who knew about his drug habit or saw him using. He'd even use the gear in front of cops. They never hassled him over the personal use – they were looking to catch him on a much bigger hook.

Eventually, Rab had me drive us to see this man who would know where the wanted one was. Sure enough, we were given an address and off we went. Not for the first time on that journey, Rab started to nod off to sleep.

'Waken the fuck up, Rab,' I shouted and shook his shoulder.

'What? What?'

'We're almost there,' I reasoned but, in truth, I didn't have a clue where we were going.

'Tell me, Paul, can you do me a favour?' he asked.

'Of course.'

'When we get to this place, can you just control things and I'll have a wee nap?'

Rab really wanted to take whosoever hostage, at gunpoint probably and then he'd just stretch out on a bed and have a doze. I knew he hadn't slept for days but we were about to go into a very dangerous situation here. As his last sentence trailed off, his eyes were shutting, his head bobbing, his breathing deepening.

That was it. No way was I going into a possible confrontation backed up by a partner in crime who couldn't stay awake. Besides, I didn't like the feel of this at all. By stopping off at the wrong addresses, at least two people knew that we were looking for a certain party. If Rab resorted to bloodshed or worse to resolve the conflict, there were two folk out there who knew what we looked like, what car we were driving, the way we spoke and who we were looking for. Fuck that. Job abandoned.

Rab wasn't stupid or careless – far from it. Since the death of his son, he had just stopped caring whether he lived or died. You'd think I'd have known better but I'd my own ghosts to deal with at that time.

Bobby and Joe's murders lay heavy on my mind. I'd been in Barlinnie jail at the time, in the segregation unit. Some of the screws were treating me badly – sticking burning cloths under my door, keeping the lights on all night, that kind of game. Then someone pushed that day's newspaper under my cell door and there was the headline telling me my pals had been murdered. I was totally devastated and I never thought I could hurt that much again. I was wrong. As time passed, my grief for the guys was actually getting worse. Most nights, I'd dream of them, waking with a start as a gun went off. Most days, they were always there in my thoughts. They say time heals but I couldn't wait, could I? Instead, I had to go and reach out for something else – drugs.

Around Rab Carruthers' house, there were drugs everywhere. No way was I going to touch smack but cocaine? Now that was something else. Coke was considered a recreational drug – something that very disciplined people would take a few lines of on a night out. The type of gear that didn't befuddle your thinking, make you hallucinate or send you crawling up the wall with withdrawals. It was, then, a rich person's snort, much beloved by successful media types, artists and actors. If it was good enough for them, it was good enough for me. A few days into the snorting, the Charlie was certainly dulling my pain and making me feel positive a lot of the time. All right, I knew then, as I know now, that it was the drug's effect but it beats the shit out of aching inside all the time.

Rab noticed my new habit – well, I was doing lines of Charlie right there in front of him – and he slagged the hell out of me. 'You haven't a fucking clue what you're putting up your nose there,' he said.

'What d'you mean?' I was a bit miffed. 'I thought you only buy the best of gear.'

'Fucking right I do but it's still cut with crap.'

Right on the spot Rab taught me how to freebase cocaine and, using his highly sensitive scales, demonstrated to me that what you cooked was a lot less heavy than the white powder you snorted. The crap had been removed. Freebase – the pure cocaine crystals that you smoke – shouldn't be confused with crack which is often cut with speed and other drugs. This was coke at its finest and its deadliest. That would do me nicely.

Freebase was Rab's habit. He cooked it up on the kitchen stove producing vast quantities of crystal just for his own consumption.

'Help yourself, Paul,' he said and he meant it. So I did – big time.

Within a week I had a heavy habit and was already beginning to go without sleep. Still, I reassured myself that, most of the time, I felt alive, positive and full of energy – and, besides, I was taking coke the 'healthy' way, without running the risks of it being cut with rat poison or Vim.

Healthy? If only I'd known.

46

SLEEPLESS CLYDE NIGHTS

Forget that Verve song, the drugs did work – too fucking well.

Down in Manchester, I knew I had to try and break the freebase cocaine habit or I was going to end up addicted for life. I'd been around Rab Carruthers off and on for two years and could see the effects the coke was having on a guy who was a top player in the premier division. The coke buzzes you up high as wire and as taut as a bowstring. If you only take cocaine, you stay sleepless, alert, fed up and sick from being awake. One way to deal with that is to smoke some heroin as a countermeasure, to take you down. Rab had been taking both for years. Anyone who knew Rab at all knew that you never told him what to do. At best you could offer a word to the wise, a suggestion or certainly a warning about something he didn't know. But tell him how to lead his life? No bloody chance.

Yet, by this time, his brother and close friends like Bobby Dempster were literally pleading with Rab to chuck the drugs. Rab was a hard man, used to disciplining himself, with a high capacity for physical pain. I reckoned that, even after years of the drugs, he could chuck them whenever he wanted. The trouble was he didn't want to come back to reality and face his great grief for his dead boy. Rab chose the zombie state of the narcotics instead.

But I knew I had to wean myself off the freebase. The last place on earth where that would succeed was anywhere near Rab Carruthers so it was back to Glasgow for me – for the sake of my health.

That was a first.

Lancefield Quay, right on the banks of the River Clyde in the city centre was where I had my flat. It was luxurious, quiet, with a peaceful view of the river – perfect for a bit of withdrawals, I reckoned, but not straight away. For a good long time, I went about my business and that included the freebase. Having decided to kick the drugs, you have to wait for the right wave to come along just like surfers. They watch the rhythm of the sea – the person kicking drugs feels the rhythm of their soul – go too early, you'll fail and be reluctant to try again. Some call this reaching your personal gutter. Whatever way you look at it, I wasn't ready for abstinence quite yet.

The flat had large windows and a spectacular view right over the south side of the city. I'd spend sleepless hours at those windows just staring out. Zonked? Not at all. Coke doesn't interfere with your intellectual abilities. If anything, it makes you sharper although only for short bursts at a time. So I was no smackhead staring at my knee, thinking of nothing but my knee – and how to get my next tenner bag. I was full of ideas and thoughts and worries – like the men watching me from bushes at the other side of the river.

The cops had been after me for years. They'd set me up with heroin, planted a paid perjurer beside me in jail, charged me with serious offences when they knew it wasn't me, tapped my phones, threatened to kill me – on and on and on. Lately, I'd been spending a lot of time with serious London firms and, of course, the bold Rab in Manchester. Why the hell wouldn't the cops be watching me now? No problem – I'd just watch them right back.

I went out and bought the strongest set of binoculars I could and set them up with a stand right at the window. For hours every day I'd watch – between pipes of freebase cocaine, of course. They were there all right.

A straight Joe good pal came to visit me one night, worried that I'd been spending too long cooped up all alone with my coke pipe. 'They're there now,' I insisted after I'd told him about the cops watching me. 'Look through the binoculars at the bushes. You'll see them. Wearing dark boiler suits.' I was so desperate to have someone else, especially someone as clean of drugs as my mate was, to see the snoopers.

Give him his due, he stood for an age at those binoculars, staring out, quietly, seriously. No complaint. No, 'You're still on that fucking freebase, eh?' No accusations. No dismissal. A good mate. 'Can't see a thing, P,' he eventually sighed and turned away from the spy glass, rubbing the strain out of his eyes.

'But they are . . .'

'I'm not saying I don't believe you,' he butted in. 'Just I can't see anything.'

'Did you watch the bushes?' I demanded. 'If you watch them long enough, they move and you can see the human shapes behind them.' By then, I was back at the binoculars, scanning the other bank of the Clyde. Sure enough, there was no movement at all. No wonder my pal was beginning to think I was losing it.

Early the next day, I was still standing at the window having not slept a wink yet again. There they were – men in dark boiler suits, arriving in unmarked vans. Others were leaving in identical boiler suits but they were different heights, different builds with different skin shades. I was staring hard at the bushes trying to spot a human shape in the foliage. No such luck. Then there it was – a glint in the morning sun from slap-bang in the centre of the greenery about three feet off the ground. I wasn't going paranoid. That was a telescope winking back at me.

There was no way I would ever convince any of my friends that I was right about being spied on. Maybe they were right and I was losing it. Just because cocaine – freebase or no – doesn't bring on chemical hallucinations, it can and does bring on exhaustion hallucinations. And God knows I hadn't been sleeping.

Maybe I was seeing the men in dark boiler suits dredged from some recess of my life. It wasn't some daft conspiracy theory to think the cops were after me. Every day, I took precautions to check I wasn't being tailed, wasn't talking within earshot of somebody suspicious. Every single bloody day for years, I had written down everything I did all day and that was on the advice of one of the most sober-minded, calm, serious lawyers in Glasgow. If he could think such surveillance likely, then I could imagine it. And see it.

Imagination? Maybe.

That's how I left it for years. Then, when I was lifted for the gun-running in London, a chance meeting opened my eyes.

47

DYEING FOR THE CAUSE

'Hello, neighbour.' I was in the exercise yard of Belmarsh Prison awaiting trial for the Mac-10 charges.

'Neighbour?' I recognised the guy as Michael Gallagher, known as Mickey. An IRA man, he had been charged with the mortar-bomb attack on Heathrow Airport and was awaiting trial himself. Sure, I recognised him but neighbour?

'Me and the missus had a flat at Lancefield Quay in Glasgow. Through the wall from yourself,' replied Mickey. That explained a lot. Mickey would have come in and out of the building by a different entrance. Flat dwellers like us can live yards apart for years and never meet. We shook hands.

'Did you like Glasgow, Mickey?' I was just trying to make conversation, the way you do.

'Aye, Glesca was fine till the fuckers started watching me.'

'What you mean?' I wondered to myself if Mickey had been doing a few pipes of freebase himself.

'I thought that place was a safe house. That's why I had my wife with me.'

That made sense to me.

'But the bastards had twigged us from the minute we moved in.'

'So why did they not lift you?'

'They wanted tae get as much from me as possible. Phone taps, walls bugged, they were even listening tae us having a shite and in

212

the bedroom. But what good taping me and me wife shagging is to the Brit security fascists I'll never know.'

Mickey didn't realise it but he was opening my eyes.

'What sort of surveillance did they have on you outside, Mickey?' I wanted him to tell me without clues from me.

'That's just it – why I wanted tae warn you. We hardly crossed the door but that didn't matter. Cunts were filming us from the other side of the river. Twenty-four-fucking-seven.'

'Thank fuck for that,' I breathed an enormous sigh of relief.

'Whaaat?' Mickey looked suddenly suspicious, hostile.

'No, no' you,' I laughed. 'Me.'

When I told Mickey Gallagher the story of me seeing the cops yet no one else could, how I thought I was going off my mind, he laughed even louder than me.

Mickey had just been trying to warn me that, if I'd been up to no good or meeting with suspicious types in my flat at that time, MI5 would have it on film for sure. But, apart from smoking too much freebase, I had been cleaner than clean. That must have disgusted the cops. I'll bet they thought they were going to catch both Gallagher and Ferris – two for the price of one.

Mickey Gallagher and I became good friends then and, later, as good friends do, he had a favour to ask me – a sensitive favour that meant we had to meet alone out in a corner of the exercise yard.

'Me trial's coming up soon, Paul,' he said, telling me something I already knew.

'How can I help?' Nice to be nice.

'It's me hair,' Mickey said, totally pole-axing me. 'It's pure grey.' He wasn't exaggerating. 'It's usually red.'

I half-expected some major request for assistance from Mickey – something entirely dodgy that I might be able to use people on the outside to achieve. But hair dye? This was a first – and a last, as it happens.

'No problem, Mickey,' I replied, trying hard not to smile.

'Bold boy you are, Paul. Bold boy.'

With a bit of manoeuvring, I promptly secured a job in the laundry room. Then I made a phone call asking a pal to send in some new clothes – just a couple of T-shirts and some socks but the socks had to be saturated in red dye and dried. No problem. When the socks arrived, I arranged for a trusted lookout man and went to Mickey's cell. With him leaning into the sink and me doing the honorary hair-dresser bit, within twenty minutes, his hair was bright red. Talk about Ginger Minger – I reckoned I'd gone too far.

As Mickey stood drying his hair and turned to look in the mirror, I took a couple of steps closer to the cell door, ready for a quick getaway.

'Fucking perfect, Paul,' he declared with a broad beamer of a smile. 'Y'know,' he said, finger-combing his hair into shape, 'I have dyed more times for the cause than anyone else.' A long moan from me. 'Now you must be the only non-political that has dyed for the cause.'

With me still groaning at Mickey's bad pun, we split up and headed down to the general recreation area. I was there before him and stood watching Mickey proudly showing off his crop of red hair. All the screws turned and gawped. I swear some of their mouths fell open.

The roar of 'LOCK DOWN!' went up. Dye is forbidden in jails, of course, because of its toxic nature and various other dodgy uses it can be put to. All of us cons were slammed back in our cells while the staff took the jail apart.

Of course, they weren't looking for a few pairs of socks, were they? A certain laundry man – me – had stashed the spare, unused pairs of socks away, in pillowcases in a room full of pillowcases. It was like hiding a needle in a box of needles – except I knew where they were and the dyeing process went on till Mickey's trial. Just as he wanted, he went to face the media and the public with his chosen colour of hair and why not?

But that was to be a few years in the future. Back in Glasgow in Lancefield Quay, I was convinced that paranoia about the spectre cops had taken me over and I believed I couldn't trust anyone, not even myself. Now there was no choice – I had to kick my freebase coke habit. But would it be cold turkey or hot steel?

48

WISH I WAS THERE

'Just one more hit.' It was the worst thought I'd had all week and that was saying something. One week, a mere seven days, without one pipe of freebase coke and I was low – as low as I could get. It was as if the spark had gone out in my spirit. Nothing tasted right. Nothing felt good. There was no humour, no hope, no light.

In my life I've had bad weeks: too many weeks in solitary confinement; weeks on trial with my freedom at stake; weeks in hospital with psoriasis, scared to see the world with my reptile skin; I've kicked my heels in jail a week before a freedom day that never seemed to move closer. They were all long weeks but that week without cocaine was the longest week of my life.

'One last pipe, that's all.' The thought wasn't going to go away. I knew one pipe would inevitably lead to another. Ignorance wasn't my problem – addiction was.

'One last pipe.' The thought was my only thought. It had taken over whatever I did or tried. Nothing mattered apart from that thought. 'One last pipe.' It wouldn't go away till I gave in, gave up.

My gear was exactly where I had left it. Slipping out one large crystal and placing it carefully on the ash on the foil, I lifted the Zippo lighter and paused. 'This could be the beginning or this could be the end,' I thought. But the beginning or end of what? Who knows? Who fucking cares? I flicked open the lighter, stroked the wheel and, as ever, the Zippo lit first time.

VENDETTA

Here we go. As I drew the smoke deep into my lungs, I flicked the play switch on the video – my favourite band, Pink Floyd. The Floyd guys are all university graduates, from well-off, middle-class families, used to the good things in life. What the fuck had they in common with me? Why did I like them so much? Who cares? My favourite band and my favourite track, 'Wish You Were Here' – just the thing for my last pipe of freebase. Just the ticket. Another deep blast of the coke, I let the music roll over and through me – nothing better. Then those haunting lyrics. Every word heard and, as the coke immediately kicked in, every word meaningful.

> . . . two lost souls swimming in a fish bowl
> Year after year . . .
> Wish you were here

The track played on but my mind stayed still, focussed, alert and aching. Those were the words I was meant to hear. Those words and just those words.

> . . . two lost souls swimming in a fish bowl
> Year after year . . .
> Wish you were here

Those words were meant to be heard by me, right there and then. Those words were the whole point of this hellhole I had dug for myself. The only way out of my pain.

It was a message from my murdered mates, Bobby and Joe. They missed me as I missed them. Together, we three were strong. Apart, we were lost. That was the problem and I knew the solution.

Going to a secret stash in my flat and pulling out the metal box, I could feel the weight inside. It was a reassuring weight. Clicking open the lid, I took out a 9mm Browning pistol. It felt cool and kind in my hand. Checking it was loaded, I went back to my pipe and to my song.

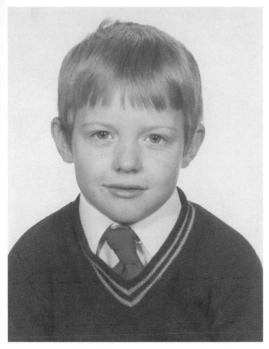

Paul Ferris, aged seven

Paul's parents, Willie and Jenny, in 1974

Willie Ferris at home in Blackhill in 1988 with
Paul Junior

Billy Ferris, Paul's brother, in 2002

Willie Ferris (bottom, second from left) in the
Merchant Navy, 1946

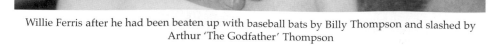

Willie Ferris after he had been beaten up with baseball bats by Billy Thompson and slashed by
Arthur 'The Godfather' Thompson

Arthur 'Fatboy' Thompson

Arthur 'The Godfather' Thompson on his way to give evidence against
Paul Ferris who was charged with the murder of his son Fatboy in 1992

Billy Thompson

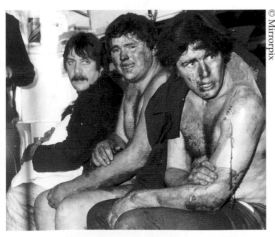

Andrew and Daniel Doyle with a fireman holding a
baby after their flat was torched in the Ice–Cream Wars

Thomas 'TC' Campbell in the Special Unit
at Barlinnie Prison

Artistic impressions of the murders of Bobby Glover and Joe Hanlon, claimed by an anonymous donor to be a police artist's impression

The pick-up

Shooting #1

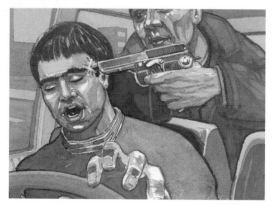

Shooting #2

Transferring the bodies

The bodies lay overnight in the yard

Car parked at The Cottage Bar with the bodies of the victims

Bobby Glover

Joe Hanlon

Joe Hanlon's funeral, with pall bearers Tam 'The Licensee' McGraw on the right and Snadz Adams on the left (face partially obscured)

Paul Ferris (with the tie) with Paul Massey (striped shirt, glass raised), leader of the Salford Team

Simon Bakerman   Michael Howard   John Haase

Tam McGraw and friends at the funeral of Gordon Ross

Tam McGraw

Tam McGraw with his wife Margaret (left), son William (back, second left) and other mourners

George 'Crater Face' McCormack

Alan Cross

Billy Mills

Billy McPhee – 3 days later he was stabbed to death

Ben Alagha

Paul Ferris leaving Frankland Prison,
January 2002

A big night out: from left, boxing champ Gary Jacobs, Rory Nicholl, Paul Ferris, Don of Dons Joey Pyle,
'Pretty Boy' Roy Shaw and Ken Buchanan

. . . two lost souls swimming in a fish bowl
Year after year . . .
Wish you were here

It was a message. My da was there too. I missed my da so much.

Everything here had gone sour. The world was full of folk I couldn't trust. People who'd sell you for the price of a tenner bag of smack. Folk with no heart and no soul. Just greed. Selfishness. Here I could never rest. Never stop watching over my shoulder and looking up every time the door, any door, opened. Never to rest – that was my purgatory. I was so weary and missed my mates so much.

Year after year . . .
Wish you were here

Tears were blinding me but I could see all I needed to see. I lifted the Browning, cocked the trigger and placed the barrel against my temple.

. . . two lost souls swimming in a fish bowl
Year after year . . .
Wish you were here

Bang, bang, bang. Somebody somewhere was rapping something. What did I care?

I wish I was there.

I was going there.

Bang. Bang. Bang. They could knock all they liked. What the fuck did it have to do with me any more? One lost soul swimming in a fish bowl. That was me.

BANG. BANG. BANG.

'What the fuck?'

Slipping the gun into the back of my waistband, I went to the door. It wasn't the cops. I knew their knock. It would be some salesman, some neighbour, some temporary interruption. Best get rid of them. Send them happily on their way. Don't want them getting scared by gunfire, do we?

'Have you gone deaf?' In breezed Sandra, my very recent girlfriend at that time. Tall, beautiful, long blonde hair, she was chatting away nineteen to the dozen. 'Pink Floyd?' She stood in front of the TV, arms on her hips, and turned slowly. 'Have you been smoking, Paul?' She didn't mean a Kensistas Club or even a joint.

'Aye.'

Disapproving eyes from Sandra.

'One last pipe, hen. Just one last pipe.'

'Right.' She was taking off her jacket, laying down a bag of stuff she'd just bought at some shop, her eyes doing all the speaking and they were saying, 'I don't believe you.'

'Sandra.'

She looked me in the face.

'I promise.'

'OK.'

And that was the end of me and freebase cocaine. I never touched the stuff again – never felt the inclination. I suppose that Browning against my skull was my gutter and Sandra coming to the door at that precise time was my wave. It was plain sailing after that as far as me and Class-A drugs were concerned. An occasional joint? Of course. A few bottles of wine? Often. A pipe of freebase coke? Never. Just as I had no intention of setting up any drugs factory either on my own or with David Santini and Blink McDonald. In fact, I've still not met David Santini again.

But those accusations were made in 2003. I'd spent most of that year working on my business as security consultant and I was doing very well in spite of poisonous stories implying that I owned Frontline Security and we were up to no good. Maybe some folk in the media believed that but the paying customers, desperate for good security, didn't – thank God.

But that wasn't to last. Events were about to overtake me yet again. This time it wasn't personal. It was political and very, very nasty.

49

THE DATE

The 6th of November. It's as good a date as any. Does it mean anything to you? Your birthday? Your mother's birthday? Your daddy's? Your lover's? The day you did something for the first time? The day you did something for the last time? The day you decided not to do something ever again and this time it worked? The day you decided not to something ever again and you failed so badly you decided not to decide not to do something ever again?

The 6th of November – an average date for most of us. If it had been four days later it would have been my birthday. Four days later in 2003 it would have been my fortieth birthday. How's about this one then? The 6th November 2003. Mean anything? No? Shame on you – that was the day Michael Howard was elected leader of the Conservative Party. What the hell is he doing in a book written by a man like me? Read on. Just read on.

50

THE LINK

Street players don't worry over what they don't know about – like when someone threatens to kill you. They're not the ones you should fret over. The ones who kill you don't tell you – they just pop you one lonely night. But sometimes what you don't have a scooby about works to your favour.

Back in the 1980s, when I was too busy working for Arthur Thompson to notice much else, action was unfolding down in Liverpool that would have a dramatic impact on my life. It started with a series of robberies as it so often does. A mob was carrying out armed raids on security vans and post offices and they were dubbed the 'Transit Van Robberies'. With the cops under great pressure to catch the crooks, two local players, Danny Vaughan and John Haase, were eventually lifted. These two young guys were handy right enough but protested their innocence right from the off. They didn't just say they were innocent or plead not guilty, they howled that they were the wrong guys. Too bad – they were held in pokey awaiting trial.

One of the guys, Danny Vaughan, had a sworn enemy in the cops. This rozzer had been after the Vaughan Family for years and particularly hated Danny because he hardly ever got caught. As bad luck would have it, the same cop was acting as the liaison officer to Danny's remand jail. As the weeks passed by, Danny noticed the cop going in and out of staff offices and he was frequently in the company of a prisoner he didn't recognise. Prisoners meeting with the cops is a strict no-no that is likely to send the other cons speculating about cooperation or worse – grassing. So Danny would've noticed. All the cons did.

Come the trial, Danny and John Haase were amazed when that same prisoner was called as witness for the prosecution. They didn't know the guy – had never even heard of him. They were soon going to learn that a viper was amongst them. At the trial, the bloke swore Danny had confessed all to him. Bad as that was, he then went on to relate his evidence in great detail and was bang on with the prosecution case. The evil sod had been briefed by the cops and was singing from their hymn sheet.

Danny Vaughan and John Haase both went down for fourteen years. They launched high-profile campaigns to prove their innocence but it was all useless. After all, a senior cop, Detective Superintendent Mervyn Davies, had sworn that the main prosecution witness was of good character, a good citizen. Shite.

The witness called himself Dennis Wilkinson though he changed his name more often than his boxers. Not only was he not of good character, he was as evil as they come. Wilkinson was awaiting trial on a case of attempted murder, kidnapping, torture, rape and robbery. He and a man called Reeves, an escapee from Broadmoor secure psychiatric hospital, had taken a young bloke, a foreign student, prisoner in his own home. They stripped, beat, whipped and then buggered him repeatedly. Bored with this, they stuck a frying pan up his arse and forced him to give them oral sex shoving their shit smeared cocks down his throat. Of good character? What do you think?

Once they'd emptied the young victim's bank accounts, Reeves and Wilkinson fled to the Netherlands. Wilkinson soon returned home, only to be arrested, while Reeves was lifted for murdering a Dutch cop. Wilkinson was looking at a lot of years – unless he helped the cops. For lying about Danny and John Haase, he was freed in a short while to go on committing similar crimes and traded the time they might have given him for more perjury in a total of fifteen trials. Then I met him.

VENDETTA

It was 1992 and I was being held in the Wendy House at BarL, awaiting trial for the murder of Fatboy, when another prisoner managed to pass me a note. 'Beware the perjuror,' it said, before explaining Wilkinson's background. He was calling himself Dennis Woodman by then but it was the same evil shit who had been transferred up from Dumfries jail to 'hear' my confession.

By luck, in the Wendy House at the time, there was a bloke called Mark Leech who'd been in a score of jails up and down the country. Mark had been around when Dennis the Menace had stabbed someone else in the back and he knew all about him. Then Woodman's own brother-in-law wrote to me warning me about his MO. Next, Danny Vaughan, Woodman's first-ever victim, contacted me. By that time, Danny was out of jail and had vowed to keep tracking the perjurer and warn those who might be his next victims. Well, you would, wouldn't you?

After a bit of dirt-digging by Donald Findlay QC and Peter Forbes, my legal team, we knew all about the man. But that didn't stop him.

Woodman made false claims that Peter Forbes, my lawyer and one of the most honest men ever, had offered him a large sum of money and a pension to withdraw his evidence. In the witness box, he sat dressed like a scarecrow in borrowed clothes and claimed that I'd confessed to the murder of Fatboy, the kneecappings and the other attempted murder charges while we played chess. Aye, right.

In spite of it being a solitary confinement unit, it was possible to play chess in the Wendy House. The opponents would shout out their moves and both players would make them on their separate boards – it was a bit like postal chess and a good way of relieving the boredom. I'd played the guy next to me a few times and won. He then played Woodman who was a few cells away from him and a hell of a lot farther from me. Over the first couple of nights my neighbour beat the professional liar easily four times out of four. So there was no way I was going to play the bastard. No challenge – except how to be heard hollering the moves through several sets of thick walls.

In court, Woodman had the gall to try and joust verbally with Donald Findlay QC. The stupid bastard – it was a no hoper. His big mistake was when he swore something on the lives of his two dead kids. To start with I thought he had just swung the jury with the sympathy vote but then, overnight, Peter Forbes did a bit of research and learned that his kids were alive and well, thank God. The next day, Donald Findlay plastered Woodman's credibility all over the wall. Game, set and match to the bold Donald.

Yet, it had been close – very close, as it always is with a paid liar set up by the state. The not guilty verdicts I got on all charges weren't the only good to come out of that trial. I had also made several new friends, not the least of whom was Danny Vaughan. His was a friendship that would give me a great deal and lead me into political intrigue.

51

THE BUSINESS

When Danny was jailed unjustly for the Transit Van Robberies, he and his family campaigned fiercely to prove his innocence and failed. The struggle almost broke Danny, a lovely sensitive bloke. But John Haase, his co-accused, was a different matter.

Haase fought the system all the way, kicking, punching and spitting. Those who knew Haase said that the fourteen-year sentence, most of which he spent in isolation and on the punishment block, changed him and, when he was eventually released, he didn't give a fuck for anyone or anything. Can't say I can blame him.

On his release, Haase went straight back to business – big time. While he had been inside, there was a new commodity on the block – heroin. Haase didn't see why he shouldn't have some of the spoils and he was going to get some help from an unexpected source – his own family. Haase's young nephew, Paul Bennett, had been busy while his uncle was away. Seeing the profits to be made from smack, he started as a small-time dealer often for an ex-bouncer and heavy called Curtis 'Cocky' Warren. Cocky was one of the biggest heroin dealers in Liverpool, the city that, by the mid 1980s, was fast becoming the distribution point for drugs to the rest of Britain and Ireland – especially Glasgow. But Bennett did more than work for Cocky – he learned from him.

By the time his uncle, John Haase, had left jail, Paul Bennett was running his own operation and had made influential contacts all over the country and further afield. This included a shady big-time Turkish operator, simply known as 'The Vulcan', who could guarantee large deliveries of good quality smack at any time. With Haase and Bennett now in partnership, the former's cunning came into play. They quite deliberately worked in partnership with Cocky Warren, only to turn on him and tax some of his team – shorthand for holding them hostage and proposing a nasty end unless £50,000 was paid up. It was and Cocky moved away sharpish to concentrate on cocaine. Smart move.

Haase and Bennett were very active in London. Whereas, down there, I associated with the traditional London firms, they made close relationships with the Turks for very good reasons. The Turkish teams liked to stay out of the limelight and weren't interested in robbery or any of the other rackets. Drugs was their game and heroin their speciality.

Within a few years of Haase being released from jail, Haase and Bennett had grown huge on the back of an international drugs racket. But danger was just around the corner.

52

THE GRASS AND THE PLANT

Liverpool, some say, is like Glasgow. I know what they mean. They're both small villages of cities, the folk have strong links with Ireland, there are two major football clubs and a scally is as recognisable as a game Glaswegian. I like Liverpool but, thank God, I decided not to hang around there.

After I was released from the 1992 trial, I wanted to get away from Glasgow for a while. I'd kept in touch with Danny Vaughan and was tempted to explore business in Liverpool. But I decided that the scenes were too similar so I moved on to spend time with Rab Carruthers in Manchester and various friends in London. Just as well I did – Liverpool was becoming a dangerous place for some people.

Paul Grimes was a well-known Liverpool hard man of the old school. He didn't object to dishing out any level of violence to anyone getting in the way of business but one thing he couldn't stand was drugs. Or so he'd say later. Grimes's son, then serving in the Royal Navy, died from a heroin overdose. The father went crazy but quietly so. He got it into his brain that the drugs must have come from Cocky Warren so Cocky would have to pay.

Working undercover while signed up as an informant, Grimes helped the cops nab Cocky. (He's still one of the largest drug traffickers ever caught anywhere.) Somehow Paul Grimes managed to pull off this stroke without blowing his cover. He went on with his usual business as a heavy, living in the same house, in the same community, and no one sussed him at all. It was a one-off act of revenge for his boy, he told the cops – now it was back to as you were. But the police wanted more.

Buzzed up by their success in catching Cocky and all too aware that Liverpool was the drug distribution centre of Britain, the rozzers decided on another target. Maybe, if they grabbed a few of the big boys, they could kill off the city's drug business once and for all. But who? That was easy – Haase and his nephew, Bennett.

A tail was put on Haase and Bennett but that wasn't the only threat to them – not by a long stretch. Through Paul Bennett, Haase had been introduced to the London-based Turkish dealer, Yilmaz Kaya. Little did they know that a certain woman, Saffia Abrahams, was watching and writing. Saffia Abrahams was a good-looking young woman who had been raised in Turkey but she had lived a double life for years. The girlfriend of heroin baron, Yilmaz Kaya, she was also a police informant registered to DS Peter Williams of the South East Regional Crime Squad.

The original plan for breaking one of the biggest drugs rings in the UK would have worked fine if DS Williams hadn't got personal – very personal. He didn't just seduce the young woman but forced her to participate in sadomasochistic sex. When she complained, he threatened to blow her cover with her drug-trafficking boyfriend and that would have been her death sentence. Saffia couldn't take any more and went to Williams' superiors who promptly charged him with something like twenty-six offences, ranging from corruption to rape. Saffia was immediately taken into protective custody and started talking. That's where Haase came in.

Saffia Abrahams had been involved directly in the drugs scam and kept a detailed daily diary about her dealings with DS Williams and all the players in the team. There were repeated references to some man she called 'The White Haired Monkey'. That, she explained to the cops, was John Haase from Liverpool. Where Saffia had grown up, there was a large colony of monkeys with a distinctive streak of white hair on their nappers. Haase always had jet black hair but it was dyed. Legend has it that, when he was a very young man, Haase's hair went white overnight.

The Liverpool cops increased their surveillance of Haase and Bennett, tapping their phones, bugging their homes and following them night and day. In London, the Turks were getting the same treatment. The police's efforts produced results as they photographed millions of pounds exchanging hands for huge loads of heroin. The Conservative government had been calling for a few scalps of Mr Bigs in the drugs world and now they were going to get some for sure.

In July 1993, Customs and the cops decided they had more evidence than they needed and hit both the Liverpool and London ends of the scam with armed squads. In the Walton area of Liverpool, in one safe house alone, they recovered 55 kilos of heroin. That was worth more than £15 million on the street and it was around fifteen times larger than other big drug hauls at the time.

With Michael Howard as Home Secretary, the hang 'em and flog 'em brigade was in control. Howard was throwing more folks in jail than ever before and making sentences longer and parole harder to get. Time and time again, he declared that prison worked in tackling crime. Now he was publicly promising to hammer the drug traffickers. Who were the first to be nabbed under this new hard-line regime? Haase and Bennett. They were in deep shit.

Or were they? Someone with other plans was about to pay me a visit.

53

THE DEAL

'It's a sensitive one, Rab.' The man looked handy and ready to take care of whatever anyone threw at him but, just then, he also looked edgy, nervous. We were sitting in Rab's house in Manchester, some time late in 1992 or early in 1993, when two Liverpool guys came to visit.

'No problem,' replied Rab, 'you know that fine fucking well.'

'Yeah. Sorry, course I do.' The bloke spoke in a Scouse accent but soft and not too fast like they often do.

'Just spit it out, eh?' demanded Rab. He caught the guy looking at me, wondering who I was, not sure of saying anything in front of a stranger. Rab caught his look. 'This is Paul, by the way, Paul F . . .'

'Oh, right,' breathed the bloke, butting in. 'Sound. How you doin', mate?' He'd obviously heard of me somewhere and didn't need any further explanation.

'Doing OK, pal,' I answered and stuck out my mitt to shake the way you do.

'It's about John and Paul, Rab,' he went on, 'we need a bit of advice.' They weren't talking about John and Paul of George and Ringo fame but John Haase and his nephew, Paul Bennett.

If the Scouser had heard of me, I'd heard all about John Haase through Danny Vaughan and from hanging around Manchester. Liverpool and Manchester might be two separate cities with different teams and set-ups but they watch each other – very bloody carefully.

'Advice to Haase and Bennett? Get a fucking good lawyer,' laughed Rab, 'that's the only advice I have for them.'

The bloke smiled at Rab's wisecrack but clearly didn't find it funny.

'John has, don't worry,' Scouser replied without humour. 'But they've a chance of a deal.' Now he had our full attention. 'He's been told, if he gives information leading to guns being recovered, the cops and the prosecution will go steady on him – lenient, like.'

'That sounds a bit fucking dodgy to me,' said Rab. With his love of shooters, he probably thought giving them away with no guarantee was unthinkable. 'Have you heard anything like that before, Paul?'

'As a matter of fact, yeah,' I replied. 'It's very common in certain parts of Glasgow.'

Rab Carruthers looked sceptical as I started to explain how McGraw, The Licensee, through his cop contacts, could arrange to have quite serious charges dropped or just overlooked in return for a bundle of illegal arms. It made the cops look good by increasing the number of illegal weapons 'recovered' and so they let some players off the hook. The routine was that a deal was struck on the amount of firepower to be handed in and then it would be stashed at a certain headstone in the old graveyard, next to where The Caravel used to stand, at an agreed time. That was all it took.

'Does it work though?' Scouser asked.

'Aye,' I laughed. 'To my knowledge, it's been used to blind a polis eye or two to a bloke being caught driving without a driving licence and in another matter with regard to a certain shooting.'

The last one impressed them. No matter how important some guy's driving licence might be to him, it's not exactly in the same league as drug trafficking though a double shooting was getting close to it.

'John's just a bit concerned it's too much like . . . well, grassing, I suppose.'

I knew what he meant. It smacked too much of cooperating with the cops – always dodgy in this game if you want to live. So I explained that the guns were bought directly from dealers and exchanged. There were plenty more weapons where they had come from. No one had their guns taken away, the men in the hot seat got a deal, the cops looked good and the dealers made a profit. So, no one lost and everyone gained. It was difficult to see what was wrong with that.

'It looks like it's worth a go,' said the Liverpool bloke. 'You'll help us get the guns, Rab, if John agrees to go ahead with the deal, la?'

With Rab's knowledge of illegal gun suppliers he was an obvious choice. 'Yeah,' Rab replied, 'of course I will as long . . .'

'As long as no one goes down for handling or dealing them right?' said the other Scouser who was there on Haase and Bennett's behalf.

'Yeah.'

'Goes without saying.'

'Aye, I know, it's just that I had . . .'

'Had to say it, sure,' the tight-lipped Scouser replied. 'No problem.'

A couple of weeks later, Haase and Bennett's representative bought around £50,000 worth of weapons through Rab Carruthers. Believe me, that was enough to start a war. But his people didn't stop there and bought more from various sources. Some even managed to find their way out of a Customs and Excise weapons dump in North Wales where they had been stored, waiting to be decommissioned.

Haase and Bennett's stash wasn't just handed over to the cops or Customs. They were planted in the boots of some cars so that they looked like they were about to be delivered some place. At other times, they would be left in safe houses. They collected sub-machine guns, pistols, Semtex, rifles, detonators, machine pistols, shotguns, hand grenades – the list went on and on.

If the goods I knew about were enough to start a war, the entire haul could have started World War Three. However, in crime terms, it was to be a bigger bombshell than that.

54

THE PARDON

'Eighteen fucking years.' I couldn't believe the sentences that Haase and Bennett had just been thumped with. OK, they'd been caught with a load of smack and the Tory government and their Home Secretary, Michael Howard, had been calling for heavy penalties for traffickers but they could've murdered some guy and escaped with less. 'Some deal, eh?'

'What a fucking waste of good shooters,' said Rab Carruthers, almost wistfully.

'Aye and money,' I agreed. 'How much do you reckon they spent on arms to trade with the cops?'

'Difficult to say,' replied Rab, 'but, from what I've heard, it must be at least 150 grand.'

'No way.'

'Listen, Paul, I know of at least fifteen raids that I reckon were down to Haase and Bennett. Just guns found, nobody arrested. Too fucking fishy, man.'

'The cops will be running out of storage space soon, eh?'

'Nah. They pass the guns on to Customs who have these big fuck-off arsenals out in the wilds – usually disused army camps.'

'Like the one raided in North Wales a wee while back,' I added with a grin.

'Aye,' Rab replied, as if the thought had occurred to him for the first time. 'Just like that one and the one in the Midlands.' He knew fine well that some of Haase and Bennett's guns had been liberated from those very camps. 'Dirty bastards, but.'

'Who? Oh, the cops. Well, what do you expect from them? That they'll keep their word?' I'd had enough run-ins with rozzers setting people up, threatening to kill me, bribing some halfwit to make up evidence against me. Bottom line – I expected the worst of them every time. Why? Because that's exactly what I'd experienced.

But eighteen years was a lot. I never thought that trading guns was enough to get them off such serious charges altogether but I did think it would win them a bit of leniency, a bit of a reduction. Instead, they'd been hammered.

Haase and Bennett weren't the only ones to suffer. The Turks – Suleyman Ergun, Mehmet Ansen, Yilmaz Kaya, Bulent Onay and Manuk Ocecki – all went down big time. And Haase and Bennett's Scouser partner, Edward Crocker, was slammed in the pokey for fourteen years.

As well as eighteen years each, Haase and Bennett had £840,000 of their dosh confiscated. It was a sore blow on the money front but it was the years in jail that was the stiletto thrust. Bennett was only thirty-one years old and would still be reasonably young when freed. Haase, on the other hand, was forty-six and had already spent too much of his adult years locked up. Given that John Haase had a habit of fighting the screws all the way, he could look forward to the full term, maybe more. Or could he?

A few months after their trial and sentence, John Haase and Paul Bennett were sensationally pardoned and freed – not the Turks or Crocker, just Haase and Bennett. It was like Scotland winning the football World Cup or me being invited to the Police Ball and accepting. It just didn't happen – not to guys like us.

When it did happen, it was to innocent folk who had been jailed unjustly – like the Scot, Paddy Meehan, who was jailed for a murder he didn't commit. In Meehan's case, it took a long campaign by lawyer Joe Beltrami, Nicholas Fairbairn QC MP, Malcolm Rifkind QC MP and broadcaster Ludovic Kennedy. These guys were heavy hitters and, besides, Meehan really was innocent. That's not what was being said about Haase and Bennett – they weren't even saying it themselves.

Michael Howard, the hardest Home Secretary in living memory, had just decided to let two guilty men walk free. That was the same Howard who, in a blink, would have reintroduced hanging and probably pulled the drop lever on the gallows himself. What the fuck was going on?

A short while after Haase and Bennett's release, a statement was issued from the Home Office. It explained that the two men weren't pardoned as such but released under the royal prerogative. This was the royal right to release guilty parties who'd previously given great service to their country. Haase and Bennett? Two scallies? Convicted drug traffickers? What service had they given to the country? It wasn't anything to do with the guns, was it? No chance.

The official release thanked the two for being such a great help in smashing a massive Turkish drug ring. Ordinary citizens, over their morning tea and toast, might nod some sense of approval then promptly forget about the statement but, on the street, only one word was heard – GRASS.

What could Haase and Bennett do? Say it wasn't them that did the Turks in but Saffia Abrahams? The public would say, 'Who?' She'd been kept under wraps during the trial and even more so after it. And they couldn't say they traded in guns. The street players would assume that they had shopped someone again, even if the men denied it.

The Home Office had just let Haase and Bennett go free with one hand and served a death sentence on them with the other. Or had they?

'What the fuck?' A well-known Liverpool face had just bumped into John Haase on the street. It was July 1996, only eleven months after he had been sentenced to eighteen years.

'What the fuck's up with you?'

'What are you doing out, you fucking rascal?'

'You not seen the papers?'

'Naw.'

234

'Got freed, didn't we?'

'What?'

'Howard let us out. Me and Benn.'

'No way.'

'Fucking royal pardon, kiddo.'

'Ye're jesting. How did you pull that stroke, John?'

'Bribed the cunt, didn't we?'

'Bribed? Who?'

'That fucking Michael Howard.'

But did they? Haase was having the same conversation all over Liverpool and telling anyone who'd listen and several who wouldn't. He had a message to spread – one that said he wasn't a grass but he had got one over the Home Secretary.

Liverpool players believed him. Why wouldn't they? Michael Howard carried some luggage that was a bit embarrassing. As they say, you can choose your friends but not your family. Howard must have wished he could.

55

THE RELATIVES

'How the fuck do we know they're good for the cash?' The speaker was tall, rough looking, his cheek carrying evidence of old knife wounds.

'Of course they are,' replied a smooth-headed man, wearing a more expensive suit and no facial scars. 'My old man's an accountant.'

'Yeah, la, but does he get on with you, like?'

'Mmm, the old dear will cough up.'

'She soft on you then?'

'Yeah,' the smooth man laughed nervously, 'and she's related to money.'

'What sort of money?'

'Michael-Fucking-Howard sort of money.'

'The cunting politician?'

'Yeah,' smooth man nodded and smirked. He knew that would impress that mob. Who'd expect a man like him, with gambling debts, a collection of bad habits and who kept company with every scally in Liverpool, to be related to a big-name Conservative Party politician?

'Nah! No you're not.'

'Fucking am,' all indignant tone from smoothie.

'Prove it, ye prick.'

Smooth features tutted and ceremoniously removed his watch, handing it to his colleague.

'Good bit of gear but so what?'

'Look at the back.'

'To Simon . . . from Michael.'

'He's my second cousin or something like that.'

'Gen up?'

'Yeah, fucking gen up.'

'OK, we'll give it a go.'

It was 1985 and a deal had just been struck between Simon Bakerman, Michael Howard's cousin, and the huge Fitzgibbon Family. Known as The Fitzes, they were notorious throughout Liverpool. (It was a member of the Fitzes who would later tackle Darren Mulholland, the fresh-faced Real IRA man, in Frankland Prison.) But this was no ordinary deal.

Simon Bakerman had bad debts to the wrong people, including The Fitzes. If he didn't pay up in cash, they'd take it out of his hide. And they didn't mess about. The Fitzes, like almost every other street player I know, would prefer to pocket the dosh rather than dish out the hurt so Bakerman had come up with a plan. He and The Fitzes would fake his own kidnapping. The Fitzes would take him to a safe house out of the way, where he'd phone his mother and tell her he'd been beaten up and was being held till the money was paid. If the cash wasn't forthcoming, his kidnappers would get more and more vicious.

'If the old bitch doesn't cough up, we could send her one of your fingers,' laughed one of The Fitzes. Then, grabbing Bakerman's hand, added, 'Choose one.'

Even at that stage, Simon Bakerman must have had his misgivings about getting into such a scam with that mob but he was desperate.

Bakerman wasn't lying about his relationship to Michael Howard. Not only were they cousins, Howard would drop by the family home and have tea with his mother, Freda, and his father, Warner. This was a fairly regular occurrence, particularly when Howard travelled to watch his favourite football team, Liverpool FC, at home matches.

Simon Bakerman's father was an accountant but business wasn't great. The debt the son owed was no more than £2,700, worth a lot more in 1985 than these days but still not an enormous fortune. Surely an accountant could find that kind of dough easily? Simon Bakerman and The Fitzes were about to find out.

'Where the fuck are you taking me?' asked Simon Bakerman from the back seat of a car as it travelled the deserted road down to the Merseyside dockland.

'A safe place,' said the driver who was accompanied by three of his male relatives. They all laughed and turned round to sneer at Bakerman.

'We agreed a safe house,' protested Bakerman.

'Yeah, we know, like, but we should try and keep this as realistic as possible, la.'

Ten minutes later, The Fitzes and Bakerman were inside a big, dark, dank warehouse. The place stank of engine oil and something rotten, like old potatoes. When they spoke, their breath curled into white wisps in front of them. There were three or four grease-smeared hard seats, no toilets, no drinks, no water, no kettle. This was too realistic for Simon Bakerman but, if The Fitzes said this was how it had to be, then Bakerman would comply. No choice.

'Another thing,' said one of the huge Fitzgibbon Family.

'What?' Bakerman turned to face him and was punched square on the face, sending him sprawling back on to his arse with a crunch. 'There's no need . . .' A boot caught him in the ribs. Bakerman rolled over and groaned.

'Up you get, la.' One of the men hoisted him by the collar, dragged him a few feet and dumped him on to one of the chairs. Another pulled his slumped torso back and bound him to the chair with strong cable. Ties round his ankles to the chair legs completed the process.

'That's more like it,' scoffed one of the men. 'It'll help you get into the role of victim when you phone your ma.'

'An' if that doesn't work, serves you right, you prick, for owing us money.'

For a couple of hours, they kept Simon Bakerman tethered to the chair. Occasionally, one of the crew would stand in front of the 'hostage', taunting and slapping him.

When they eventually released him, they gave him a drink of lager from a carry-out they'd brought and drove him to a call box nearby. Speaking to his mother, Freda, Simon Bakerman blurted out the tale. Sure enough, The Fitzes were impressed by the authenticity of his pleading voice. They almost believed him themselves.

'No probs,' said one of the mob, 'that money's a dead cert.'

However, he hadn't heard Freda Bakerman at other end of the line ask, 'How much?'

'Three thousand,' advised her son adding a little interest for himself.

His mother's reply amounted to long seconds of silence. Financially, things weren't great in the Bakerman household and three thousand was beyond their means. Besides, Simon had always been a difficult child. It was never possible to entirely believe him.

The farce went on for three days till, eventually, The Fitzes had to concede that the Bakermans weren't going to pay up. They gave Simon Bakerman another slapping and then sent him to the door of the warehouse.

'You can walk it, ye prick,' one of them spat.

Bakerman headed slowly out the door.

'Just a minute,' another of The Fitzes screamed. He went up to Bakerman, lifted one of his wrists and removed his watch, the only thing of value in his possession.

A short while later, Simon Bakerman was arrested and charged with deception by faking his own kidnapping. How was he sussed? Maybe it had something to do with a certain member of the Fitzgibbon Family standing in pubs showing off his new watch with the inscription 'from Michael'.

Bakerman didn't blab on The Fitzes and was given a six-month suspended sentence for his pains. It wasn't the last time he'd get into trouble with the cops and he wasn't the only one of the family either.

A few years later, his father, Warner, then aged sixty-two, was arrested and charged after a large consignment of cannabis was found in a lorry-load of oranges. At the cop shop, Warner complained of chest pains and provided evidence that he had heart problems. That was the official line at least. He was released and charges dropped but, as Liverpool faces would all report, Warner Bakerman seemed to make an instant recovery.

It was just as well really because, if he'd gone to court and been found guilty of drug trafficking, it could have been very embarrassing for his relative, Michael Howard. By that time, Howard had become Home Secretary – the most hard-line Home Secretary on crime in living memory.

It wasn't Michael Howard's fault that he had dodgy relatives. I'm sure some of my cousins, nephews and nieces don't advertise the fact that they are related to me. But you can't give men like John Haase a death sentence and expect no retaliation. It wasn't finished – not by a long shot.

56

THE POLITICS

Did Haase and Bennett bribe the Home Secretary? Or, by the Home Secretary, did they mean some high-ranking civil servant? Or someone in Customs? The cops? Or even MI5?

Word on the street spread like a forest fire. We knew that Michael Howard had some dodgy relatives. We also knew that he kept in touch with them. It was our business to know. Knowledge is power and never more so than on the wrong side of the law. Yet it seemed to stretch credibility to suggest that Howard himself had been compromised. If it was at all possible, what would it take? Millions of pounds? Several millions of pounds? Haase and Bennett could afford that, for sure. After all, they had been nabbed with £15 million of smack and that was only in one of their safe houses.

If the street knew all about Howard's bent relatives, the politicians knew that something was far wrong with this royal pardon. In particular, it annoyed the hell out of Peter Kilfoyle, the local Labour MP when his party was still in opposition, who stood and watched Haase dealing on the street the day after he was released. Haase was flaunting his freedom and his return to criminality, Kilfoyle decided. Haase had been released by the top authority in the land to sell drugs to his constituents and the cops seemed to be ignoring him. Sod that. Late in 1996, Kilfoyle decided to raise questions in an interview on Sky TV. Then he got an unusual call.

That Michael Howard, Tory Home Secretary, phoned Peter

Kilfoyle, opposition Labour MP, was unusual in itself but so was the reason for his call. It was the night before Kilfoyle was to raise the Haase/Bennett issue publicly and Howard asked him not to, claiming lives would be put at risk. Assuming that the Home Secretary meant the lives of police or Customs, Kilfoyle immediately agreed. It was a decision he later admitted that he regretted, saying, 'It seems the only people at risk from publicly airing this issue were Haase and Bennett. Strange that the Home Secretary was so concerned about the well being of two convicted drug traffickers.'

Eventually, many months later, Kilfoyle did ask a question, only this time it was in Parliament. He got little back from the government in terms of a reply except that Howard's deputy, Ann Widdecombe, had not been consulted by him on the royal pardon – that was a strange one. Everyone knew that Howard and Widdecombe didn't get on. So what? A royal pardon is exceptional at any time especially when it relates to two guys still considered to be as guilty as sin. Was Howard hiding something? Even from his colleagues?

Kilfoyle didn't get the answers he wanted so, later, he asked more questions in Parliament and did some finger-pointing at me. In this statement, he claimed that one Paul Ferris knew about the guns that were exchanged and knew all about the ones that came from the Customs dump in North Wales. Great! At that time, I was being held for the gunrunning. I was trying to keep out of trouble and planning on getting out of jail as soon as possible so that I could spend a long, free – and straight – life with my kids and he goes and names me in Parliament. He made no mention of Rab Carruthers who supplied the shooters and made not even a whisper about Haase's Scouse delegation who bought the guns – it was just bloody me and all I'd done was to give some advice on the matter.

Kilfoyle's finger-pointing could well have resulted in me being held back in prison and, as if that wasn't bad enough, he repeated it a few months later. This was getting to be personal. In 1997, when Labour gained power, Jack Straw, the new Home Secretary, appointed Kilfoyle to a junior ministerial post with a roving remit. He was expected to look at any and every aspect of the Home Office and draw anything that he felt needed to be looked at urgently to Straw's attention. If I was Peter Kilfoyle, I would've headed straight for the Haase/Bennett file. What about you?

A short while later, Kilfoyle went to Straw seeking urgent action on something he'd found. Straw refused. Kilfoyle resigned. Kilfoyle has never revealed what he found that was so important as to be a resignation matter. What is obvious though, and he has never denied it, is that untangling the royal pardon fiasco remains high on his agenda – so high that he went public again in Parliament. That night, Michael Howard stormed up the corridors of the Home Office and straight into Jack Straw's office. For hours, the two men's loud, angry voices could be heard echoing through that dusty building. No minute-taker and no civil servants were present. It was just Straw and Howard and they weren't very happy.

Kilfoyle might have taken some satisfaction in rattling Michael Howard's cage but he had done something else – named me yet again. This was now personal and no doubt so I decided to find out some answers to the royal pardon saga. I didn't have too long to wait.

57

THE BOX

One minute, there were allegations that John Haase had a licence to commit crime without arrest – the next, he was in jail. If it surprised the rest of us, it must have been quite a blow to him.

The licence wasn't just a rumour. Some associates of mine got nabbed in a large-scale raid in Liverpool. One minute they were exchanging goods – the next the street was full of Customs and cops hefting shooters. It was pandemonium with bodies running everywhere, motors trying to take off and everyone reaching for their guns. Slap-bang in the middle of this was Haase, innocently using a call box and accompanied by one of his team.

'Leave him,' shouted the Customs gaffer as his troops went to arrest Haase, 'he's one of ours.' And they left him.

But, unknown to John Haase, there had been a change of heart. Paul Grimes, the grass who had brought down Curtis 'Cocky' Warren as revenge for his son's death from a heroin overdose, wasn't a happy man. Another of his sons, Heath, had found work in Haase's firm which was called Big Brother. While Big Brother officially dealt with security services and provided bouncers for doors, Grimes knew what Haase's real racket was – drugs. Furious that his son was being implicated in Haase's business, Grimes duly signed up with the cops to bring him down.

Grimes infiltrated Big Brother by also getting a job with the firm and he was able to keep a note of all the comings and goings. Haase trusted him. Why shouldn't he? On a day that he knew Haase was to be involved in uplifting some shooters and carrying load of dirty money, Paul Grimes made the call. He did so knowing fine well that his own son, Heath, would get nabbed too. That's a grass for you.

Haase and his team were in the pokey awaiting trial when my search for some answers took a turn for the better. Down in Liverpool, sniffing into some story, Reg's mobile phone went off at three in the morning as he snoozed in that great old hotel, The Adelphi. It wasn't anyone he knew – just some guy calling himself Matt and asking for a meeting right away outside some nearby shopping centre. The place would be deserted and dark. It was definitely a dodgy call.

All sorts of people had taken to their heels in terror from this tale. The first was an old-time journalist working for a local newspaper – the kind of guy used to dealing with threats from wild men. He was paid a visit one day and resigned the next. When he was last heard of, he was working on a market farm some place in Yorkshire and had changed his name.

An ambitious and pushy young whiz kid had come up from London intent on researching a documentary on the case. For months, he worked on the story then was given an address near Newcastle where he was promised some crucial evidence of bribes. Off he set, full of optimism, but he was never to be seen or heard of again.

Now Reg was on his own in a strange city in the middle of the night, being promised 'the goods' if he dared go to a dark shopping centre right away. Fuck it, he went anyway. Good call. The man calling himself Matt handed over a cardboard box stuffed full of papers and documents. Wishing Reg the best of luck and telling him to watch out for himself, Matt disappeared into the night.

Back in the safety of The Adelphi, Reg couldn't believe his eyes. The box was crammed with Customs, police and court papers on John Haase and Paul Bennett.

Now we were going to get some answers.

58

THE REAL DEAL

There had been some shenanigans and no joke.

The guns, explosives and so on had been exchanged all right. They were listed by Haase and Bennett's Customs handler, Paul Cooke, in a report he had sent to their original trial judge, David Lynch, recommending that he consider some degree of sentence reduction for the two men.

The guns, ammo and explosives had been seized in around twenty operations and found in cars and so-called safe houses around Liverpool. Some were suspected to be en route to Ireland while others were thought to be earmarked for big firms in London and Scotland – no evidence just 'suspicions'.

It was also true that no one had been arrested in connection with any of these raids – not one person. Reading the official reports, it still didn't seem to be to be enough reason to release Haase and Bennett from their eighteen-year spells. But, of course, there was more. There were other goods recovered and attributed to Haase and Bennett. A skunk den was broken up and a heroin factory seized. Though there was a quantity of drugs recovered, yet again, no one was arrested. So still no big deal. Among the long list of shooters recovered, it was almost too easy to have missed the line in Cooke's report that referred, somewhat vaguely, to assistance given in recovering a gun in a prison and possibly averting some serious incident. That's when Reg went on the hoof and discovered what that was all about.

There was a bloke called John Lally. Although he was a local hard man, he was not involved in the organised crime lark. Instead, John worked up a business running bouncers on doors – a dodgy game but it was one he was good at. Liverpool has to be one of the toughest cities in the world to be a pub bouncer but John did well and his reputation was sound. Many big-name pop stars doing gigs in the city and staying over would hire him to be sure they were safe. It was a far cry from the days when you could pop into The Cavern and listen to The Beatles, eh?

Haase knew John Lally very well. The security man had given Haase a job when he first emerged into the light from The Transit Van Robberies sentence. It's part of the code of the street – helping a guy out when he's back from jail. Lally sounds like a good bloke.

After Haase and Bennett had been packed off to prison awaiting trial for the drug trafficking, a lawyer approached Lally saying he was from Haase. There was no surprise there – it was what came next that was the bombshell. The request, allegedly from Haase, was that Lally should smuggle a gun and bullets into Strangeways Prison – like you do. A small tape recorder is one thing, some dope is no problem but a gun gets you the modern equivalent of a hanging offence. You couldn't just breeze through the prison's reception on your way to a visit with a shooter in your boxers. Well, you could try if you were well mental. John Lally wasn't that.

To make matters worse, Strangeways housed a hell of a lot of IRA prisoners at the time. They were deemed the number-one security risk and perfectly capable of getting weapons smuggled in and blasting their way of jail. The lawyer didn't tell Lally what the gun would be used for, just that arrangements would be made to hand it on to a screw. Sod that. John Lally declined the request.

A short time later, a man called Tommy Bourke was on trial for a double murder. It was an unusual case. Bourke was a non-player who owned a garage and he was alleged to have blasted two Customs and Excise men to death with a shotgun. It was the job of these Customs and Excise boys to inspect and register garages to allow them to carry out MOT tests. At his trial, Bourke pled not guilty but described how the two officers expected big-money bribes to issue the necessary certificates. Without them, a business like Bourke's would go bust. They had him by the short and curlies, in other words.

In court, the prosecutor claimed that Bourke had been driven to distraction by the Customs guys and, in a fit of temper, lost the place entirely and killed them. It was a straightforward story with an air of realism about it but the trouble was it was weak as hell. The killing was meant to have taken place in a small brick room. The killer would have been saturated with the men's blood and no amount of scrubbing would have removed the forensics from his body. None was found. One of the chief witnesses was a dull-witted young guy who contradicted himself a number of times and so no one believed him.

With the main proceedings of the trial over, the court retired for the day. The next morning the judge was due to give his summing-up to the jury who would then go off and make their minds up. As the lawyers tidied their desks, the prosecutor approached the defence lawyer and told him that he considered it a hopeless case and he had lost – in other words, Bourke would walk free. That night, a loaded pistol was found in Tommy Bourke's cell in Strangeways Prison. Bourke was slammed into solitary. The jail was then locked down and the place searched from end to end. It was a major security crisis and no doubt.

The next day, Tommy Bourke was driven to court in a bulletproof van filled with armed police. The van was surrounded by out-riding motorbikes and there was a procession of cop cars with their lights flashing and sirens blaring. At the courthouse, he was marched in wearing handcuffs and surrounded by armed cops. The gun-toting bizzies stood there looking mean as the judge gave his address to the jury but they listened more to the non-verbals of the glowering armed rozzers. Message received loud and clear – guilty and sentenced to twenty-five years.

There were immediate appeals and Tommy Bourke's sister, Jo, and brother, Wally, tried to publicise the case with no luck. Yet, the law actually caught the screw who had smuggled in the gun hidden inside a toaster of all things. He got rapped across the knuckles and transferred to another jail. Mind you, it might have had something to do with the fact that his father was a governor in the prison service. Even the head of security who had allowed the breach just got transferred and was soon promoted. All the while, Tommy Bourke was rotting in jail.

Customs have been challenged over the gun in Tommy Bourke's cell being their responsibility – that they set him up to make sure he went down for killing their mates – that they ensured someone went down for the murders whether they were guilty or not. Customs deny it, of course. When John Lally heard of what happened to Bourke, he went to the cops, choosing one he thought was honest. He's still waiting for some action.

Was that gun in Tommy Bourke's cell the same gun the lawyer had asked John Lally to smuggle in for Haase? Was that another part of the deal that Haase and Bennett had settled with Customs? Or had Customs really bribed someone?

Street players like me and the media alike were making the same mistake for once. We all thought the royal pardon and bribes issue mainly concerned John Haase – that he and not Bennett was the main player in this game. Or so we thought.

Yet some dirt-digging was to reveal that Bennett had been very busy and was very well travelled. He was about to spend time with an old enemy of mine in Glasgow as people would learn to their cost.

59

THE NEPHEW

Thomas McGraw wanted a word with local Glasgow player, Ian McAteer. A favour was needed. A man needed some place safe to stay for a while. Some place no one noticed. Some place in Glasgow. McAteer agreed, of course. The man's name? Paul Bennett. As his uncle John Haase lay in prison awaiting trial for the guns and dodgy cash, Bennett had just returned from Belfast where he'd been a very busy man indeed.

Bennett's travels had started a few years before when his lawyer received a phone call from his Customs handler, Paul Cooke. His client was wanted in connection with smuggling £1m worth of cannabis and could Bennett come in for interview? Like you do. So it was no surprise when, the next day, Bennett had disappeared from his family home and wasn't seen in the Liverpool area again for a long time. A short while after he went away, his house was sold and his family moved out of town – destination unknown.

About a year later, one Saturday, a duty solicitor was asked to attend Manchester Airport. A guy had just landed from Ireland and was discovered with a bag of drugs. Large scale, they said, and he needed a lawyer. When the solicitor arrived at the airport, Customs and the cops apologised and told him he was no longer required despite the fact that they had already named the man. There was no explanation – he was just told to go away. That was a strange one, he thought, so made a point of scanning the court schedules for

Manchester and Liverpool for many, many months, looking for the bloke's name. It never appeared. The name? Paul Bennett.

Bennett had been in Ireland setting up drug-trafficking deals with Loyalist groups. It was at the time when Loyalist groups like the UDA and UVF had started fighting among themselves. There were splits and, with former leaders like Billy 'King Rat' Wright shot dead in the Maze by Republicans, the civil war turned bloody. Guys like 'Mad Dog' Johnny Adair were fighting for control and one issue underwrote the whole squabble. Paul Bennett's expert subject – drugs.

Some Loyalists, like Adair, argued that they should use their firepower and underworld connections to earn money from drug trafficking. Others disagreed, saying they were freedom fighters and should have no truck with the trade. They fought out their dispute on the streets of Belfast with bullets and bombs. Terrorists were killing each other and they were becoming weaker every day – the authorities loved it. You might even suspect they made it happen. Maybe they did.

Some say it's significant that Bennett – a long-established heroin trafficker – was seen around Belfast at the precise time the Loyalists were shooting each other over heroin. As the situation disintegrated into all-out civil war, it eventually got too hot for him and he had to leave town fast. He needed a safe house. Where to go? Glasgow, of course, and to Thomas McGraw, The Licensee.

McGraw and his brother-in-law, Snadz Adams, had been big supporters of the Loyalist cause for years. When, in the early 1980s, they were both members of the Barlanark Team robbing post offices, they sent many tens of thousands of pounds to the cause every week. Mad Dog Adair and his wife, known as Mad Bitch, were frequent visitors to McGraw in Glasgow. A few years later, when Adair's mob was kicked out of Belfast, it was Scotland and McGraw they first went to.

When Paul Bennett headed to Glasgow he needed a safe house. However, it wasn't the authorities he was on the run from but the Irish mob who were on his tail. The Licensee isn't in the habit of taking such risks himself so asked a trusted east-end face, Ian McAteer. McAteer was well known in the city and had served time for various crimes. He knew the scene, could handle himself and was known to be able to keep a secret – perfect in other words.

Bennett was put up for about ten months by Ian McAteer. In that time, McAteer had been making a good living on cars. Some straight deals and others ringed – stolen and their identities altered. He was up and down the country delivering these motors and was often around the Liverpool area. Many times, Bennett suggested certain jobs to McAteer. Cautious, the Scot always declined. It got to the stage where McAteer's intuition screamed that Bennett was trying to set him up and the two split up.

A short while later, Warren Selkirk, a Liverpool associate of McAteer, was having an access visit to his kids who lived with their mother. As he drove the young boys, his mobile phone had rung and he explained to the kids that he had to go and meet someone. Parking the car, he reassured the children he wouldn't be long. He never returned. Warren Selkirk's body was found a hundred yards away, down by a marina. He'd been shot at close range and a symbolic bag of dog shit stuck in his hand. The kids were still in the car, howling their eyes out.

It was a murder that drew the sympathy of the people of Liverpool and the cops were under great pressure to get the killer. Ian McAteer went down for it but only after a trial full of more games than the Olympics. During the trial, an unknown terrorist group from Ireland contacted the press, taking responsibility for the murder. Immediately, the cops claimed that McAteer's friends had set that up to lay a false scent. Yet Warren Selkirk had contacts in Ireland and been there frequently before his death. Selkirk also had a big gambling problem and owed money to some very dangerous people – some very dangerous *Irish* people.

Then the cops claimed that McAteer was a feared gangster whose street name was Little Hands. This was news to me and any other Glasgow street player who'd known McAteer since childhood. But it sounds sinister, right?

Ian McAteer could prove he was nowhere near the scene of the killing at the crucial time but he'd be accused of conspiring to murder – setting it up. The case against him still looked weak till one of his workers, George Bell Smith, agreed to give evidence against him. Glaswegian Bell Smith was a low-level player McAteer used for nothing more arduous than delivering cars. But Smith claimed that, one night after the murder, McAteer had shown him a gun and more or less admitted to the killing. That'll be Ian McAteer, who is so cautious as to be almost paranoid, confessing then? No bloody chance.

What McAteer didn't know was that Bell Smith was a very jealous man. On more than one occasion, he'd attacked former girlfriends' new lovers with hammers and blades. At the time of Selkirk's death, McAteer was going out with a former girlfriend of George Bell Smith. Bell Smith also had a secret – underage sex charges. He and a friend had cruised a small town near Glasgow, picked up two girls aged fourteen and thirteen, taken them to a house and had sex with them. In Bell Smith's case, the fourteen-year-old girl claims she said no but he just did it anyway. Is that rape? Sounds like it to me. As Bell Smith was helping the police prepare for McAteer's trial, the underage sex charges were suddenly dropped. No explanation given. No explanation needed.

Ian McAteer had come close to revealing to the street what he thought of Paul Bennett – that he set people up and worked for the cops, much like McGraw, The Licensee. Now McAteer was in jail and too busy fighting to prove his innocence to worry about either of them.

During the murder trial, one of McAteer's co-accused was being taken care of – his mortgage was being paid and his wife was given money. Who was the benefactor? Paul Bennett.

One year later, in 2001, Customs and cops seized a massive load of cannabis that had come into the country directly from Spain. Nine different parties were involved and the only man who had met them all? Paul Bennett. The only man not arrested or charged? Paul Bennett.

An internal Customs and Excise memo dated 3 August 1998 and signed by Steve Rowton, the boss of Haase and Bennett's handler

Paul Cooke, was circulated to all operatives warning them that there was increased political interest in the two players and so all contact should be cut off. The key phrase was, 'In order to safeguard our position, we must maintain our distance.' That word 'distance' meant different things for the two men. For Haase, it meant his Customs and cop minders were called off. For two years, they had tailed him wherever he went, making sure he was OK and not pulled in by other forces. The officers were compromised frequently as Haase dished out the damage to whoever got in his way. For Bennett, it meant continuing to use him as a plant. Paul Bennett's not alone. Last year, in England, approximately seventy-five people were released from prison, pending appeals against very lengthy jail sentences for drug trafficking. They were all released for the same reason – evidence that they'd been set up by Customs and the cops who had used agents provocateurs to befriend them and trick them into trafficking. No doubt the appeal proceedings will be held in secret to protect the identity of the Customs officers involved and maybe that of their helpers too. Protect the guilty, as per usual.

Bennett is now, once again, openly seen around the Merseyside area, the investigation into that £1 million dope smuggling long forgotten. The nephew has never boasted about any deal with guns or hinted at bribes or flaunted claims about conning Michael Howard. His uncle John Haase wasn't so quiet. And he was about to pay for it big time.

60

THE PRICE
2001

'You can't try me, you old cunt!' Haase was screaming at the judge
and spitting with fury from the dock in the Crown Court in Liverpool.
'Get me the fucking Home Secretary. The fucking Prime Minister.
Only they can try me, you pricks.' It wasn't the best start to a trial.
The court was immediately closed and three armed cops put on the
door.

Haase and his mob had been caught red-handed with a load of
illegally obtained weapons. The delivery included a Smith & Wesson
Magnum revolver – the so-called 'Dirty Harry Special' – an Uzi sub-
machine gun and a stack of ammo, some of which were dumdum
bullets that explode inside the body. Heath Grimes delivered the
guns on his motorbike to one Walter Kirkwood, a Scottish guy who'd
been paid by one of the Glasgow teams to courier the shooters up
north. Kirkwood, an ex-soldier with no criminal record, was on his
uppers and had accepted £400 for the job – buttons. He didn't even
make it to the motorway before the armed squad arrested him.

A few weeks later, Haase and a Liverpool bloke called Ken Darcy
caught a train at Liverpool's Lime Street station. What they didn't
know was that the ticket seller, the cleaners, the guards and the
inspector were all undercover cops. Haase and Darcy were watched
all the way as they travelled first class to Euston Station, London.
There, they were followed as they travelled by hack to the north of
the city and a Turkish restaurant. So much for smashing a Turkish

drugs ring – Haase was still well in with that crew, something that would never have happened if they suspected him of being a grass.

Armed cops jumped them. Darcy had a Bhs carrier bag with him containing a kilo of smack. Haase had nothing more sinister than £3,000 in cash – not much for a man of his means. The trouble was it was all Scottish notes. It was payment for the guns and ammo delivery that Walter Kirkwood was supposed to make – gun money and hot too. Haase was in the shit.

After his outburst at the opening of the trial, the court was closed to the public and armed cops put on the door. The authorities said they feared for the safety of the accused, witnesses and the officials. Stories ran through Liverpool of certain teams planning an armed raid on the court with guns blazing. Bullshit. The authorities simply wanted to keep everything about John Haase secret. They had pulled him in precisely because he talked too much and Haase wasn't going to shut up now. The dealings of the court were hit with Public Interest Immunity orders (PIIs) – that's jargon for confidential. That didn't stop certain parties getting the paperwork out to us – just as the armed cops didn't stop Reg walking straight into the court. The three polis were too busy talking about Gary McAllister's sparkling form for Liverpool FC that year.

Word was circulating that we had more on this case than anyone else and, one day, Reg got a phone call from a guy claiming to be part of a team of private detectives working for Harrods' owner Mohamed al-Fayed. Al-Fayed, of course, has been denied a British passport for years. According to this guy, his boss thought there was some Jewish plot at the highest level against him and he'd be willing to pay big money for anything on Michael Howard. No thank you, Mohamed al-Fayed, it's not our style.

But, behind the scenes at Liverpool Crown Court, deals *were* being struck. Haase had threatened repeatedly in court to reveal the secrets behind the deal that led to his royal pardon. That got their attention. They knew Haase had secretly recorded the negotiations in jail that eventually led to the royal pardon. On the tape, senior Customs officers were heard talking about giving the men a 60% reduction on their sentences in return for their help and also suggesting that maybe it was best if they served at least four years so it didn't look bad. Haase stated he had other tapes about the taking of bribes – tapes that would bring political parties to their knees. He'd done it once – he could do it again.

Back in court in 2001, Haase eventually pled guilty to money-laundering charges. When he was brought in for sentencing, he got the agreed six years for the money and seven added on for selling the guns. He went ballistic, claiming he had been deliberately cheated to shut him up. The court didn't listen and he'd serve thirteen years.

The Scot, Walter Kirkwood, got three years for the guns. Heath Grimes got four years thanks to his supergrass father. Ken Darcy took the full weight of six years for the smack. One of the accused, Barry Oliver, got a not guilty and walked.

Haase is now being passed around between top-security jails, a Category-A high-risk prisoner who is never allowed to settle in one place for too long. True to form, he refuses to work or cooperate with the screws in any way so, although he's due to be released in 2009, it's likely that John Haase will earn himself extra time inside. Now and then, he sends messages out to certain parties saying that he is ready to release recordings that will blow our minds. Recordings that will prove he hasn't been spouting hot air. Recordings that will show he was cheated into extra jail time. Maybe one day we'll see and hear those recordings.

At the time of writing, Michael Howard is, of course, the Tory leader but he's said he'll stand down towards the end of 2005. That he'll stay in public life and the limelight is for sure. Does he think about Haase as often as Haase obviously thinks of him? Only Howard can answer that.

The gangster or the politician – I know which one I trust. How about you?

I was about to be reunited with an old friend who promised me a new world. I trusted him totally and too much trust was about to bite me in the arse big time.

61

THE EVIL GENIUS

2002

'My brother.' It was a warm greeting. The handsome, suave man walked towards me smiling, his arms wide open for an embrace. I walked forward and clasped my arms round him, as you do with someone who has been close to you and yours for twenty years.

'Good to see you, Ben,' I replied and meant every word of it. I had just been released from prison a few weeks before and had made a point of arranging to meet up with Ben as soon as possible. He had always opened doors, trying to give me lucrative and straight income opportunities, and now I intended to take them up. The meeting was taking place in his luxury flat at Riverview Gardens in Glasgow, overlooking the River Clyde from the south bank. It was a plush setting and Ben's natural habitat. As he demonstrated in his many other houses in Britain and abroad, Ben was a multi-millionaire and no doubt.

Ben's full, formal name was Seyed Muhammad Benham Nodjoumi Qajar Alagha but we called him just Ben for short or Ben Alagha for long. He was certainly a man of many names and I wish I'd known then just how many faces he also had. But Ben had given us clues about the faces. In fact, that's how I came to meet him.

The Shah of Iran was his grandfather and Ben was brought up in luxurious palaces there and schooled in the art of diplomacy from an early age. It seems to me that that's the art of saying what the listener wants to hear while meaning and doing something else –

what you want. The SAVAK was the Iranian secret police and they had a reputation for terror that puts all similar organisations to shame. When Ben was a young adult, the Shah was fighting a revolt by the fundamental Muslim mullahs and the internal battles were fierce. A qualified lawyer, Ben became a torturer for SAVAK, an expert at inflicting pain a thousand different ways. He used to say that, when all else failed, he'd stick a newly boiled egg up the victim's arse. It never failed and no surprise.

By 1979, the Shah had lost the struggle and the Ayatollah Khomeini took over. Years later, I watched Khomeini's funeral on TV. Millions of men turned up, distraught and weeping. They totally lost the place and the coffin was overturned and the stiff's clothes were all ripped. That day, I got a sense of the extreme terror men like Ben must have inflicted to keep that kind of passion under control. But, in 1979, with Khomeini on the way in, the Shah and his family took refuge in countries all over the world. Ben chose Britain and was welcomed with open arms. Well, he was royalty on the run, after all.

Ben didn't return the open-door hospitality with respect – well, not in the authorities' view. By 1981, he had embarked on a career of crime. Big time. Along with three British accomplices, including one of the Arif Family from London, he set about conning the Iranian government out of $52 million in a bogus arms deal. Iran was at war with Iraq at the time and there was a worldwide embargo on selling Iran weapons. It must have been like having a knife fight with your blade arm tied behind your back. The Iranians were desperate for arms and Ben took full advantage.

Posing and dressing as an arms dealer, Ben offered to sell the new Iranian government 8,000 anti-tank TOW (tube-launched, optically tracked, wire-guided) missiles but planned to deliver thirty-four crates of useless machinery in their place. The 'arms' were to be made available in Antwerp for inspection by three Iranian colonels. Instead, Ben and the Arif bloke posed as Iranian colonels, carried out the inspection themselves and forged the clearance signatures.

Back in London, the rest of his team had taken an Iranian diplomat and two bank managers hostage, just to ensure that the dosh was paid over. What they planned to do with these guys after the job is unclear. I suspect they weren't going to be around long enough to collect their pensions but we'll never know for sure.

The political situation in Iran and Iraq was as sensitive then as it is now. MI6 had been watching Ben very carefully and had sussed his plot. One hour before the cash was due to be handed over, a crack cop team armed with sub-machine guns hit the gang's London HQ.

At the Old Bailey, Ben claimed it had been a political act against the government of Iran. Aye, right. The judge called him 'an evil genius' and he wasn't wrong. Ben Alagha was one very bright man – so bright that the $52 million remains frozen in a Swiss account to this day. I wouldn't be a bit surprised if he's worked on a few ploys to get his hands on the dough. Ben was sent down for twenty years and had a deportation order slapped on him. As soon as he was finished serving time, he was to be sent packing out of the country. Well, that's what they said then but there I was meeting him in 2002, years after he had been released from jail, and he was still happily resident in Britain. That was the type of game Ben was good at – manipulation. But that's not a game you play with family and friends, right? Right.

My brother Billy, serving time for murder in England, was in Wormwood Scrubs at the same time as Ben. The Iranian sweet-talker had got caught up in an escape plan involving explosives and guns and it went belly up. He was in big shit not just from the prison's point of view but because he'd landed a couple of IRA men in trouble too. So Billy, who's scared of no one, stepped in and took the blame. Even back then, Billy reckoned that the authorities would never let him out so what the hell? He'd do extra time and the spell in solitary that went with it. The only trouble was that the IRA wanted to talk to him. Twenty years later, when I was serving time for gunrunning and I was moved to Full Sutton, I was approached by an IRA man who said they hadn't forgotten Billy and still wanted a word. That's Billy.

Ben was all gratitude to Billy. He sorted him out with regular goodies and promised him that he'd take care of him when he left jail – they'd be brothers for life, that type of thing. During my late teens, I visited Billy in jail regularly and was introduced to Ben. The Shah's grandson took a shine to me and asked if I would carry out some work for him on the outside – all legitimate, of course. The main earner was to take possession of two ships. A family owed Ben millions and had decided to ignore the debt since he was locked up. All I had to do was turn up at a certain port on a certain day, slap some notices on the sides of the ships and accompany an engineer aboard who would then disable both vessels.

My cut was to be substantial. Overnight, I would become a very rich young man and there was other similar work where that came from. At that time, I was working with a group of pals, robbing jewellers' shops and the like. Would I stick to that or accept a legitimate get-rich-quick card? What do you think?

Even as a kid, I was like every other street player I met. We break the law for one reason – money. Would we rather get loads of dough and be legal? Bet your bottom dollar we would.

But I had broken the law and got nabbed at the wrong time and place. Days before those two ships docked, I landed in jail. Bastard! If I had been jailed one week later and had managed to seize those ships, most likely I wouldn't have gone on to work for Arthur Thompson and all the rest that came after. Most likely.

From that early age, I'd always been grateful to Ben for giving me a chance to break away from crime, even if I didn't make it – being jailed at the wrong time was my fault, not his.

When I found out that, after being jailed on the bogus arms deal, he had also been found guilty of raping his secretary, I had serious questions to ask. No matter how kind someone is to me I have no truck with rapists. When I visited him in jail one time, Ben said he understood how I felt and that he also considered rapists to be worse than the lowest life form. He had been having an affair with the secretary, he explained, but she'd been planted by the Iranian government and she wasn't really a secretary but a call girl willing to be hired out for almost anything at a price. After love making one time, she'd faked the rape and called the cops.

'It's political, Paul,' he'd said. 'It is my curse for the rest of my life.'

It sounded like a dodgy James Bond plot. But Ben had been a torturer for SAVAK. He was the Shah's grandson. There was a movement to have the Shah's family reinstated on the Iranian throne. A part of Ben Alagha's life was full of spies and dirty tricks. I gave him the benefit of the doubt.

In the early 1990s when both Ben and I were free, he gave me a gift that had nothing to do with money. Ben introduced me to his father-in-law, Arthur Suttie, and his family. What gems. Arthur was an old London face who was known and respected by all the senior players in London like Joey Pyle and Frankie Fraser. A small man with the heart of a lion, Arthur reminded me so much of my own old dad. From a working-class family in London's east end, Arthur had worked himself up to a wonderful standard of living. He had this big fuck-off ranch at Epsom, with a massive house surrounded by field after field, most of which were full of horses. No one would have blamed him for taking a bit of pride, showing off a little, but there wasn't an ounce of that in him.

Arthur dressed like he didn't care and smoked roll ups. His wife Sheila and his daughter were some of the most welcoming folk I've ever met. Ben, with his expensive suits, gold watches, silk shirts and that silver spoon in his mouth, didn't quite sit properly with the Sutties. But Arthur was no fool and, if he accepted Ben, that was another good sign as far as I was concerned.

In that same period of the 1990s, Ben gave me some contracts to do with my security business. Just after the Americans and Brits liberated Kuwait from an Iraqi invasion in 1991, Ben smelled oil. There was a worldwide ban on buying Iraqi oil so he intended to steal it. Along with some Kuwaiti and Pakistani businessmen and politicians, he was plotting to access Iraqi oil from a supply that ran underground into Kuwaiti territory. My company, Premier Security, guarded the meeting where these plans were being discussed. Within minutes, it was clear that there was an orchestrated and highly skilled watching brief going on. When I was absolutely certain, I alerted

Ben by writing him a note. He just smiled, wrote on the note and passed it back to me with a broad grin. It said, 'I've seen them too. Don't worry – it's MI6. What did you expect?'

When my brother Billy was eventually freed from his life sentence, I was inside serving time for the gunrunning. One of the first people to greet Billy on his release was the bold Ben. Right away, he fixed him up with some money and a job with him – a business job with loads of prospects. Ben openly repeated that he had a debt to Billy that he would continue to repay for as long as Billy was alive. He assured him he would never have to worry about any problems he or his family might face since he, Ben, would fix them.

'I am a man of honour, Billy,' Ben had said. 'With me, your future is assured.'

Lying in Frankland Prison, I had been delighted that Ben was free and helping Billy. My brother had spent twenty-four years in jail. After that length of time, it's one hard job adjusting to everyday life in the free world. Ben had been busy, by all accounts, and he'd kept Billy busy too.

But now, in 2002, as I stepped back into that free world myself, I was about to find out just how busy Ben had been. I was about to have my eyes opened and risk paying the ultimate price for showing too much trust.

62

JUST ONE JOB
2003

'Have you ever been to South Africa, Paul?' Ben asked as we talked in his flat. Behind him, the Clyde flowed on towards the coast carrying what? Too often, it was too many dead bodies. But did they jump or were they pushed?

'I've never been to Africa, Ben,' I replied. Well, it had never occurred to me to nip across for the summer hols.

'That might change if you are interested, brother.'

It was early 2003. I had been released, recalled and released again from jail. Still on licence, I wasn't allowed to go for a fortnight to Skegness without permission. But that control would end soon and here was Ben dangling a big juicy carrot of a trip to South Africa.

'Go on.'

Ben told me about a business prospect he had. Some scientist had invented what he reckoned to be an effective end to malaria. I knew that malaria was mosquito-borne and it killed far too many people – especially kids in poor Third-World countries. There endeth all I fucking knew about malaria. According to Ben, mosquitoes need bodies of water to breed and thrive. What the egghead had come up with was a treatment that went over the surface of lakes and stopped the insects getting on to the water. It prevented them from breeding and so killed them off. Rather than trying to treat the mosquitoes' targets, humans, this would stop the problem before there was one. According to Ben, previous attempts to control the spread of the

264

disease had worked for a while but then the hardy mosquito adapted and started to spread malaria again. It would be hard for the buggers to adapt if they were dead. Made sense to me.

The boffin with the patent was having problems getting the chemical marketed. It had to be tested and no one was too keen to allow him to test the gear on their waters. It might kill the fish, poison the birds, turn the water black. Can't have that so the people will just have to keep dying. That was Ben's tone. I was already on his side. Who wouldn't be if you could do something to stop such a killer as malaria? And maybe make a few quid while you're at it.

'If this works,' continued Ben, as if reading my mind, 'it will be a huge phenomenon. A massive amount of money to be made and it will belong to us.'

I could see those two ships coming in to dock again. Same singer, same song – this was just a different version.

'There's only one little problem,' said Ben and I knew there had to be.

To get the chemicals tested, Ben had set up two companies, Surfqil and Dayfield Technology plc. He had teamed up with a millionaire entrepreneur we'll just call Owen who had good contacts in South Africa. Given legal guarantees that the chemical treatment would be produced there, South Africa was quite happy to allow the trials to take place there. Lakes and swamps had been identified but they were in a remote territory that was full of armed bandits and dangerous as hell.

A sizeable laboratory would have to be built and a staff of about fifty bodies sent out, including some top scientists. Protecting those folks would be paramount and that's where I came in. I could just see myself riding shotgun on a jeep through the jungle – it was almost like my days with Arthur Thompson except it was legal. It sounded like good fun to me but I couldn't do it on my own – I'd need a team.

The fiercest gangsters I knew couldn't cope with the job. They lived and breathed in a different kind of jungle. With a bit of asking around and pulling in contacts, I located a bloke, ex-SAS, who now ran a personal protection agency. Very discreet to the point of secrecy, this guy was keen to take on the work. Personal protection versus jungle warfare? Bodyguards versus soldiers? They didn't seem to tie in to me. That's when he revealed that a wee sideline of his was supplying mercenaries to places where they were needed. It seems that he hired former soldiers, all Brits and preferably ex-SAS, who would go and kill anyone, anywhere, if the right price was on offer. These guys had played a role on almost every side in every conflict in recent times. Often they changed sides halfway through simply because the opposition made them a better offer. It wasn't something he wanted to advertise for obvious reasons. The South Africa job was right up his street and, on my word alone, he started recruiting bodies right away.

This was better. After a year of grief from the cops and certain quarters of the media, I was getting into the kind of business I knew I could make work. My security consultancy was going well and, Frontline, the company I had encouraged to be set up, was going from strength to strength. All of that was great but I was looking for bigger challenges, more exotic settings, a more meaningful impact. Eradicating malaria in South Africa would do me nicely.

Then Billy called round and that's when the trouble broke out.

63

MICKEY MOUSE AND THE MAFIA

'I'm not fucking having it, Paul!' Billy roared as he can do when excited or angry. This time, it was the latter.

'Calm down, Billy, and just tell me about it,' I coaxed and he did.

'That cunt Ben's let me down time for the last time.'

'Let you down?' As far as I knew, they'd been working well together for a couple of years.

'Aaaye,' Billy drawled, sounding exasperated, weary and very pissed off. It was not good. 'He's fucking owed me money for ages and just doesn't cough up.'

'Money? What for?'

'My wages. Money I've worked for.'

I looked at him sceptically. Ben was loaded – had more dough than I would ever see. One man's wages would be like small change to him. But I believed my brother so I asked, 'How long's this being going on for?' expecting Billy to say something like a couple of weeks or months.

'Best part of two fucking years.'

'What? Why did you not tell me?'

'And give you added grief when you were in the jail? Like I fucking would.' Billy knew all about jail time. 'Then there's the motor . . .'

'What car?' This was losing me a wee bit.

'Precisely. What fucking motor?' Billy rubbed his big handsome face.

I always marvelled at how fit and strong he looked at his age in spite of all those jail years. But that day he was tired or maybe just fed up putting up.

'He's been promising me a company car for about a year. No show. Now mine is fucked and I've no fucking wages to pay for another.'

'We'll sort that out, Billy,' I said, feeling heart sorry for my brother. After twenty-four years, you come out of jail with less than nothing. All his energy and hope he'd been investing in Ben and, it seemed, he was not getting much back.

'Thanks, Paul, but it's worse than that.'

Silently, inside, I groaned. Billy had a way with money – a very quick way. His attitude was to spend it and spend it fast. Had he spent his way into major problems? No, it was worse than that.

As a convicted murderer, Billy would be on licence for the rest of his life. That meant, if he farted at the wrong time and the wrong place, the cops could send him winging back to jail for years. Not long before I had been released from prison, the silly bugger got nobbled one night in a car with a nail gun and a cattle prod under the seat. It was a bit like The Licensee's golf club – perfectly legal items that could also be deadly. For Joe Soap, this would be no problem but, for a guy on a life licence, it was a ticket back to the pokey.

On his first night in Kilmarnock Prison, Billy called Ben and asked that he pay his wages to his wife, Carol Anne.

'Of course, Billy. Don't you worry yourself,' Ben had reassured him.

A couple of days later, Ben had visited Billy in jail, all sweetness and light, and told him he was going to drop by Carol Anne's after the visit to give her his wages. But there was no visit and no dough – in fact, there was nothing for the whole time Billy was away. This didn't sound like someone who was repaying a lifetime's debt to Billy – someone grateful to my brother for saving his life. This sounded like someone who was taking the piss.

'Billy, are you sure you've earned wages?' I asked, knowing the question would anger my brother, but I needed to ask it. My experience of Ben's generosity wasn't tying in with Billy's information. I needed to reach out for an explanation.

Billy grinned. 'And more,' he replied.

'Give me an example,' I said.

'How about the Mafia, the Teamsters and Al Gore, fucking Vice President of America?'

'You're kidding.' He had to be.

'I'm fucking not.' And he wasn't.

The Teamsters are the trade union in USA that represents truck drivers and other transport workers. Given the scale of America, it is a huge organisation and one that has a history of corruption and Mafia links so hot that they would melt glass. From day one, the Teamsters have had to fight against the private traders, the strike-breakers and the competitors and they didn't do so through politics but with baseball bats and bullets. Their most famous president was Jimmy Hoffa. By his time, the Teamsters were so big and rich that the Mafia wanted to get them onside. At the same time, Hoffa knew that the Mafia's methods and political connections would serve his organisation well. The partnership worked out fine till Hoffa wanted to break away. One day, he was called to a meeting and has never been seen again since.

But the Teamsters still go from strength to strength. Around 2002, they decided that there had to be better ways to check on union membership and whether all the dues were up to date. Their traditional methods involved roadside checks – usually armed roadside checks. Old-fashioned membership cards could be forged so it was decided that technology was where the answer lay. The wealthy Teamsters threw some money at a couple of boffins who invented a smart card – the kind of thing we're all using more and more for clocking in at work, ID cards and so on. But it so happened the Teamsters had stumbled on the mother and son of all smart cards – one that could hold pictures, medical records, bank details, travel history, DNA and a whole stack more. They decided to make some money out of it and that's where Ben and Billy came in.

Ben had set up a meeting in New York with the Teamsters' top bods to discuss a business agreement to market and sell the smart card worldwide. There was just one problem – Ben had a deportation order hanging over his skull and there was no certainty he could get out of the country. He found ways round the restriction often enough and carried out business all over the globe but it didn't work every time so he asked Billy if he would go. The deal was worth millions and the Teamsters had also managed to persuade Al Gore to endorse the product so of course Billy would go – even if he was under the restrictions of his life licence. However, in the event, Ben managed to go too. Both were taking risks but certainly Billy was risking more. Just being seen with Ben, a known offender, could be enough to send Billy back to jail.

At the meeting, Billy thought he had stumbled into a club of failed assassins. Every man round the table carried the facial scars of street violence and worse. The guy chairing the meet started talking about the bad old days and how they had lived by their wits and their muscle. To demonstrate the point, he rolled up his shirt sleeves to expose his arms which were covered in deep, permanent welts and their crooked bones indicated old breaks. Billy felt right at home.

For some reason, the Teamsters took to Billy and addressed him as if he was the one with the money, the power. Mind you, he had been given some fancy title like 'Director' for the show. The deal was struck that day and Ben caught the flight home a very much wealthier man.

'How much does Ben think that deal is worth?' I asked Billy.

'Fucking millions, Paul, and pounds not dollars.'

'From just one deal?'

Billy nodded his head.

Now I understood his anger and frustration at Ben not paying him his wages. 'Is there anything else I should know about what Ben's been up to?' I asked.

'How long have you got?' replied Billy with a sigh.

That judge had been spot on about Ben Alagha. That he was a 'genius' I already knew but just how 'evil' he was I was about to discover.

64

BOLLYWOOD DREAMS

'Ben is . . .' the young woman hesitated, looking for the right words, 'sexually depraved.' Then she laughed.

I guessed it was at herself for being so polite in her language. Usually she wasn't that uptight. 'What's so funny?' I asked.

'Well, I get them all. Judges that want you to shit on their chests, big tough guys who pay you to whip them, one shopkeeper who dresses in his dead wife's clothes . . .'

'I get the point,' I butted in. If I hadn't, she could still be talking – reeling off the sexual tastes of her clientele. She was a working girl, one of the higher-class ones, and we'd been introduced by a third party who knew that she knew about Ben.

'Compared with that lot, he might seem almost normal,' she explained.

'So what does Ben get up to?' I blushed, asking such a question.

She didn't blush in responding. 'Young lassies – very young lassies.'

'You mean kids?' This would be too much. I'd have to stop the bastard.

The young woman went on to explain that Ben preferred prostitutes who were short, of small build, had all their pubes totally removed and the younger the better. He had turned away from her in favour of a sixteen-year-old – at least that's how old she had claimed to be – who was brand new to the game. 'I meet bastards

271

like him all the time,' she added. 'As they're shagging you up the arse, you just know they're pretending you're twelve years old. Dirty fucking bastards.'

The way she looked on it, if they were paying for sex with her, a grown woman, then they weren't going after the kids – not that day, anyway. It was almost a social service and Ben had been an enthusiastic, regular consumer of that service.

Ben had separated from Arthur Suttie's daughter and was living with another woman at his Riverview Gardens flat. She was beautiful, sophisticated and took care of all his needs. I'd always suspected that he would screw around but prostitutes who looked like underage girls? That threw me.

Later, I was to be thrown even further when a man who knew all about Ben's private life revealed that young male prostitutes were regulars to his flat and not for tea and biscuits. 'This is a man whose great grandfather was the Grand Ayatollah,' he explained, 'who ruled all the Muslims in all of Persia.' A devout Muslim himself, he was shaking his head in disgust. 'A man who is descended from the Prophet Muhammad fucking men? Not just men – fucking boys.'

I had heard enough. Billy not getting paid the money he owed had been bad enough. There was something rotten about Ben Alagha and I decided there and then to find out what. I'd be very careful when I dealt with him but go on as normal and not reveal that anything had changed. That would buy me time to dig deep and find out about the real Ben Alagha.

The first link was much closer to home than I thought – right on my doorstep, in fact.

The east end of Glasgow has so many characters that it's almost impossible to know them all. I'm lucky in that I have a few friends who seem to have an encyclopaedic knowledge of the whole place – the people, the history, the politics. One young straight guy in particular I call 'The Man Who Knows Everything But Says Nothing' – The Man Who Knows, for short. It could be catchier, I know, but it sums him up perfectly.

One day, The Man Who Knows was sharing some snippets with

me about Gordon Ross, The Licensee's number two who was stabbed to death outside The Shieling Bar. It seems that, in happier days between Ross and The Licensee, the latter had been investing in property abroad. Ross was his front man in many of these deals and he worked through this Asian businessman from the area. No surprises so far. The Man Who Knows – a successful businessman himself – was intrigued by the Asian guy's background and it seems, at one point, he had been well loaded, making a lot of his money in the movie industry, Bollywood in particular. The bloke made the mistake of putting too many of his eggs in one basket and, when the BCCI bank collapsed, it wiped him out. Careless.

To build himself up financially, this guy had been doing all sorts of dodgy deals with very dodgy people, like Thomas McGraw, The Licensee, but, apparently, he had amassed his pot of gold again and was back into Bollywood and even Miramax.

'Do they call him Dr Mo?' I asked my pal.

'Aye. So you know him then?'

'No, not yet.'

Miramax had been the give away. At one point, after our first book had been published, a guy had contacted Reg saying that the book would make a wonderful film. The bloke had ranted on about films he'd been involved in before and mentioned Miramax. And he claimed he already knew a very good friend of mine, Ben Alagha. Ben, Gordon Ross, The Licensee – this Dr Mo was worth a look.

Dr Mo and Ben had been friends for years. At one point, they discovered that a male relative of Dr Mo owned a huge tract of land north of Cumbernauld. The bloke was old, a bit blind, going deaf and getting confused. Dr Mo managed to get access to some of the old boy's files and pulled the information they needed. Then, an appointment was made for the old man to see his lawyer. He turned up and signed the property over to Dr Mo and Ben. Generous? Stupid? Neither – it wasn't him. Ben had been at the dressing-up again.

The pair set up a company called St Denys Marina and hatched business plans to develop the land into a luxury leisure resort with a large five-star hotel and a custom-designed golf course, marina and equestrian centre. The land alone was worth £30 million. Billy knew about Ben's plans for St Denys Marina but not how he and Dr Mo had conned the old guy out of it. Billy would have seen that as taking a liberty and not on. But he was aware that Ben, or at least the company, had borrowed millions on the back of that land – loans that would never be repaid, of course, as companies would fold, office addresses would be abandoned and bank accounts would be emptied.

Through some London contacts, I learned that Ben hadn't stopped to take a breath after being released from jail in 1993. He had gone round a load of London faces as well as rich business people offering to sell bearer bonds on behalf of some mysterious American. Bearer bonds carry a marked value, much like banknotes, and the country that has issued them will pay an agreed interest rate. These bearer bonds were very old and carried substantial additional interest. Flogging them at less than the full value was a great way of raising money fast. They were also an ideal way for certain people to hide money they didn't want to declare at that time to the Inland Revenue or the cops.

After some checks by potential customers, it was agreed that the bonds looked genuine. Ben did a brisk trade. He always had more available, never seeming to run out. Some of his customers began to speculate on who the un-named American was and what scam he had pulled to have them in his possession. A few years later, some of the customers came a cropper when they discovered that some of the bonds were forgeries. Ben was cornered and in danger of big grief but he was ready for them and started weeping and moaning that he had also lost a fortune on the bonds. Of course, the Yank had disappeared – if there ever was a Yank.

Then there was a mystery. Ben's in-laws knew that he'd been arrested soon after his release from jail in 1993. The charges related to bribing screws at different prisons during his long sentence. In my world, there's no harm in that and it happens in every prison. The prosecution must have had a good few confessions backed up by hard evidence. That's the only reason that Ben would plead guilty as he did. The thing was he was found not guilty. Now how did he get off with that? Having pled guilty, how the hell did that happen?

I wouldn't have to wait long for the answer. It started with a call from Arthur Suttie passing on the bad news. Ben and some others had been arrested, charged with large-scale smuggling and massive financial irregularities. The Shah of Iran's grandson was in serious trouble. Or was he?

65

JUST EVIL

Ben Alagha had been keeping quiet about it. He had first been arrested and charged in London in June 2001 yet just got on with life as if he wasn't worried. Maybe he wasn't.

The charges he faced concerned massive cigarette smuggling and a whole heap of financial irregularities over many years. In one raid alone, 4,990,000 Benson and Hedges cigarettes were recovered. We're talking about millions of pounds here. This was one huge operation and I'd be worried if the cops were on my tail for that kind of thing – but not Ben.

The team had set up around twenty companies as fronts for the scam. They would order goods from one country and arrange delivery to bases in former Soviet-bloc countries, particularly Russia and Lithuania. There, the goods would be off-loaded and reloaded on to, say, two ships, this time with added dodgy ciggies. Using the same papers from the original orders, the loads would then find their way mainly to Britain where cigarettes are so expensive their profits were high.

Big warehouses in the south of England were used to store the smuggled goods. Orders were set up and teams would arrive in their own vans and lorries to pay for and uplift them. To work, it needed a great deal of coordination, contacts and brains. Ben had all of that but he wasn't the only one. He was also in cahoots with the Russian Mafia – or so he claimed.

The main man for the Russians was Darius Descera, known on the street simply as Darius long before the singer by the same name was launched. Darius worked closely with a Scottish player, Jim McCaffrey. These two were backed up by other Russians – Edward Pashiiskis, Robert Sinica, Alexander Maslianikaite and Paul Maslianikaite. This was a top team and no doubt. The Russians and the Scots have always had a lot in common for some reason. In crime, it's no different. Since the Berlin Wall came down the two mobs have moved closer still. Why do you think Afghan heroin is so cheap and plentiful on Scottish streets? Because the Russians were in there for years and have it stockpiled in huge quantities in Moscow and elsewhere.

Ben wasn't just charged with serious offences. Even though the Russians weren't lifted, Ben was also deemed to be in their company, bad company. That combination usually results in one heavy treatment by the courts.

In 2001, when Ben first went to court, he had to fight to stay out of custody. Needless to say the lovely Arthur Suttie, his father-in-law, stood bail of £750,000 security. Who has that type of spare cash lying around? Damn few. Arthur had to put his house up as a guarantee but he didn't think there was any risk. Although Ben was separated from Arthur's daughter, it was an on-off situation and everyone was still close. Ben even often stayed with the Sutties in their summer-house – it was that type of place – and he had even promised to pay for a kidney transplant abroad for a male relative of theirs. He had also promised to do the same for Mickey Carroll, a close pal of mine. Ben was a generous man. He wouldn't cheat Arthur. Would he?

Every now and then, Ben would have to appear in court at Ipswich, where the case was raised, for a bail hearing. The prosecution always argued for him to be held in custody since he was at risk of running away abroad. When Ben's lawyer pointed out that, as someone under a deportation order, he had no passport, the cops then alleged that he had been travelling abroad using someone else's passport – one belonging to a Dr Mo. That's how he got to the States for the meeting with the Teamsters, as well as several other countries. Luckily for

277

Ben, the only proven cases of him slipping abroad illegally were before he had been charged with these offences. Since then, he'd been of good behaviour so the magistrates continued bail. Big mistake.

Armed cops arrested Ben just before he boarded a plane at Heathrow Airport. Two days before his trial was due to start in 2003, he had gone to the airport and almost smooth-talked his way on to the short haul to Dublin, using nothing more official than an Irish driving licence. If the computer system hadn't gone ballistic on spotting his name, he would have been up, up and away. And not only would Ben have been free, Arthur Suttie would also have lost his home. Doing something that would force Arthur to start over again at his age was a very cruel and selfish act. And what about the two men who believed he was going to save their lives by paying for kidney transplants for them abroad? I suppose they could just die as far as Ben was concerned. Ben had just lost some of the very good friends he had. No decent person would trust him now.

We now know from a few of his ex-friends, bitter at having been betrayed by him, that Ben had a house in Dublin and lot of dough – around £1 billion – stashed there. That would be tempting for anyone but that wasn't the reason he had tried to skip to Ireland. Something had spooked Ben. But what?

On the phone was a man with a thick Turkish accent promising me secret papers on Ben Alagha. When I got the call I thought it was a joke but I took a chance – and thank God I did.

We call him Genghis Khan because both were great warriors – just in their own different ways. Genghis had an arrangement with Ben – if he did several years of work for no pay, Ben would pay for essential surgery for one of his relatives back home. Of course, Ben had broken his part of the agreement and now it was payback time.

The bundle of papers Genghis handed over mainly concerned the smuggling rap – orders, shipping numbers, faxes with Ben's writing and signature, warnings to other members of the mob and so forth. It was a gold mine and it easily displayed that Ben hadn't just been involved but was, in fact, the ringleader. But there was more – an affidavit, signed and initialled on each page by Ben. It was a duplicate of one handed in by Ben to the trial judge in the hope he would be freed. Fat chance? Not really. Ben's statement revealed that he had been a police informant since his time inside for the hostage-taking, arms-deal scam – he had been officially registered as a grass by the National Criminal Intelligence Service, MI5, the National Crime Squad and Customs since 1994 and had been active ever since. The National Crime Squad had intervened at his trial in Bristol where he had pled guilty to bribing prison officers and they don't do that unless the grass is worth it – and he was.

By his own admission, Ben gave crucial info leading to the arrest of a heroin and cocaine mob in London in 1995. The two gang leaders, Raymond Hill and James Ward, he claimed, figured out his role and had him beaten to a pulp. In his sworn statement, Ben states he was asked to infiltrate the Russian mob by Customs and NCS and that was why he was involved in the smuggling scam or so he claimed. But, around that time, I met someone with a very different view of his motivation. This Scottish player had been recruited by Ben for some undercover work. Ben explained the smuggling set-up and how most of the tobacco ended up in large warehouses in the south of England. So he knew about all those goodies lying around and, if he chose his time right, there would be a lot of dough too. A little sting should do the trick.

Ben would kit the player out in a Customs officer's uniform and give him high-quality ID. Along with a squad of others, he'd raid the warehouse, demand papers and, when they weren't forthcoming, hit them with a confiscation order – again the genuine article – and a bill for unpaid tax on the goods. This is standard procedure when smugglers are caught and most cough up the tax. All it would depend on was the quality of the ID and the confiscation order. The player still had the ID and showed it to me – it was, indeed, very high quality, with a picture of him in uniform.

'Ben said it was the name of a real officer and his number,' explained the player.

Now that was clever. I read the name out loud, 'James McLean.'

And the penny dropped. That was Ben's Customs handler as stated on his affidavit.

This hadn't been the first time Ben had conned his own team, according to the player. Apparently, he had boasted to him about quietly arranging for one load to be taken off a boat in a French port. The smuggled goods were removed and then the much-emptier crates were loaded back on the ship to go on and finish the journey.

What the guy didn't know was that the bundle of papers I was now sitting with referred to the theft of a whole consignment by persons unknown. The Russians clearly weren't happy about it and who could blame them? What they didn't know was that it was an inside job.

It seemed to me that all the agencies must have stepped back from Ben for some reason or another. Why else was he going to court? Were they aware of his double-dealings and deciding to let him hang? Just stand back and let justice take its course and then kick him out of the country on his release?

Was the evil genius finally in big trouble?

66

TRUST THE TURKS

Ben Alagha's smuggling trial collapsed – no explanation, no pack drill, no retrial.

At least the smuggling charges collapsed while he was sentenced to next to nothing for the attempted escape to Dublin. Well, they could hardly ignore that, could they? Ben had been held in Belmarsh after his attempted flight. Now there would be no jail time for him and he walked out of court a free man – again.

Jim McCaffrey wasn't so lucky. He faced serious smuggling accusations but pled guilty to reduced charges and landed three years in the pokey – different court, different outcome, different relationship with the cops. At that time, the law still hadn't caught up with Darius but would they? If they did, it would be through Ben Alagha's backstabbing.

Ben's trial had suddenly halted and he went scampering from the court, a free man again. They didn't even stop him to apply the deportation order that had been hanging over him for two decades. They're not so generous to poor souls just trying to escape mayhem back home and seeking asylum here. They get the boot out double quick. For the first time in my life, I was almost disappointed that someone walked away from court. But Ben had befriended me only to betray me and mine and abuse a hell of a lot of folk. In his affidavit, he even admits that NCS and MI5 asked him to keep close tabs on me when I was released from the gunrunning sentence. He felt bad about this, according to his statement, but he had to consider his deportation order so he decided to cooperate. Self-centred prick. Ben felt so bad about it that he went to his NCS handlers with some crock of shit about me talking to Irish Loyalist groups about some scam. Not only was that not true, if those lies had got into circulation in certain quarters, my name would top their wanted list. And they don't take prisoners. Some pal, eh?

I thought Ben was being friendly when I got out of jail yet all he was doing was setting me up. Being a fucking snake in the grass. A grass. Simple as that. I can just about understand greed, anger, jealousy – most things, in fact – but never will I understand betrayal. Nor will I stand for it. The old Paul Ferris would have paid Ben Alagha a visit. The new Paul Ferris just decided to let him rot. Shame he didn't act the same way.

The bold Genghis Khan was back at my door. Genghis is the kind of guy who puts a lot of time, effort and energy into his family and his community. Some of his reasons for being angry with Ben had concerned smaller acts of what he called dishonour against his community. Seems that Ben left a trail of minor unpaid debts, owing people Genghis had introduced him to. Then there was the mosque he had cheated out of £45,000. When I told Genghis that the papers he had passed to me proved that Ben had arranged for pretty young women from Lithuania to be brought in for the sex slave trade, he was livid. In other words, he was good man who was known and respected among Turkish communities the length and breadth of Britain.

One Turkish guy had called Genghis from London with important information.

'Ben, the bastaaard, has been trying to get me killed,' growled Genghis.

I wasn't surprised. Genghis knew too much about Ben.

'Asked two different Turkish families in London to take on the contract – top dollar,' he said, his head shaking with anger. 'But there's worse. He has a list.' He shouted those words and banged the table. We were sitting in a very open and public coffee area at the St Enoch's shopping centre in Glasgow. I could hear his voice echo through the cavernous halls. 'His Scottish girlfriend, her poor little boy . . .' Genghis looked as if he would cry but with pity or fury I couldn't tell. Ben's Glasgow girlfriend had a disabled son who needed constant care. Why the fuck would anyone want to kill the boy? How could he even think of it? 'Your brother, Billy,' Genghis continued, his voice back to normal volume. 'And . . .'

I knew what he was going to say before the words left his mouth. 'Me,' I smiled.

'Yes, brother, you,' he said quietly and reached and gripped my wrist.

I nodded, still smiling. This wasn't the first time someone had tried to take out a contract on me but it *was* the first time someone I had considered a friend had tried to do such a dirty deed.

'And what did your London friends say to him?' I had to ask the question yet, depending on the answer, I might just have to come out of retirement and fast.

'They told him to fuck off or they'd kill *him* for free.'

Both of us laughed out loud. I knew the families he was referring to as well as he did and I trusted them. For lesser reasons, they'd take great pleasure in killing Ben and would do so slowly, with great expertise – the torturer tortured to death. Now wouldn't that be justice?

'Maybe we should tell them that he's a registered grass?' I suggested.

'Too late, brother,' laughed Genghis, 'I already have.'

That'll be one part of London Ben Alagha will not be visiting in a hurry.

Why did Ben go so corrupt? He states in a sworn statement it was to combat the deportation order hanging over his head. Did it work? Well, he's still here. And he'd try again to get me and mine.

But next time, it would be murder.

67

PUB CRAWLS AND CURFEWS

5 February 2003

'Where the hell are you, Billy?'

I was standing outside the Morvern Bar in Glasgow's Barmulloch area. It was a place full of character – some would say too much character. Some time before, Tony McGovern had been shot dead outside there. The McGovern Family were well-respected players from the nearby Springburn area. The McGoverns and I went way back. Not as partners or anything but as parallel people, developing our hold of the streets at the same time. There was mutual respect and more. A good pal of mine, Russell Stirton, had married Jackie McGovern and so became part of the McGovern Clan.

Russell had once been told by the cops to set me up with heroin – they threatened him with various outcomes, all not good, if he refused. He agreed but instead came straight to me. On the night they handed over the smack at Lenzie Station, we had them filmed by a crew from Scottish Television. We were going to expose their corrupt ways on national TV. The whole deal went belly up when STV went to the cops rather than show the film and we were charged with conspiracy. But Russell stood firm – a good man.

Billy has a low boredom threshold but I expected him to be waiting at the pub. OK, the Morvern had shut already because it had had conditions put on its opening hours by the Licensing Board but he could've phoned me or waited. I knew he'd been in the city centre earlier that night so suspected he'd gone on a bit of a pub crawl.

Fine by me but business should have come first.

Irritated, I got a good and sober friend to drive me down to Ayrshire, to Irvine where Billy lived. We'd sort the business out that night. As we drove up to Billy's house, there he was standing in the street talking to a man and a woman.

'Where were you?' I demanded.

'I was there – where were you?' he replied.

'We were supposed to meet at the Morvern.'

'Aye, at half nine. If you'd been on time, it would've been fine.'

'You could've waited, Billy.'

'I did – till the place shut at ten.'

He had a point. The man and woman Billy had been talking to weren't for shifting and I wasn't for discussing my business in front of people I didn't know. Besides, Billy had had a few drinks and so had I – better if we both chatted when we were sober the next day.

I told Billy I'd stay at our mother's house that night. She didn't live too far away. But my ma is old fashioned – come a certain time of night, the door is locked, always, and she's off to bed. Any movement or knock on the door after then upsets her and I wasn't about to do that. So I had to rush to beat Jenny Ferris's curfew.

As we drove out of the street, I could see Billy chatting with the couple and then walking with them away from his house. 'That'll be a late night, Billy,' I thought, assuming he was heading to their place. As it happens, I was right about that but, if only I'd known what else was happening nearby, I wouldn't have left my brother alone for one second that night.

68

LIFTED
February 2003

'Oh, the poor wean.' It was my mother, speaking to me in the front room of her flat as she sat reading the newspaper.

'What, Mum?'

'That fifteen-year-old boy. Terrible.'

It was two days after that bad-tempered meeting with my brother Billy. That same night, late at night on 5 February or early morning of 6 February, Jason Hutchison, just fifteen years old, had been beaten and stabbed several times in his family's house in Irvine – murdered. And, as he sat slumped and bleeding, someone had torched the flat. Like everyone else, I took in all the media reports with a mixture of disgust and disbelief – disgust that a young boy could have met that such a horrible end and disbelief that Irvine, a small Ayrshire town, seemed to have turned as nasty as any Glasgow scene.

My own mother had moved out of Glasgow for some peace and quiet. Billy and his wife, Carol Anne, had happily lived down in Irvine enjoying being out of the way – easier to get on with their lives. What the hell had they walked into?

After the murder of Jason Hutchison, I asked about a bit. It becomes force of habit when you've lived the kind of life I have – always expecting to get blamed for everything. Then there was the issue of Billy – a convicted murderer, a Ferris and living just round the corner from the death scene. Billy had been pulled in and questioned on seven murders, all gang-related, over the previous year. The cops would eye him for this too if they got half a chance. Knowledge is power so I was going to find out a bit about the boy and his family.

It wasn't difficult. Originally from Cranhill in Glasgow, the Hutchisons were well known in the Irvine area as local drug dealers – a tenner bag here, a wrap or two there. They were very slow in paying their own debts but they'd cut you in a flash if you failed to pay the bill. I recognised their style – lowlife. There was Jason's father, James, the kingpin of the crew, and his brother, John. They had four sons between them and all four of them acted like any young team from the schemes and worked the drugs market with their old boys. Local opinion was that the ringleader of the sons and their hangers-on was David Hutchison, who was aged about eighteen. They all thought they were hard men but, apparently, David Hutchison was the most violent of the lot. Then I learned something that made my heart sink with dread.

A couple of years earlier, while I was still in jail, Billy's wife Carol Anne had been out at a party near their home. In the street, just yards from where she lived, Carol Anne was attacked and severely assaulted by some young lads. No one seemed to know why. Carol Anne was very badly injured. After the physical damage began to heal, she was left frightened to go out – she was sometimes scared of her own shadow. Carol Anne is a lovely, gentle woman. She and Billy got married when he was released from prison and she has two teenage sons from a previous relationship. They are fine, law-abiding boys with steady jobs. They were the type of family who don't know street life, who don't go around picking fights and who would be good for my big brother.

Carol Anne insisted she didn't know who had attacked her. The common view locally was that it could have been local kids – or maybe this dead boy's older brother, David Hutchison. So no one knew for sure and, to this day, Carol Anne says she can't remember. She had, after all, been on the sharp end of one hell of a doing. A short while after the attack on Carol Anne, another Irvine woman had her jaw smashed in an unprovoked attack by a young man.

Gary Donaldson got seven years jail for that and the robbery of a petrol station.

Most men would want to avenge an attack on their woman. Even straight Joes – never mind convicted murderers like Billy – are likely to have a go especially if the cops don't nab anyone and no one had been convicted of the attack on Carol Anne. So, when the cops pulled Billy in to interview him in connection with the murder of Jason Hutchison, I wasn't surprised or worried. David Hutchison's name would surely be on anybody's list of Carol Anne's possible attackers and that was all the bizzies needed by way of an excuse – a revenge attack on someone close to the suspected attacker.

But this would make it the eighth murder Billy had been interviewed about since his release from jail. It was getting to be a bad habit for the polis. Besides, stabbing and torching fifteen-year-old boys isn't Billy's style. When the cops released Billy, I wasn't surprised and just got on with my life. He wasn't surprised either and not worried at all. He had the carefree air of the innocent about him. Then, not long after Jason Hutchison's body was found, Billy was charged with murder. He had a co-accused, Lance McGuiness but known as Lance Goudie around Irvine. I'd heard Billy mention the name Lance a couple of times before but knew sod all about him. He hadn't been important to me before. Now he was.

'Who the fuck's this Lance Goudie?' I asked Billy in the visiting room of BarL jail where he was being held on remand.

'Lance Goudie? Fuck, where do I start?' replied Billy.

As I sat back and listened, I couldn't believe my ears.

69

DRUGS AND DRUNKS

One of Billy's close and trusted pals had introduced him to Lance Goudie. A bad move.

Billy knew that Lance was heavily into drug dealing locally. People like us, even when going straight, have contact with and an understanding of the underbelly of the streets that an investigative journalist would give their eye teeth for. So what? That Billy was associating with a known dealer doesn't mean that Billy was dealing drugs. The drug market works in layers. The top guys pay others to traffic huge quantities. They sell on large consignments to big-time dealers who, in turn, sell on to the more local dealers. They sell on to very local dealers who sell on to the merchants flogging tenner bags on the street. Billy knew about the layers above and below Lance Goudie and below Lance was one of his best customers – Jason Hutchison's family. The two men had known each other for a couple of years – not great mates, just occasional drinking partners.

Earlier on the night of Jason Hutchison's death, Billy had driven Lance Goudie into Glasgow city centre, in Carol Anne's car, for a few drinks before Billy was due to meet up with me at the Morvern Bar. Billy's first intention was to try to track down a guy called Raymond Sinclair. On my request, Billy had done a piece of work for this guy but the trouble was it was meant to be a favour and my brother had taken money for it. I'd already told him that wasn't on so Billy had hoped to meet up with the bloke to straighten things out before he then met up with me.

Lance tagged along as Billy went to the Tolbooth Pub at Glasgow Cross, the Counting House at George Square, the Inter Mezzo on Renfield Street, Thomson's Bar in Springburn and the Morvern Bar in Barmulloch before finally heading back to Irvine. It had turned into a right pub crawl and Billy hadn't met Raymond Sinclair or me but he'd had a good time looking.

Back in Irvine sometime after 10 p.m., Lance Goudie had asked Billy if he could borrow Carol Anne's car. Apparently, he had to see someone who owed him money. This was no problem to Billy who is generous that way. Lance drove off having arranged to meet Billy in the nearby Redburn Hotel later on. Billy went to check in on Carol Anne first – just to make sure she was OK. When he was almost at the house, he met his neighbours, Derek and Jennie Taylor, and got chatting. That's when I drove up and we had some brief words before arranging to meet the next day. I went on my way to my mother's house and, just as I'd thought, Derek and Jennie invited Billy to their house for a beer. Billy was on a roll and accepted without hesitation.

Fuelled by large quantities of cheap wine, Derek and Jennie blethered on and on about some neighbour they had a dispute with and Billy drank the can of beer they'd given him and listened. They actually had a serious drink problem – he was just on a night out. That night Billy didn't think much about their booze problem but, before long, it would have tragic consequences for them and disastrous ones for him because, many months later and some weeks after Billy was charged with the murder of Jason Hutchison, Derek and Jennie were found dead in their house. It was very sad because they had been lying there for weeks, unnoticed, uncared for and ignored but it also made things very difficult for Billy – dead defence witnesses were not going to be able to corroborate anybody's whereabouts.

But that night in February 2003, with Jennie and Derek very much alive and in their cups, Billy heard the chimes of an ice-cream van. The couple said they needed cigarettes and, remembering Carol Anne had asked him to bring her back some cigarettes too, he offered to nip out to the van. One person was in front of him in the queue – Dawn, the girlfriend of Darren Hutchison. Darren was the cousin of Jason Hutchison and he was known to Billy as the local hash dealer who peddled his wares from four closes down from where he lived. Dawn got some goods but she asked for them on credit. It was a no-go and she was far from chuffed.

'Can't be many drugs getting sold around here, eh?' Billy had said to the ice-cream man, having a dig at the Hutchisons' reputation for dealing – everyone knew what they got up to.

Billy returned to Derek and Jennie's house with cigs for them, had another beer and split for home around 11.25 p.m. Just as he was at the door of his house, Lance Goudie turned up in Carol Anne's car. Billy invited him in and Goudie started going on to Billy and Carol Anne about his wife having fallen out with him. Refusing the offer to sleep over, Lance was then loaned Carol Anne's car to drive home. Shortly after Goudie had left, Billy decided to return to Derek and Jennie's place. On the way there, he discovered he didn't have his mobile phone with him so he went back to the house to get it. One frantic search later, he realised he must have left the phone some place. Given his pub crawl earlier that night, it could have been anywhere. There was only one solution – call the mobile from the landline in the house. Lance Goudie answered. According to Goudie, Billy had left his phone and his jacket in the back of the car. He must have slung them on the back seat – as you do.

A few minutes later, Goudie met Billy at a bus stop. Billy had arranged this to save the man the trouble of driving into the complex maze of streets to get to his home as he could get to the rendezvous point easily on foot using a pedestrians-only path. Goudie drove off in Carol Anne's car and Billy went on to Derek and Jennie's for one last can of beer before getting home and hitting the sack at the back of midnight. It had just been an ordinary night in an ordinary small town. Except, of course, it wasn't – especially not for young Jason Hutchison.

'What did you think when you heard about the kid's murder?' I asked Billy in BarL's visiting room.

'First I thought it was a fucking shame,' he replied, 'for a young kid like that. Then I tried to place him. Couldn't. I knew a few of his family by sight – every fucker did – but he was too young.'

'But was there nothing else?' I asked.

'Aye, that the area was becoming as rough as fuck. We'd be safer back in fucking Blackhill.'

'No theories or even threads about why or who might have a reason?'

Billy looked thoughtful, rubbed his chin and then said, 'Just the one thing.'

'Yeah?' I was having to drag this out of him.

'I knew that the Hutchisons owed Goudie money for drugs. He'd been moaning about it for ages. Asking me to back him up.'

'What?'

'No worries, Paul, I told him to fuck off. Do you think I want to be back in jail?'

I was working through the events of that terrible night that Billy had told me, step by step, line by line until . . .

'And he borrowed Carol Anne's car because . . .'

'he had to see somebody that owed him money,' I said, finishing off his sentence.

Billy twisted his head to the side to say that he knew and that was his point. 'You asked what I thought then, Paul, and that was it.'

'Fucking . . .'

'But now's now and I know a lot more about Lance Goudie.'

He wasn't exaggerating either.

70

DIRTY TEXTER

When you are dealing with a brother you love, there's always some doubt by the outside world that, if you stick up for him, you're simply biased.

In the public eye, who would be more likely to claim innocence than Billy, a convicted killer, and me who some still thought was up to my neck in organised crime? When a call came from an outside source, I was greatly relieved even though it was from a most unlikely source – a child murderer.

In 2001, Alexander Ness had killed his own son, Caleb, when the poor wee boy was only eleven weeks old. He was not the kind of guy I'd cross the road to piss on if he was on fire and nor was he the kind of bloke I was likely to know. But, still, he put a call in to David Leslie, the top crime man at the *News of the World*.

Ness, from Edinburgh, was in the protection unit at Saughton jail. If he had been put anywhere near mainstream prisoners, he would have been dead inside a week. The protection unit was also where Lance Goudie was being held. Why was he there? Alexander Ness knew.

Ness and Goudie chatted a lot. Goudie was forever boasting that he'd soon be out of prison. He'd made a deal with the cops and the Crown that he'd make sure that Billy went down for the murder of Jason Hutchison. Goudie and Billy were jointly accused of murdering the boy, torching the place and stealing some goods from the house

– just some tapes and the like. It's an old trick of the Scottish criminal justice system to turn one accused against the other. It's especially useful when the authorities are desperate to nail someone and just don't have enough evidence. It was useful information that had been freely given by Ness and, from Billy's knowledge of the man, it would be totally in character for Lance Goudie to trade lies for freedom. But how could Billy use Alexander Ness? What jury would believe a child killer?

It transpired that Ness had a long history of drug addiction, psychiatric problems and violent outbursts. The man shouldn't have been anywhere near a baby. He should have been given medical care – been treated for his problems – and, maybe, that tragic death wouldn't have happened.

If Billy couldn't use Ness's evidence, it alerted him to the games Goudie was playing. Soon a whole package of fabrications emerged. Two weeks before Jason Hutchison was killed, Goudie had approached a local drug dealer known to him and asked him to go with him round to the Hutchisons' house to collect a lot of money they owed him. The guy refused, saying that it wasn't his problem. Soon after Hutchison's death, Goudie had approached the same dealer and offered to sell him a stack of smack cheap. He'd said to the guy, 'I done that murder – the Hutchison boy – and need to get out of the area fast.' The drug dealer told him to fuck off or there'd be another murder.

On the night of the murder, another drug dealer had seen Billy hand over the car to Goudie who then drove off. The witness knew Goudie well from the drug scene and had also been in the Hutchisons' house a few times when Goudie was there, selling them gear. Goudie did a disappearing act shortly after the murder, first to Carluke and then south to Stevenage. Later, when arrested, he'd claim he had run away to save his life. He claimed that Billy had killed Jason Hutchison and had threatened to kill him too in order to keep him quiet.

Even after he fled, Goudie claimed Billy still threatened him by mobile phone texts. To back up his story he showed the cops one text with a picture of a gun. The cops checked it out by using tracing masts and signals. It turned out that Goudie had sent himself the text from one phone to another down in Stevenage. There was an even easier way to check. Billy's phone couldn't send that kind of message and he probably still wouldn't know how to do that.

When he was arrested, Goudie had told the cops that Billy had already set about him and he had the injuries to prove it – knife scars on one arm – but, when he was examined by the forensic doc, he wasn't forthcoming to her about how the wounds happened. Her scientific conclusion was that they were self-inflicted.

The cops already knew Lance Goudie as a drug dealer and now they knew him to be a liar – maybe a murderer. Still, he was to be their star turn. Well, there was a Ferris to punish, wasn't there?

71

DUE DILIGENCE
December 2003

The High Court in Edinburgh is one of my least favourite places. Not that I've appeared there myself but it is a High Court and it looks like it. But that's not why I stayed away from Billy's trial. I was doing him a favour – if I had appeared at court, the journalists would have been happy to snap away at me on the way in or out, ask me questions and make me the centre of attention. They'd bill me as a terrible gangster, of course. That would tell the world – and, if they didn't already know, the jury too – that one of the accused was related to the man behind organised crime in Scotland. It didn't matter that I'd been keeping straight. What sort of prejudice would that lay on Billy?

When they announced Billy's trial would be in Edinburgh, I was a bit hopeful. Glasgow and Edinburgh are only fifty miles apart but the people of those cities have a different approach to some things. In Glasgow, it's hard to find someone who isn't well schooled on the history of the streets but, generally, Edinburgh folk aren't quite as au fait with such things. However, the majority of them would probably know the Ferris name and I was still worried that Billy wouldn't get a fair trial. So I stayed out of the court and arranged for two trusted friends to attend every day.

Each lunchtime, we'd meet up at the Castle Arms pub and they'd brief me thoroughly on events. It was a nice place – very welcoming and it served a good lunch. Better still, it was free from media folks.

I reckoned the staff had sussed who I was early on but there was never a mention or any phone call to a newspaper. Good people.

Billy was represented by Donald Findlay QC togged up in his usual frockcoat and with his handlebar moustache even more luxuriant than ever. Simply the best, Donald hadn't lost any of his skill or his amazing ability to cross-examine or speechify without using notes. Scotland has many fine criminal lawyers – we need a lot – but I reckon he's the best.

Lance Goudie had made a statement to the cops that spelled things out. He admitted that he was in the Hutchison house when Jason was murdered. He claimed that he went with Billy to give the family payback for the assault on Carol Anne. He had only agreed to go along because he was frightened of Billy – so far, so bad. Then the expert witnesses started to be called. The Hutchisons' flat was full of Goudie's DNA. In his statement, he had admitted being in the flat so there would traces of his DNA and he also said that he'd pissed on the carpet while the assault was taking place. Blood was found on Goudie's body and clothes but he'd thrown away his expensive Cat boots that night. The place would have been dripping with blood and the floor would have been soaked in the stuff. No boots, no forensics on the boots.

Billy, on the other hand, was relatively free of forensics except for Carol Anne's car and his jacket which he had said in his own statement had been left in the back of Carol Anne's car on the night of the killing. It had taken them a second check to find blood in Carol Anne's car and two spots were found down either side of the passenger seat. Billy's jacket was stranger. After he was arrested, the cops removed certain items from his house. The jacket in question was hanging up on the wardrobe and yet had a lot of blood around the buttons. Careless – very careless? Or innocent – totally innocent?

As the cops gave evidence, it was apparent that Lance Goudie had changed his story about where he was in the house that night numerous times. First, he was in the bedroom where the murder happened but then he said he wasn't and then, finally, he claimed he watched it all from the hallway. From there, he seemed to have seen a lot. He said he watched as Billy lay on top of Jason Hutchison, knifing him numerous times. He said he then saw Billy setting him up on a chair and, at this point, the boy's head fell limp to the side. There was more that added up to a graphic and detailed description of the killing and it all tied in with the medical reports on Jason Hutchison's death. It looked like Billy was sunk.

Then a fireman took the stand, one William Davidson, and he was very experienced in these tragic scenes. To him, it was quite clear. Given the layout of the flat, no one could get a view of the murder from anywhere in the hallway. To have seen what was happening to Jason Hutchison, you would have had to have been in the bedroom, very far into the bedroom. Maybe up close to Jason Hutchison?

Lance Goudie would not give evidence. His statement to the cops, his lies, his motive against the Hutchisons, his self-inflicted wounds, his sending himself threatening texts, his exact position in the flat that night and the amount of forensics found on him – none of that could be tested out.

The bold Donald Findlay was in a positive mood. He reckoned they had won every day of the trial so he decided to make a risky call. Billy had had a clear alibi for where he was that night but, with the subsequent deaths of Derek and Jennie Taylor, the couple he had been drinking with at the crucial time, his alibi was dealt a severe blow. Where once there had been two people able to testify to his whereabouts, now there was a great big gap. But he had had an alibi, he denied being at the murder house and he denied being the killer. Goudie, on the other hand, admitted being there and knowing, in detail, how the young guy was killed. Findlay decided he wouldn't call any of Billy's witnesses, many of whom had convictions. It was now up to the jury.

In her summing-up to the jury, the judge, Lady Smith, warned them that, given Goudie had not given evidence or made the statement in a way that allowed Billy's lawyer to cross-examine, none of the things he'd said in his written statement, blaming Billy for the murder, could be used. It was a clear, well-explained piece of guidance and the jury were asked to show due diligence in excluding such claims by Goudie from their deliberations.

That last day of the trial, I met up with my guys on the inside of the courtroom at the usual pub, the Castle Arms. We couldn't get our normal booth – it was one that guaranteed privacy – because two men were sitting there. The hairs went up on the back of my neck – the old radar was telling me we were in the presence of the filth. We found another seat and my pals chatted while I listened. It was all good news and they agreed with Donald Findlay – Billy was going to be a free man soon. Then the two men who had been sitting at our usual booth got up to leave.

'Fuck sake,' whispered one of my mates, 'isn't that one of the jury?'

'Aye, aye, you're right,' whispered the other. 'Who the fuck's he with?'

Who indeed?

As I was paying for the lunches, one of the regular female bar staff came out – an older woman with a great, warm personality. She was chatting away and apologising that we couldn't get our regular seat.

'No problem,' I reassured her, 'no problem at all. Any idea who the dastardly seat thieves were?' I asked with a laugh.

'Didn't recognise one of them,' she said, with a smile, 'but the other's police.' She pulled one of those fake sour looks saying that would be the last person she'd want to have lunch with.

'Ach, even the bizzies need to eat,' I smirked, 'and your home-made soup's famous, eh?'

Billy was found guilty – Lance Goudie not guilty. One decision wasn't right as far as I could see. And the other was technically wrong if nothing else because, in Scotland, you are deemed to be guilty of a crime if you are there with the person who carried out the act – art and part, we call it. In Goudie's own statement to the cops, he had admitted all that and he knew, in detail, how Jason Hutchison had been killed. Unlike his statements against Billy that couldn't be used, the judge had made it plain to the jury that statements he made about himself could. These were admissions and didn't need to be corroborated.

The decision to convict Billy should also have convicted Lance Goudie but he walked free to go back to his lowlife drug dealing and lies. Another Judas walking the streets who sold his soul to escape his punishment. Walking free so the cops could settle an old score. Against me.

Billy was sentenced to a minimum of twenty-two years. If he serves all of that time, he'll next be free at the age of seventy-five and, in total, he will have spent forty-six years of his life in jail.

He's appealing, of course but I fear he's in for the long haul. Think of all the men who have been unjustly imprisoned and how long they're kept in jail – TC Campbell, twenty years, and Robert Brown, twenty-four years, are just two typical examples. The system makes it hard – it takes its time, hoping the men will get worn out and take refuge in drugs or just give up. For those who don't submit, the men in suits, who used the lies of perjurers to get convictions, are long since gone, dead or retired.

Billy Ferris is my brother. They'll not want to give him a chance of freedom soon.

Since the day I walked out of Frankland vowing to go straight, they have tried everything from recall orders to hit contracts to get me. But I'm still here, still straight, still free. So, if they can't get me, they'll get my brother – simple as that. It's a heartbreak seeing Billy locked up for something I believe he didn't do but, if they think we're going to lie down now, they've got another think coming. Billy Ferris will be free again, sooner than they think.

As I visit Billy in jail, my life goes on. But, not long after he was sentenced, I was about to meet some real crooks in the most surprising of places.

72

NEW COMPANY

2003

It was an invitation that I couldn't refuse. When Joey Pyle, Don of Dons, asks to meet you for a meal and a few drinks, you go along. It's an honour. Besides, I liked Joey and I owed him. Big time.

A while before, a guy called Rory Nicoll had tracked me down. Rory was making a film called *Fight 'n' Talk* and it sounded interesting. He was interviewing people who were used to violence – mainly faces and sportsmen – and asking them how it happened, what their worst experience was and so on. And he asked me if I would I take part. Usually, I'm wary of getting into any filming venture with people I don't know but a couple of things about Rory interested me. To say he was a Walter Mitty character is no exaggeration. There was no harm in his lurid tales such as the one about him singing with Take That before Robbie Williams joined the band. In fact, they made me laugh. But he left you totally confused about what was real and what wasn't. One time he chatted about how his father was a millionaire, living in a big castle in Ayrshire, and I just wrote it off as another tale. Then Reg put me right.

Rory's old man is Watt Nicoll, one interesting bloke who has reinvented himself more times than I have convictions. Watt started as a folk singer in the days when Billy Connolly was a banjo player with a sense of humour. The folky mob seem to have been close and people like Connolly and Gerry Rafferty would regularly share a couple of fish suppers at the Nicoll household. As some from that world were making it huge, some were dying and even more were taking to too much strong drink, Watt Nicoll left the folk scene and set about a series of reinventions. He became a scriptwriter for Norman Wisdom, a zoologist, then a stage hypnotist and, finally, a motivational therapist. I reckon that lark is all smoke and mirrors but it has made Watt Nicoll wealthy.

A few years earlier in 1998, he had published a book, *Twisted Knickers and Stolen Scones*, that has to get ten out of ten for the title alone. In fact, it sold extremely well. Watt Nicoll has motivated people like Hillary Clinton so he doesn't come cheap. His most audacious move came when he worked with the English football team, helping them to thrash the Poles in some key game. Now, he's small, bearded and very obviously Scottish and there he was working with the Auld Enemy. He got pelters for it but I liked his style.

I could see a lot of his old man's nerve and creativity in Rory Nicoll. If nothing else, working with him on a project would be a laugh. So it turned out.

For his film, *Fight 'n' Talk*, Rory had already interviewed upfront guys from the street, like 'Pretty Boy' Roy Shaw, Frankie Fraser, Joey Pyle and Charlie Bronson, as well as wannabes, like Dave Courtney. From football he had blokes like Frank McAvennie, Gordon Smith, Chic Charnley and Andy 'The Goalie' Goram. Frank played for Celtic and West Ham and he had taken on Terry Butcher, Graeme Roberts and Chris Woods all at the same time when they played for Rangers. He also became the first man in Britain to be charged for a criminal offence on the field of play. Gordon Smith famously missed a sitter for Brighton in an FA Cup Final against Manchester United in the last bloody minute and could have sealed the match, the score at that point being 2–2. Some say Chic Charnley was the most gifted player never to have pulled on a Scotland top. While he was playing for Partick Thistle, an armed gang wandered on to their training ground one day, waving blades. The bold Chic took a sword off one of the mob and chased them away. The last time I saw Andy Goram, he was being hunted at Victoria's nightclub by some guys whose wives he had got too close to.

Then there were the boxers, Freddie Mac, world champion Ken Buchanan, Gary Jacobs and Ernie Shavers. If you want hard, those guys are hard. So, with the interesting selection of bodies and the good fun that was to be had from Rory's patter, I was convinced I should give it a go – anything for a laugh.

Rory was also arranging a benefit year for the boxer, Ken Buchanan. The former World Lightweight Champion was the first Brit to be entered into the Boxing Hall of Fame. Still worshipped for his skill the world over, Ken is one of Scotland's unsung heroes. After his career ended, a couple of bad business moves and an expensive divorce left Ken broke. Rory was trying to raise him some dough. That's when Joey Pyle asked for a meet.

We were to meet and we wouldn't be alone.

73

TOP TEAM

2003

Joey Pyle, Don of Dons, was himself an ex-boxer and he was pretty handy with those mitts but, early on, he chose crime as something where he could earn a lot more for much less effort. Judge him if you like but feel the honesty.

In 1961, Joey got lifted for a murder in the Pen Club in London. Found guilty, the death penalty was still around and it looked certain he'd face the gallows. Fortunately, he won a retrial and lived. Joey Pyle not only lived, he prospered as his contemporaries, like the Kray Twins, were nobbled and spent their lives in jail. He'd become so successful and so well known that, in the 1970s, during a visit to New York, Joey Pyle was approached by the Mafia and told that he was the only man they'd work with in London. He had been declared the Don of Dons of one of the largest cities in the world by the biggest mob in the world. Mess with Joey Pyle and you'd mess with the Mafia. No one did.

Joey Pyle isn't just powerful, he's caring. When 'Pretty Boy' Roy Shaw got jailed in 1964, all the faces in London paid attention. Well, he got eighteen years for the armed robbery of a security van and he did the job all on his own. No one is meant to rob security vans on their own, believe me, and the eighteen years he got for it was one long haul – the normal would be eight or ten. Roy couldn't stand the prison system and fought it every inch of the way. His legendary strength and brutality were things I'd had first-hand experience of.

Eventually, the system admitted they couldn't handle Roy and 'mentalled' him – that is, they declared him insane and dumped him in Broadmoor, the state psychiatric hospital. There, they pumped him full of drugs just to make him quiet. You wouldn't get away with treating an animal that way but that's how they treat prisoners they can't control.

Years later, when Roy was released, he was still as fit as a fiddle and easily up to being a boxer again. Of course, the British Boxing Board of Control wouldn't give him a licence because of his criminal record. So, is it only good boys they allow to knock lumps out of each other? Crazy. Joey Pyle thought it was wrong and so he set up unlicensed fights – what they call 'on the cobbles' – just for Roy. The pair of them went on to make a good few quid. Some of Roy's bouts against Lenny McLean were legendary – bloody but spectacular. Some say Lenny McLean – The Guv'nor – was the top man but I'm not so sure. Just look closely into Roy's eyes even today and you tell me what you reckon. Either way, Roy made a good living at boxing. He became a businessman and is doing very well, thank you very much. Or should that be thank you, Joey Pyle?

One time I'd told Roy Shaw that the only way I'd go in the ring with him was with a gun. The giant just laughed and said it had almost come to that once in a bare knuckle bout when his opponent was backed by the IRA. The IRA had put out the word that their man should win but Roy Shaw never fights to lose. Never. In round one, he just went straight at it with a head butt followed up with a boot in the guy's balls. Roy went crashing out of the ring with the ref hanging round his neck, trying to stop the massacre. The IRA guys weren't best pleased but no one messed with Roy Shaw.

Sitting at the meeting that night in Glasgow late in 2003, he looked the meanest and the fittest of us all – not bad given the company he was keeping and the fact that he was over seventy years old.

Joey has a habit of taking care of people in prison. He's a major support to Charles Bronson, the most dangerous man in the English prisons, who is now stuck in the system and doesn't look as if he'll ever get out.

As it happened, Joey also made sure I was treated all right when I was jailed in London for the gunrunning. At that time, the bogus letter Arthur Thompson had circulated claiming I was an informant was still doing the rounds. It was a dangerous time but with Joey's support it wasn't so dangerous after all. So, when I got the message that Joey and Roy were coming north for Ken Buchanan's fundraiser and wanted a meet, I was straight there.

At the Holiday Inn in Dundee for the fundraiser, I was in select company. There was Joey, of course, and Roy Shaw, Ken Buchanan, Rory Nicoll, Arthur Suttie, Gary Jacobs and Freddie Mac. You wouldn't mess with that crew.

The huge, American ex-boxer Freddie Mac was tickled by the Lord Provost of Dundee, who was swanning around with his impressive chain of office. Freddie said, 'Woweee, man, look at that flash motha fucking dude with the gold chain.' Freddie just assumed that the man was wearing some impressive bling-bling and compared the Lord Provost's class with that of Snoop Dog or 50 Cent. I'm not sure the Provost would have been chuffed to be compared to rappers.

Early doors, before the drink kicked in, I had decided to tell Gary Jacobs a few home truths. Gary had been the Middleweight Boxing Champion of Europe and a world contender. He was the first Jewish boxing champion Britain had produced in 100 years. He was good, very good. Early on in his career, I was asked by Arthur Thompson to do a favour for his pal, Alex Morrison. Morrison was a boxing promoter and manager of Gary Jacobs. According to Thompson, Gary was thinking of leaving Morrison for a London-based manager. At that time, the young boxer hadn't made it big but it was obvious he was destined to. Morrison wasn't happy.

'Just a slash or two on his mug,' I had been told. 'Try and get his eye and his mouth. Turn the ungrateful cunt into a bleeder. Finish him off as a fighter.'

I had never refused any job from Arthur Thompson no matter the odds or the opposition. I refused that time. It wasn't my place to ruin some young sportsman's career – now, that was immoral. Joey, Roy Shaw and Ken Buchanan were listening with particular interest and disgust. In their own different ways, they all had been sportsmen and the thought of deliberately killing off a career out of spite appalled them.

But now they were about to be impressed. As is the norm at such fundraisers, there was an auction of donated goods. Someone had contributed a big sword that had been used in the film *Braveheart*. Joey Pyle was particularly struck with it so I arranged with the auctioneer to slap a reserve price on it but not reveal I was responsible. But, bugger me, in the bidding Joey just kept going higher and higher, forcing me to pass notes to the man with the hammer upping my bid. We played cat and bloody mouse for ages. The trouble was I was buying it for Joey. Later, we got Ken Buchanan and a piper in full regalia to present it to him. A small mark of my respect and he was chuffed – so chuffed he was singing.

Later that night, we had Jocy Pyle, Roy Shaw and Arthur Suttie, Londoners all, belting out 'Flower of Scotland', the Scottish national anthem. It was one weird experience listening to it in those cockney accents – so weird, I had it videoed for posterity. Mind you, I think all working-class Londoners are just Scots with strange accents.

'Do you miss the boxing?' Ken asked Roy Shaw at one point.

'Yeah, of course,' big Roy replied, taking a sip of brandy. 'It was real useful for getting rid of my temper and I got paid for it as well.' Roy's furies were famous.

'Do you still get as angry as you used to?' asked Ken, who didn't say it but meant now that Roy was old enough to collect his pension.

'Oh yeah,' Roy replied earnestly, his muscle-thick neck nodding his head slowly, 'but I'm working on it, mate. If I feel like going to war on someone now over some little thing, I just do this.' He picked up his heavy, crystal brandy glass and bit a huge chunk out of it. Growling, he took another bite sending shards and slivers all over the carpet.

'Mental,' giggled Rory.

'Mental? Me?' roared Roy Shaw. 'I'm the only bastard here certified sane.' And he was. He has the certificate from Broadmoor to prove it.

A short while after that night, Rory had organised a Scotland versus England seniors match at Dunfermline. It was great night with guys like Gazza, Ally McCoist, Frank McAvennie and Andy Goram. I was in a buzzing mood and buying a load of drinks as were the organisers but I can tell you it's now official – Frank Macca can drink champagne faster than anyone can supply it. Shame guzzling bubbly isn't an Olympic event.

Next day, some newspaper really upset Arthur Suttie by mistaking him for Mad Frankie Fraser. Though they're around the same age and good mates, Fraser, of course, dyes his hair. That's too much for our Arthur. A short while later, I made a point of meeting up with Frankie to set one record straight. I had met Frankie Fraser before in the days when I worked with Arthur Thompson. Whenever we were in London, we'd drop by the Tin Pan Alley, a pub run by Frankie's family, to meet up with him. Thompson and Fraser were very good friends. Glasgow's Godfather would visit Mad Frank in prison a lot. Now over eighty years old, Fraser has spent more than forty years in jail and had been 'mentalled' to Broadmoor twice so Thompson had had plenty of visiting opportunities.

Before the strong drink took too much hold, I decided to tell Fraser about how his friend Arthur really was – about the bogus letter, giving evidence against me and him being too pally with the cops. He didn't like what I was saying – who does like hearing bad things about a mate? – but he listened quietly and respectfully. Frankie Fraser might be over eighty years old but he's still game and would take me on if he thought I deserved it. But we had a quiet chat – that was all.

Now I was about to experience some madness of my own and a lady with sinister connections.

74

THE LANDLADY

'Have you borrowed some money from a woman?' I was on the phone speaking to Rory Nicoll.

'A woman?' he replied, as if borrowing from females was something beneath his dignity. Aye, right.

'Rory, I wouldn't ask you if it wasn't serious.'

'Of course, Paul.'

'So have you? And would that be Ken Buchanan's landlady?'

There was a long silence at the other end of the line. Rory was trying to work out how I knew about the borrowing. 'Eh . . .' He was uncomfortable admitting the truth that he'd borrowed £30,000 from the woman to help fund his film, *Fight 'n' Talk*, so I thought I'd help him out.

'Her family aren't too happy, Rory – they want the money back now. In fact it's not even her money. Belongs to big Giovanni, a cousin of hers, and he says she should never have passed the cash to you. You'll have heard of big Giovanni, eh?'

'Noooo.' The word was spoken softly, almost inaudibly, dripping with worry.

'He's a bit of a player. Owns some restaurants and pubs around Glasgow, couple down south. Problem with Giovanni, problem with the landlady is they're part of the fucking Olivio crew.' I let the name sink in. 'You'll know they're Mafia.'

'Fuck.' Clearly he didn't. It wasn't the landlady any more but The Landlady.

'Think it would be safer if you paid back the dough pronto, Rory.'

'Paul, you know I'm heavily committed to a number of projects.'

'Look, Rory, this is a bit serious.'

'How serious?'

'As serious as it gets.'

If you can read silences, I was reading FEAR over that telephone line. Eventually, he said, 'Paul, I do have business with The Landlady but her turnaround isn't till next November.'

'Look, Rory, you're lucky we found out about this. We can maybe sort it out. Get the contract on you lifted.'

'Fuck, that would be great.'

'I'll see what I can do,' I said in a reassuring voice. 'Are you in a place where The Landlady would know to come looking for you?'

'No.'

'Good, stay there,' I instructed.

'I can't, Paul, I have to go home,' I swore I heard his voice breaking.

'Right then, does The Landlady know where you live?'

'Aye.'

'Well, don't go there and sort it out before you go home.'

'I'll have to call some people for advice,' said Rory.

'Fine, pal, you do that and call me when it's sorted.'

'OK,' he said, with a long, deep sigh. 'And, Paul?'

'Yeah?'

'Thanks for the warning, mate.'

'No problem.'

Of course it was all one big wind up. Ken Buchanan had let slip the business Rory had with his landlady – by all accounts, a lovely, gentle woman – but I decided to have laugh.

Whenever I was around any of the London faces with Rory, people like Joey Pyle would talk of him as a player. By that I mean someone who is or has been actively involved in crime at an organised level. Joey's far from being anyone's mug so fuck knows what old palaver that Walter Mitty part of Rory had been spinning him to give him that impression. Either way, Rory always corrected Joey at great length but it never seemed to work. The idea of a Mafia family chasing Rory seemed even funnier somehow. Maybe the whole world thought of him as a player?

A few hours later, in the early hours of the morning, Rory called me again. Since he and I had spoken, he had been on the phone to Reg. Fuck, I hadn't told Reg there was wind-up going on. What the fuck had he 'advised' Rory?

Reg told me the next day. 'You bastard, Ferris,' he growled, 'I had fucking Rory on the phone for two fucking hours last night.'

I was pissing myself laughing. 'What did he say?'

'That he owes The Landlady money and now the Olivio Mafia Clan are out to get him.'

'What did you advise him,' I could hardly get the words out for laughing.

'Well, what I didn't tell him was there is no Mafia clan named after fucking margarine.'

I'd just made the name up on the spur of the moment but now I realised he was right.

'But what advice did you give him?' I asked.

'Two fucking hours' worth.'

In reply, I just laughed.

'After I got the story out of him,' Reg went on, 'I asked who he had spoken to. He wouldn't say. Kept talking in some daft code. When I eventually worked out it had been you, I advised him to pay back the money or maybe consider he was having the piss seriously taken out of him.'

'What did he say?'

'He wasn't convinced he *was* having the piss taken out of him.'

I knew he hadn't been.

'I advised him to go home and relax. If he was going to associate with players on any kind of creative project, then he had to learn how to sleep at peace when someone had a problem.'

The night before, Rory had phoned me from his car. He had left wherever he was when I'd first spoken to him and was heading back to his place at Perth. The trouble was he kept thinking he was being followed by a black BMW for some reason. He had applied all

311

his knowledge of Hollywood gangster films and tested out the tail by pulling off the road and seeing if they followed.

That's how Rory Nicoll came to be sitting in his car, at night, in a shopping centre long since shut for the day, phoning me. As a precaution, he noted the car number and texted it back to his wife. But paranoia is a terrible thing. Think one car is following you and . . .

'How many numbers have you noted, Rory?' I asked.

'Why?'

'How many?'

'About forty.'

'Rory, go home to bed,' I said. 'Nothing's going to happen tonight.'

When I came off the phone, a pal who was round for a drink and who knew Rory well had gone soft and suggested maybe we should tell him it was a joke. I decided it could wait till morning.

'You bastard,' the voice growled at me down my mobile.

I was barely awake and already Rory was on the prowl. He'd phoned Ken and The Landlady, gently enquiring if everything was OK. Of course, it was.

Rory doesn't play-act the player any more. Well, not when I'm around.

Through Rory, I met his brother Rod, a bit of an entrepreneur who knew a bit about technology. With Rod's help and a bit of cash from me, I was able to do something I'd been thinking about for a long time. It was time for payback but using a new style.

I set up a website, www.ferrisconspiracy.com. Sound less innocuous than a loaded gun? The site has one purpose – to tell it how it is. Corrupt cops, bent officials, flesh-trading players – I'd out the lot. Newspapers running stories based on a tissue of fabrications – I'd publish the truth. Some guy done for a crime he didn't commit – I'd shout it to the world.

All my adult life, I had been a sitting target for anyone to write anything about me but I had no right of reply. This often had severe repercussions like me getting sent to jail wrongly and, if the editors decided, as they have done, not to print that I'd been freed pronto by the Home Office, people thought I was still in jail. Some people still think that. The power of the pen, eh?

With newspapers, it's possible to get stories corrected, as I have, but it takes a long time. By then, people already believe the original load of nonsense. A website allows an immediate response and it's good fun.

All Rod was involved in was setting me up with the technicians, advising on design and the like. He had nothing to do with content. No one else has. If you look at the site and it makes you want to have a go at someone, have a go at me.

The authorities won't leave me alone, of course. I know that and have made sure that, if they close down the site in one spot, it will open instantly from another base some place else in the world. If the blue serge mob want to play cat and mouse, I'm ready. Come to think of it, it's not much different from my old world – just different weapons.

As I got the website up and running, another door was opened for me. I was going undercover. Or was I?

75

FISH SUPPERS ON THE FRONT

2004

'*MacIntyre Undercover*? Are you serious?'

'Not undercover, Paul. He wants to do a different type of film,' replied Reg.

'Can we trust him?'

'I think so.'

That was good enough for me. Donal MacIntyre had made a name for himself as a TV presenter by going undercover and exposing a few cons. His big breakthrough came when he joined a group of Chelsea boot boys who were into football violence and even had his arm tattooed. It involved some well dodgy stuff like sitting in a car full of these guys, secretly filming them. The Chelsea team swore revenge and life was a wee bit awkward for Donal for a while. How do you hide when you earn your living by being on the box? He did what I would do and just went on living.

By the time Donal's Extreme Productions team – commissioned by Channel 5 – had approached us in early 2004, he had also been involved in *The Secret Policeman's Ball*, exposing racist cops in Manchester. With that and a few other ploys, he wasn't on any cops' Christmas card list and that made him OK in my book. But he had also done a series conning and exposing some really stupid, low-life cons. Drawing them into a situation then turning them over. Now that made him bad news.

An assistant producer, young Sam Emmery, had contacted Reg

about the prospect of making a crime film in Glasgow. When he arrived, it was to be a half-hour film in a set of ten. When he left Glasgow the next morning, he had a raging hangover and a new plan – now they'd make only three films, each an hour long, with one concentrating on Manchester, one on Liverpool and one on Glasgow. That was better.

The first time I met Donal was in a warehouse in Govan. It seemed fitting somehow. Even before we had shaken hands, we had slagged each other off – him in his Irish brogue me in my Glaswegian street patter. Different sounds, same origin. I instantly recognised Donal as a chancer – a guy with a sharp brain and sharper tongue who would take risks, having total faith in his ability to talk his way in and out of most things. Like many a chancer, Donal had turned it into a profession and made a good living. I liked him.

Along with Donal and Sam there was Kirsty Cunningham, the young producer. Kirsty was clearly very bright and ace at her job but she had hidden talents. One time we were filming and she was on the camera, a heavy-looking beast that she had hoisted on her shoulder. For some reason, they wanted me to go up this long flight of stairs and fast. No problem. Off I skipped with Kirsty right behind me. It was a multi-storey car park and it was high. By the time I got to the top, the old lungs were feeling it and, turning, I was shocked to find Kirsty right behind me. I tried to say, 'That was some climb.' But all that emerged was breathless gasps.

Kirsty, with the camera still rolling, replied, 'Yeah, it was, wasn't it?' and then started chatting about something else – which was just as well because I was still trying to draw breath. Heavy camera, sprinting up all those flights, not even out of breath at the top? Take my advice – don't mess with Kirsty.

Over a fine lunch at L'Ariosto in Glasgow's Mitchell Lane, we got chatting about their other projects. They were hoping to cover the Arif Clan in London. No chance we told them and we were right. One of their other films was on the Noonans from Manchester. I was good friends with Dessie Noonan – a real hard man and old fashioned with it – but I warned them that they'd find Dominic

Noonan surrounded by the young boys and he would play to the camera. Right again.

Their third film featured Paul Grimes, the Liverpool grass who had shopped Cocky Warren, John Haase and even his own son. Within two minutes, it was obvious that Reg and I knew more about the Liverpool situation than they did and more than whoever was helping with their research. The chat with the filmmakers helped me confirm what I already believed. Cities used to be islands in crime terms and few players travelled from one to another. But Glasgow was part of the world now and, just because Reg and I live there, it doesn't mean we don't know more about what is happening in London, Manchester, Liverpool or Newcastle than most people and most journalists.

Then the filmmakers planned a very local visit – to a place that held only bad memories for me. They wanted to go doon the watter to Rothesay. Rothesay is the main town on the Isle of Bute which lies well down the Firth of Clyde. It's a beautiful place, right in the middle of wild sweeping hills and surrounded by the broad mouth of the river. Before cheap foreign travel, this was where Glaswegians who could afford it went for a summer break. It was easy to understand why.

The last time I'd been there was twenty years before. On the run for numerous attempted murders, Arthur Thompson, The Godfather, and his son Fatboy had arranged for me to hide out at a flat they had in Rothesay. I had only been there a few hours when a team of armed cops burst in. One of the cops had an unlicensed gun that night. I was meant to be a dead man. Only one thing saved me – my very pregnant girlfriend Anne Marie had come along. No one else knew that she'd be there – not the Thompsons and certainly not the cops who were very pissed off when they saw her. So, instead they planted some smack on me.

'Whose is the little brown bag?' this big copper had asked.

In court, I'd prove it wasn't mine – I hadn't put it in my pocket and so it must have been put there by the bizzies. But what the raid that night was mostly about was betrayal – the Thompsons were the only ones who knew where I was hiding. And it was an eye opener – the cops would kill me given half a chance and, if not, they'd jail me for something, anything, even if I didn't do it. That wee flat in Rothesay marked a significant change in my life and it made me the person I still am today as I write this book. And I was going back there.

It was a top-floor tenement flat over a jeweller's shop. As I walked upstairs the sense of that terrible time came flooding back. I could hear the cops' footsteps as they ran up the stairs, guns in their mitts. I could hear Anne Marie's screams as they kicked in the door. I could smell the bad breath of the polis who put the gun into my face. I could feel the acid anger in my stomach as I remembered the treachery of people I trusted – people I'd risked my life for. The visit was surprisingly moving and it left me zapped but, if I thought I was in for some rest and relaxation after it, I was to be disappointed.

Reg had warned the Channel 5 people that, in Rothesay, a hotel wasn't necessarily the same as what they would class as a hotel – a B&B would be a better description – and he'd also told them that the town closed early. The Londoners didn't seem to understand and booked us into just such a hotel. It was nice enough but, if you expected a meal, you were out of luck. So we trawled the town for some grub. It was only early evening but already every place was shut. Eventually, a couple of locals told us the town's one Italian restaurant would still be open and gave us directions towards the far end of town.

Donal and Reg went off to buy some wine – the place where we were staying didn't have a licence – and the rest of us went ahead. One long walk later, we realised that we'd been hoodwinked by an elderly couple from the sticks. I'm sure they'd watched us from a distance, real tickled at conning the outsiders. And that's how we came to be eating fish suppers washed down by a couple bottles of wine in the pitch dark on a bench at the front on Rothesay. The cameraman, Sam, Donal the top TV presenter, Reg the best-selling crime author and me, top gangster or so they would tag me. If only a local had had the gumption to take a snap, they would have been well rewarded by a Scottish tabloid and no doubt. The event remained unrecorded but, for this record, please note – it was one of the tastiest meals I've ever had.

The filming was carried out on a day here and a day there, over several months. One thing all journalists have in common – be it TV or newspapers – is that they always want more. Could they just film me going about my everyday business? Sure. What did they want? An occasional site visit to assess security. A meeting with Reg some afternoon during which we drink three bottles of wine as we chat. Me adding material to my website. None of that would make great TV, would it? So, as usual, they devised other plans.

Reg had bought a painting off this young Glasgow artist, John McGlynn. It was called *Don't Shoot the Messenger* and it featured two pairs of hands, one with a shotgun the other handing over a letter. Appropriate, eh? I liked the painter's style so agreed that he could paint my portrait. One point I made to the film crew – there was to be no hint of Dave Courtney, The Great Pretender. Courtney had a massive, fuck-off mural painted on the gable of his house with him togged up in armour like St George and sitting astride a white charger. Aye, right. In the event, they played another trick. As I let John into the house, the crew filmed and, while he set up his gear and we chatted, the crew kept filming – not saying anything, just filming. The bastards just left me to get on with it to see how I behaved without any instructions from them. As it happened, I had a very relaxing few hours.

Next was to be a game of badminton with Donal. I play a bit to keep fit but Donal is an ex-international rower for Ireland, fit as fuck, and he plays badminton. But I reckoned I could take him on. The night before the match, we were sitting having a drink and he told me about a trip to Colombia. He was out in the wilds, living and filming with a small army of bandits who specialised in cocaine trafficking. The guy in charge of this mob was a one-eyed, one-armed general, his body parts having been lost in conflict. The bloke only challenged Donal to a game of badminton. After his troops had cleared and roughly marked a court out of the jungle, they kicked off. First shot from the general flew over Donal's head and landed at least three feet beyond the back line.

'Out,' shouted Donal.

'No, no – in,' the general shouted back.

A competitive bastard, Donal was about to argue the toss when he looked around. About one hundred of the bandits had gathered to watch – every one of them armed to the teeth and every one of them shouting for the general.

'IN,' shouted Donal. He'd decided to lose a game of badminton and leave alive. Smart move.

Working with Donal and the team was a pleasure. They'd make the film as they saw it, of course, but they allowed us some input too in things like suggesting the music and commenting on and criticising the cuts as they pieced the film together. Very open, very fair and very much worth trusting. In fact, just the way you imagine the BBC would behave, eh?

I was about to find out differently and a good man would pay the ultimate price.

76

HEADS IN THE SAND?

In the middle of filming with Donal and the Extreme Productions team, a call came in from the BBC. A woman called Sam, as in Samantha, Poling wanted to interview me for an investigative documentary series on BBC TV called *Frontline Scotland*. What about? My involvement in the security business.

We had known for some months that some media mob was trying to run a sting fronted by a fake company in Glasgow by inviting security firms to tender for contracts. This was the mob. While I don't approve of those methods – you can't always a guarantee the accuracy of the results – I had nothing to hide. Ever since my release from jail, every bad news story of gangsterism and the security business had my name in it. Not only that, the reports always claimed that I owned the security company called Frontline. (Sorry about the names of company and TV show being so similar but there it is.) I was an independent consultant and Frontline was then owned by an experienced businessman by the name of Jim Methven.

Having had a chat with Reg, we decided that the BBC's approach could be a chance to set the record straight. On the day of the interview, we were driven to an address in Maryhill. From the outside, it looked like any other industrial estate apart from the big signs advertising the kids' programme *Balamory* – but this wasn't going to be child's play. At our insistence, Reg sat in and witnessed the interview. We knew the BBC might play editorial games, missing sections out, putting them next to others and making me sound as if I said something I did not. All TV programmes have to be edited to make them sleek. The question here was would they be honest?

The interview was fine although the interviewer, Sam Poling, repeatedly asked me if I owned Frontline. Towards the end, she started demanding how much I paid Reg McKay to be my PR agent. The way we work together upsets a lot of mainstream journalists who assume there's more to it than joint projects, many shared views and friendship. Why is that? The idea of Reg being my PR man and me paying him fees was so ludicrous that both he and I began to laugh. But what had those questions to do with the security business? Had I been too tight with my answers? Was she trying to rattle me? If so, it didn't work, Sam.

As Reg and I left the BBC studios we knew the results weren't going to be good. The interviewer had given every sign of making the story she wanted rather than what was actually happening. She wasn't that unusual – just disappointing.

While I'd been in that studio-cum-warehouse being interviewed by Sam Poling, half a mile down the road in Maryhill a plastics factory had exploded, causing many deaths and injuries. Now that was harsh reality, not the games that had been played in front of the TV cameras.

Jim Methven, the owner of the security company Frontline, and Joe Lilley, the finance man, invited the BBC team to their office and gave them free access to all the paperwork, files and financial records. This was to settle once and for all that Jim owned the company and it was run well, legally and was very successful. Their offer was declined. Well, we don't want facts to get in the way of a good story, do we? The BBC reckoned they had Frontline and me in the shit and that suited them just fine. They'd hooked one of Frontline's staff, Nancy Jones. Nancy was the sales executive and very good at her job. Like every successful salesperson I'd ever met, Nancy would do and say almost anything to make a sale and get her commission. And they call me the crook?

The BBC had secretly recorded Nancy who thought she was

meeting with a prospective client. This bogus client was offering a fat, juicy contract and securing it would be worth a lot of money to Nancy – I could just imagine her planning to buy her next Louis Vuitton handbag on the proceeds. In a very positive tone, the so-called client asked if it was right that Paul Ferris owned Frontline. Nancy said I did and waxed lyrical about me. Nancy had been reprimanded twice before for telling clients that I owned the company. This was because, firstly, it wasn't true and, secondly, while many clients like the idea that I did own the company, some didn't. The only reason Nancy ever said that I was the owner was to make a sale. Some business people believe that they'd rather have an ex-gangster like me making their goods or property secure than a layman or even an ex-cop – guys like me know how to rob, after all, and ex-cops only ever come in after the crime. Poor Nancy – she had done very well for Frontline but now she was for the sack. Bloody shame. She was only trying to do her job but she just took it a bit far while being secretly filmed.

If what they were after was an exposé of the security business, the film itself was pretty poor. They had an ex-player by the name of Frank Carberry spouting forth. Carberry looks and sounds the part but he is strictly third class and he knows it. A brutal, cowardly bugger, Carberry had tried to throw his weight around in the security business but found that he simply wasn't up to it. Now here he was singing like a birdie, making up tales and getting bitter payback on others.

Carberry had tried to reinvent himself by hooking up with a millionaire's daughter who was obsessed with horse jumping. The trouble was he kept getting himself into bother. One time, he even tried to resolve a argument by slapping a woman on the face with a severed horse's ear. You can take the man off the street but . . . By the time the *Frontline Scotland* documentary was released, Carberry was more infamous for his taste in young men and being a regular informant for a journalist called Russell Findlay. Findlay had written numerous untrue, fanciful stories about me over the years and, with Carberry feeding him stuff, it probably reflecting how much Carberry hated me. Russell Findlay and the BBC should choose their sources more carefully if they want to get near the truth.

Nancy Jones wasn't the only victim of this farce. Joe Lilley, Frontline's finance man, had suffered from depression all his life. A warm, bright, intelligent man, depression was his illness just as psoriasis is mine, diabetes is someone else's, epilepsy Reg's and so on and so forth. Joe couldn't believe that the BBC, that institution of the truth, could refuse an open offer to examine the company's books and records, only then to do a story that they would have known wasn't true if only they had taken up the offer. Joe took it personally and he took it bad. A few days after the programme was broadcast, he committed suicide. What a hellish waste of a good man.

A week or so after the broadcast, Reg wrote his column, 'The Gutter Sniper', which then appeared weekly in the *Big Issue*, and, in it, he was very critical of the BBC's programme in terms of accuracy and methods. The BBC went ballistic, blazing on to the editor of *Big Issue* in Scotland, demanding that Reg be given the boot and implying that they'd get their lawyers on to the magazine. The biggest corporation in the world, the BBC, was threatening the Scottish edition of a magazine set up to help homeless people earn some money and get off the street – David and Goliath didn't have a look-in. The *Big Issue* told the BBC that they ran their own magazine and Reg stayed put – small magazine but big balls. What Reg wrote certainly upset them but there was no legal action. Funny that, eh?

A while later, I almost choked when I learned that the BBC's *Frontline Scotland* had won a national award for that film on the security business – that film which I knew to be full of misrepresentations and inaccuracies. I'll bet the BBC team and Sam Poling didn't even blush when picking up the award. And I'm meant to be the con merchant.

The serious stuff was soon forgotten when I got a call one morning. How would I like to make a film? A big film? Hollywood maybe?

The sharks were circling.

77

CROOKS AND KRAZY HORSES
2005

'How's it going, Bobby?' It was the familiar voice of my pal, Mickey Carroll at the other end of the mobile line.

'What are you on about, Mickey,' I replied, laughing. Mickey has a zany sense of humour. The year before, Celtic-mad Mickey had gone off to watch Celtic play in the UEFA cup final in Spain. He had hired a car there and it was a very long drive from the airport to the venue. Two other fans hitched a lift from him – big mistake. Mickey is such a bad driver that the hitchhikers' story made it into a book – the chapter it featured in was called 'Driver from Hell'. Well, Mickey had been an armed robber not a getaway driver.

'Bobby,' he replied. 'Bobby Carlyle. Have you no' seen tomorrow's *Sun*?' Mickey always bought the first editions of the papers late the night before.

'No.'

'You'll need to get out and buy it. Robert Carlyle is playing you in a film of *The Ferris Conspiracy*.'

'You're fucking joking.' Mickey wasn't and neither was Robert Carlyle.

Ever since we had written *The Ferris Conspiracy*, anyone who said that a film should be made out of it always added that Robert Carlyle should play me. That suited me swell. Carlyle is a great actor, a Glasgow boy and, by all accounts, he knows how the streets work. Of course, Carlyle had made it big playing the head-case Begbie in the film of Irvine Welsh's *Trainspotting* but he'd played loads of other roles like the Highland bobby, Hamish MacBeth, and, more recently, he'd portrayed Hitler. He should have no problem in handling me, then, eh?

A few months before I'd met a guy called Paul Kerr. Paul was the brother of Jim Kerr, lead singer of Simple Minds. Paul had been involved as tour manager for Simple Minds but was now on his own, bobbing and weaving on a number of projects. He hired out luxury chauffeur-driven cars to big-name rock stars while they were in Scotland, promoted music and told me he owned part of a group just then being launched, El Pres!dente.

In December 2004, I had created a company, Real Productions, with the aim of producing a couple of films. The initial two films were to be about TC Campbell's unjust conviction for the Ice-Cream War murders and Britain's greatest perjurer, Dennis Woodman. I was looking for some music for these films and that's when I was introduced to Paul Kerr. Before I knew what was happening, he had started brokering deals for making a film of my story. He'd got Simon Cowell's music company, BMG, interested in providing the soundtrack and there was a queue of production companies wanting the movie, as well as a sniff that Robert Carlyle might be interested. But that late-night call from Mickey was the first I knew about any of it. Within days, we were meeting for lunch at One Devonshire Gardens, one of the plushest restaurants in Glasgow, with the press crowding outside.

Carlyle and I met privately for lunch while Carlyle's PA, some people from one of the interested production companies and Kerr talked financial turkey in another room. I had a list of questions for Carlyle to test out his commitment to keep the film real, not glamorise crime and tackle the issue of the impact of early bullying on guys like me. Turned out he had exactly the same questions for me. He was a cool guy and, as mate of mine used to say, 'Forgive us for being normal.' For the rest of the lunch we just chatted. We even had a couple of friends in common. Big-time film star and street player knowing the same people – that's Glasgow for you. His wife,

Anastasia, had read *Conspiracy* a long time before and said to him that he was the only person to play my part. If everybody was saying it, surely it had to be right.

By the end of the afternoon, a budget was agreed, as was Carlyle's fee, and it looked like that movie was going to happen. Outside the restaurant, I spoke to the media and I publicly thanked Strathclyde Police – without their efforts to stitch me up, plant heroin on me and run me down, I wouldn't have such a story to tell or much of a movie to make. A short while later, two guys were sent up to Glasgow to talk to me about the film. One was Scottish, originally from Balornock, a stone's throw from my own Blackhill patch. His film partner was public-school educated and English. They were chalk and cheese but they worked well together. One of their claims to fame was that they made those famous Tango adverts where the orange genie slaps hell out of unsuspecting folk. They had imagination and a sense of humour at least.

Paul Kerr had been in trouble with the law a few years earlier. A fall-out with some DJ over a business deal had led to him being charged with all sorts of stuff including torching a sofa in the guy's house. He went to jail. While inside, he met another old pal of mine, James McIntyre. James was a criminal lawyer – literally. He had developed a fascination with guns and had gone native. Tom Hagen, the lawyer character in the movie *The Godfather*, had nothing on James. I told him once that I was the bad boy wanting to go straight and he was the straight guy wanting to go bad. And he did.

James got caught with a few shooters, went to prison and was struck off as a lawyer but he remains one of the most interesting guys I've ever known – eccentric as hell but interesting. One time, a very unhappy bunny stabbed James in the leg, causing lasting damage. Now he walks with a stick but he sometimes forgets which leg has the limp. Like you do. The same guy can quote great screeds of Shakespeare. He can drink all night and yet still work the next day. And he knows every face there is. While still a lawyer, his best man at his wedding was one of the McGovern Family who run Springburn.

So, it was no surprise to me when I learned that James had reinvented himself as a scriptwriter. Now he works on *River City* and *EastEnders*. Whatever you think of those soaps, it takes real skill to produce their scripts. I thought James would be useful in some of our film projects so I got him together again with Paul Kerr, his old cellmate. They met in L'Ariosto – they sat in one booth while a pal and I sat in another. The idea was to let them talk a bit of business then we would join them but my first drink hadn't arrived when a commotion broke out. McIntyre was livid – his face was bright red and he was shouting and swearing at Kerr. Ten seconds later, Paul Kerr walked out. Deal off. I suppose mavericks and eccentrics don't mix – except maybe in pokey.

A few months later, Paul Kerr dropped another bombshell, again without me knowing it. Liam Gallagher of Oasis was interested in playing my pal Paul Massey, the leader of the Salford Team, in my film. As it happens, all that Liam needs to do is just be his mad, outrageous self and he'll fit the bill perfectly. The item hit the news pages fast. Yet all Kerr had done was phone a friend – Liam Gallagher. The actress Patsy Kensit had been married to Jim Kerr then went on to marry Liam. But, in getting involved in this film project, Paul Kerr had dropped a cigarette butt in the woods and was surprised to find himself chased by a raging forest fire – the media.

Through my new contacts in the film industry, I was introduced to two Glasgow guys who had some impressive CVs in making docu-dramas – award-winning stuff. We agreed to work together on my Glasgow films and set up a company to oversee their production. I didn't care about the money to be made. All I wanted was the best possible films to be released and for them to be real. But other folk have to make their wages so we discussed that.

I had the funding in place. Also the bold TC Campbell had won his appeal against wrongful imprisonment and was looking at £3 to £4 million compensation. Loving the idea of the films, he immediately committed £1 million. That's Tommy Campbell for you. But, before I paid out any dough, I decided to check out some of the companies the two film guys had been involved with and what I found was a list of bad debts. I had known one of them was bankrupt but neither had mentioned this trail of mess. That's the film industry for you – full of guys talking big numbers and keeping mum about the truth. They're sharks, every one of them – more vicious than salesman and less moral than gangsters.

Then a blast from the past came back to haunt me. Most Scots probably know Stuart Cosgrove as the other half of Tam Cowan's double act on the radio football show *Off the Ball*. Cosgrove does this working-class with a uni degree sort of act while Cowan is just his outrageous self. But those in the media know him as the Head of Programmes for Channel 4. If you want a TV show commissioned or a film made, Cosgrove is very influential. He has come out and slated books like mine. He is also on record as saying that he'd never make another gangster movie based in Scotland. These are his opinions and his choices but what folk don't know is that, a few years back, he wanted to make a film of my story and I think he lost his bottle because of dead bodies under his patio.

Before my sentence for gunrunning, Cosgrove and I met a number of times, usually in the Moat House Hotel in Glasgow. I was providing him with the info I had on corrupt cops, setting people up and so on. One night, he asked me a favour. He'd just moved into a house in Dennistoun in the city and there were rumours that someone had been seen to there and buried under the patio – seriously. He didn't find it funny at all when, a couple of weeks later, I told him there was good news and bad news.

'The good news is there isn't one body under your patio, Stuart,' I said. 'The bad news is there's two.'

It took me fucking ages to convince him that I had been joking – that his back garden was corpse free. But this was the same guy who was using his influence to stop crime films based in Glasgow being made. It's not as if crime isn't a day-to-day reality of my city – a place where guys like him have to ask guys like me to find out about bodies buried in their back court. Smoke and mirrors, that's what most of these people play with. The world isn't how it really is – it's how they describe it. Wake up and smell the gun smoke, Stuart.

To succeed in an industry, you have to learn how it ticks. Six months on, the film is certainly going to happen. We haven't finished recruiting big names and we know the £14 million production budget that has already been tabled can be bettered. Watch this space – we'll make sure they keep it real.

The film world isn't the real world, thank fuck. It's now July 2005 and I'm sitting in Reg's front room, a bottle of wine between us and the air thick with blue cigarette smoke. We're musing over everything. A lot has happened since I walked out of Frankland Prison. A lot has changed but people don't like it – don't like it at all.

78

MOUSE BITES CAT
2005

What's that old Mafia saying? Keep your fiends close and your enemies right by your side? Me? I have no choice with the foes.

When I walk, I see what's all around me and I mean all around me. A long time ago, I developed the habit of stopping and looking to the side, while also checking behind me, or turning a corner and looking back, seeing every reflection in every glass pane. Those and every other trick in the book of the streets just became part of my life. A pain in the arse? It's second nature now and . . . well, I'm alive.

Who am I on the lookout for? Young scalp hunters wanting to make a name for themselves? Not really. One of the great joys of my life is that, since I've been free and going straight, the average young player treats and greets me very well. The young team seem to understand what I'm trying to do and why. They've grasped that I'm leading a straight life but, at the same time, I'm refusing to turn my back on old pals – that I'm not willing to have crap written about people but I am willing to take on the big boys in the cops and the tired old hacks who churn out clichés. Yes, the young guys are OK by me.

Should I be worried about street-player enemies? Aye, I suppose so but the only enemies I have there are the backstabbing bastards who are in cahoots with the cops. And they probably wouldn't have the balls to do their own business and would hire some young junkie to do it for them. If he was stoned enough, he might just try but the day I'm caught out by a sky pilot is the day I deserve to be caught out.

The cops? Yeah, it's the fucking cops – if anyone's going to top me it will be those bastards and it's not because I'm up to no good. I've known this ever since that unlicensed gun was shoved against my skull in Rothesay and then, later, when I listened to tapes with a detective sergeant saying, 'Wee Paul was almost taken for a walk in the Campsies. And he wasn't coming back.' So I watch out all the time – especially when driving.

There I was, out of jail for more than two years – I'd never even been interviewed by the rozzers, let alone charged with anything – when I spotted them on my tail. Again. Usually, I'd just boot it and leave them for dead but, this time, I'd a business meeting to go to in the city centre and I was running late. Sure enough, they followed me off the motorway at Charing Cross and all the way through the city centre, right down to Mitchell Lane. Those who know the city will realise the number of twists and turns that route takes. At Mitchell Lane, I drove in to a multi-storey car park, shot right in to the first free space and rushed to the wall where I could look down on the street. There it was – the same car and it was parking just up a bit. Bastards.

I went to my business meeting and, as others blethered about this and that, I thought of all the times I'd been chased. The one that stuck out was in Glasgow when I was taking my son Paul, then aged about nine, to meet a pal and his kids. This pal was known as Steve Doc and we were going to have a dads' and sons' day out at Strathclyde Park. Instead, it ended up in a 140mph car race down the M8 with one very frightened son in the back seat. As I found out later when the speeding ticket tumbled through the door, the big white Merc behind me wasn't driven by some street enemy but by the cops. Mind you, I was driving a Ford Probe 24V so they had their hands full.

As I thought back on that day, I was full of sad memories. Poor Steve Doc, a wonderful guy, killed himself over a domestic by jumping from a high flat. His enemies put it about that they had taken him out. Shite. They weren't fit to. It was that hard man with the soft centre again – what a waste, though. I miss him still.

Another sad memory was in my thoughts. What sort of a father was I to have my wee boy Paul in the car for a pleasant day out and end up putting him through those terrors? I was a shite dad. I was letting myself down and, much worse, letting him down too. Was that going to happen again with young Dean? At the meeting, I decided that that nonsense was going to stop right there.

As I drove away through the city centre, the same car picked me up at George Square – game on. I just trundled away at a decent speed, knowing exactly where I was taking them. As a street player, you get to know your territory intimately and you get to know it better than the cops – that's the point. Carntyne is a great wee scheme and that's where I took them. Losing them at one point, I did a quick handbrake turn and pulled in, engine revving, pointing their way, waiting for them to appear. Appear they did and I swear I saw the two detectives blush as our cars almost ended up nose to nose. Me? I just sat there staring right at them, noting down their registration number.

The suit in the passenger seat got out with a piece of paper in his hand and started asking passers-by for directions. I could see by the look on the citizens' faces that they'd never heard of whatever address he'd made up. Yet off he went on foot as his mate in the car did a quick U-turn and headed off.

What to do? Confront the guy on the pavement and demand an explanation or go after the cop in the motor? Fuck it, I eased the car into first and rolled off, right on the cop car's tail. This cop wasn't too sure of Carntyne. He took this turn and that and I knew he was going up dead ends or driving in circles. All the time, I could see him repeatedly look up at his rear-view mirror, eyeballing me. He was nervous. Good.

Eventually, he found his way out of the scheme and on to the link road to the motorway and I was still right behind him. It was a notoriously busy section and I knew all three lanes of the M8 would be heaving with traffic. And he must have known that too. He wasn't going to escape from me that easy. Or was he?

Trundling down the link road in second gear, he suddenly took off. I mean went flying. Screw the motor-polluted lanes, he just went straight on to the hard shoulder and belted it big time. Dangerous. Very dangerous. Me? I just let him go. No point in me breaking the law and putting innocent motorists' lives at risk. Besides, I'd had enough fun as the mouse had turned cat. The point was made to the cop that, if he was going to follow me in future, he'd better improve his skills. A word about his motor. I know all those jokes about Skodas are long dead but that was what the rozzer was driving – a Skoda. It was a two-litre turbo job and, man, that car could go.

Later that day my lawyer, John Macaulay, phoned the police to submit a formal complaint. He gave them the make, colour and registration of the car, a full description of the two cops and a very detailed account of the guy's kamikaze driving down the hard shoulder of the M8. That was my coup de grâce – having John make a formal complaint about the cop's dangerous driving. I'm sure the irony of me making that sort of grumble didn't escape the attention of the top brass at the other end of the line. 'OK, sir,' he finally sighed, 'I'll have word with the driver.'

The cops still follow me from time to time, of course, but not nearly as often as they used to. They play other games like tapping the phones of friends and associates. Other tricks they have got up to have included the time they wrote, in a report to a Lanarkshire Licensing Board, that the oriental owner of a hotel was doing business with me and I was working with the Triads. The fucking Triads? I ask you! In the sleepy little new town of East Kilbride? All I did was have a meal out there.

From time to time, guys come to me to show me legal papers in some case against them. Usually this is because the investigating cops have reported surveillance sightings of me. These are guys that I've usually never met before, let alone been involved with them in some crime.

So the heat's still on me from the cops. That's OK, I can take it.

You have to ask how long they can go on snooping into this bloke as every week, every month, every year passes and I'm without interview or investigation, never mind charge.

But then it's personal between the cops and me. Always will be probably. I'm not grumbling. At least I'm free – unlike some of my pals and some who are in very bad company.

79

DR DEATH

'I'm not going to hospital.'

'But you need to. You need treatment.'

'Fuck off – I'll die here in the jail.' It was big Grant Turnbull, down in Frankland Prison, talking to a screw. For once, I agreed with the screw. Grant did need to go to hospital But I also sympathised with Grant for one good reason – Harold Shipman.

Grant's HIV status was going through a bad stage. He'd developed immunity to his medication, his liver was packing in and his legs had swollen up so big he couldn't walk. If he didn't go to the prison hospital for constant treatment, he'd die.

He was vulnerable in other ways too. After I'd left Frankland for the second time, Essex boy Jason Vella, the guy who had waited till the second I was leaving before having a pop at me, decided to have a pop at Grant now. But, again, he waited till the big man was at his weakest.

When Grant became ill, this other prisoner approached him. He'd been given a bundle of drugs to stab Grant as he sat in his wheelchair but, instead, the guy told Grant, smoked the drugs and stuck two fingers up at Vella.

Grant had been in the jail's hospital before and hated it. The place was stuffed full of child abusers, serial killers, mental types and the terminally ill – it was a madhouse. The last time he was there, he had shared a cell with two guys. One didn't stop talking to himself night or day and the other sat in a wheelchair, chain-smoking, not speaking and just shit and pissed himself where he sat. And, if that wasn't bad enough, Shipman, one of the biggest serial killers in the world, had established himself there as one of the kingpins. Grant wanted fuck all to do with him – even knowing they were sharing the same unit was too much for him.

After a long chat with Reg, Grant agreed to go to the hospital to get the treatment. He also decided to hold back the disgust he felt for Shipman and try to get a sense of what sort of person he was – apart from being the slaughterer of so many innocent old folk, that is.

Shipman lorded it around the place and was given his own room. I say 'room' deliberately because it was not a cell. The place he called home was kitted out with fitted carpets, en suite bathroom, wallpaper, TV, sound system, cooker and fridge. It was like a luxurious wee bedsit and it was meant to accommodate suicidal patients and men called 'listeners'. Listeners are prisoner volunteers who have been trained by the Samaritans to help and support suicidal people. When such a bloke was identified, the suicidal person and the listener would move into this special room together and live there for as long as it took for the suicide notions to pass. Grant was a listener.

That crucial resource, which was there to save lives, was given to serial killer number one. Bloody scandal. Shipman would tell other prisoners what to do and very often the screws too. He had his routine every day – breakfast, newspapers, walk outside, lunch, work translating books into Braille, afternoon tea, walk outside, letter writing and chess. No one else was allowed that amount of freedom.

Grant was struggling. He wondered if the relatives of Shipman's victims knew what a cushy life he had and, if they did, he wondered what they would think of it. Then he had a good idea.

Shipman was keen to play Grant at chess. He had already beaten all the other players in the unit and he wanted a fresh challenge. Grant agreed and the two men would chat as they played, the way you do. Dr Death was always going on about how he'd win an appeal and be freed. This was at the same time an investigation was identifying hundreds more of his victims. Grant couldn't believe his arrogance because that was all his faith was based on – pure bloody conceit.

On Grant's last night in the unit, he asked Shipman, 'What happens if you don't win an appeal?'

'Oh, I'll win,' insisted the evil quack.

'But just imagine that it doesn't happen,' persisted Grant.

Shipman pushed his glasses up the bridge of his nose, looked Grant straight on and replied, 'They'll never take me. Never.'

A short time after this conversation, Shipman was suddenly moved to Wakefield Prison where he was treated as just another inmate. A few days later, he hanged himself in his cell. When the news broke at Frankland, there was cheering throughout the prison – even the screws were in a chirpy mood that day.

Grant Turnbull still has a bad taste in his mouth from his time with Shipman. His only consolation was that, on their last night together, he, Grant, won both games of chess that they played. Since then, Grant Turnbull has kept good health. He's still alive and kicking after thirty years of being HIV positive and there's a good few years left in him yet.

In 2005, the Home Office agreed to give Grant early parole on compassionate grounds – he's hardly a risk to the community any more. But, up in Glasgow, there was someone else who the cops thought *was* a risk – a lethal risk.

80

FUNDRAISING AND FIT-UPS

'The Red Rose Ball? What the fuck's that?' I had just been invited so I needed to know.

'Eh, it's just a fancy do – a good night out, Paul. You'll enjoy it.' The speaker was Justin McAlroy and he'd handed me some tickets to this ball. I knew of McAlroy but hardly knew him at all. So why the hell was he inviting me out? It turned out that Justin McAlroy was inviting almost ever player he knew and with good reason. The son of millionaire builder Tommy McAlroy, from Lanarkshire, Justin was the rich kid who'd turned bad. For reasons only he would know, he got into drug dealing and the trouble was he owed some serious faces a lot of money.

It seemed to me that what Justin McAlroy wanted was a show of strength. With a bunch of well-known faces as guests at this bash, the blokes he owed were likely to back off. And that was a good enough reason for my decision not to attend – politics of the street was in my past not my present.

Another good reason to give the Red Rose Ball a body swerve was that it was political – it was an annual event to raise funds for the Wishaw constituency of the Labour Party. Politics? No thank you. Of course, the Wishaw constituency had some powerful politicians connected to it – John Reid MP, who was then Secretary of State for Northern Ireland, Jack McConnell, the First Minister of the Scottish Parliament, and Frank Roy MP. And so these suits ended up in the company of street players that night. But the ones who did accept McAlroy's invitations weren't the big faces – it was just some of the crew from McGraw's camp, some of the south-side mob and a couple from Edinburgh who turned up and it wasn't enough.

A few days after the Red Rose Ball, McAlroy was shot dead in front of his house in Cambuslang. Seeing the gun, McAlroy had run and crawled under his car. The hit man calmly crouched down and shot him anyway. It was a professional hit and no doubt.

The cops went into overdrive. Millionaire's son ... Contacts with powerful government ministers ... This was one gang killing they *had* to solve – unlike most.

The media also went into overdrive. Who exactly was at that Red Rose Ball? Were there any links between crime and politics in Lanarkshire? Well, if there aren't, it's the only part of the country where that's the case.

The first so-called suspect they hauled in was a young east-end player, Mark Clinton. At one point, he was even charged with the killing but then he was released with all charges dropped. However, they would be back for Clinton.

The next guy they lifted was Willie Gage. Willie was a second-hand car dealer and a bit of a bad boy but in a small-time way. He also had a fascination with shooters but he was no hit man. The street knew that Willie Gage was innocent and no one even imagined he would go to trial. Wrong, of course.

A burnt-out car had been found a distance away from the murder scene and it had, at some point, been registered to Gage. But he was a second-hand car dealer and there were thousands of motors like that.

McAlroy's wife had rushed from the house that night and she caught a glimpse of the hit man. He was wearing a hood and a scarf over his gob so she only saw his eyes but it seems that that was enough to finger Willie in court. He was found guilty and went down big time. It was a bloody scandal but they had a conviction for the murder of a politically influential millionaire's son and that's all they wanted. I'm sure the First Minister and his chums will be pleased the cops are doing their jobs. If only they knew ...

Mark Clinton was soon in the hot seat again – this time he was charged with the murder of Billy McPhee. The Licensee's equaliser, McPhee had been repeatedly knifed in the Springcroft Tavern as he watched rugby on TV, surrounded by families having lunch. A bloody killing in every sense.

The hit man had worn an improvised hood made out of a black bin liner. In the struggle with McPhee, it had slipped a little so, in spite of the chaos, one or two witnesses thought they might recognise some of the man's features. However, all the people in the pub when the attack happened agreed that the hit man was very tall and slim and had sallow skin and a long, hooked nose. Mark Clinton is average height, stocky and muscular, pale skinned and, while his nose is no button, it's not long and hooked. But the cops weren't going to allow a few minor details like those get in their way.

One of the witnesses was asked to call at a cop shop for an ID parade. When he arrived, the polis put him into an interview room to wait – and wait and wait and wait. All there was in the room was a chair and a table. On that table was a copy of *The Sun* newspaper. Inevitably, the very bored witness picked up the paper to pass the time and, there inside, attached to the newsprint by Blu-Tack, was a photograph of Mark Clinton. No prizes for guessing who the witness fingered at the ID parade.

One night, a bunch of heavies who usually work for The Licensee took Clinton off the street and bundled him into the back of a car. Sitting at either side of him, two men slashed and chopped at his legs with cleavers. All the time this was going on, they were saying, 'You're going down for McPhee.'

Mark Clinton takes a lot of persuading. A short while later, he attended a formal hearing in the High Court to do with the McPhee murder charges. As the left the building later on, he sensed he was being followed. It was the snitch and his bitches – The Licensee and six of a crew.

A simple deal was put to Mark Clinton. 'I can make sure you go down for McPhee,' said The Licensee. 'Twenty-five years minimum. Unless . . .'

'Unless fucking what?' demanded Mark Clinton who wasn't scared of that pack.

'Unless you take Ferris out.'

'Aye, right. Fuck off.'

'You need to fucking remember something – Billy McPhee had a lot of friends.'

'And you need to remember that I didn't kill him,' replied Mark.

'It's Ferris or you, ye cunt. Ferris or you.'

Mark Clinton takes a lot of persuading. Instead of carrying out the hit on me, he went on trial and pled not guilty to the murder of Billy McPhee. Within three hours, the witness who had ID'd him at the parade at the cop shop had withdrawn his evidence. Another witness also said it wasn't him. Within three hours, the case had collapsed – it was the shortest murder trial in Scottish history where the accused has pled not guilty.

Sometimes the system does work. All it needs is honest people – some honest cops would help too.

McGraw had failed to have Mark Clinton convicted or to put me in an early grave. Failure was becoming a bad habit for him and life was about to become worse.

81

TOMMY NO PALS

Thomas McGraw, The Licensee, hit the deck when the bullets started flying. By the bar, a lone gunman was pumping bullets into two of his friends. The Licensee had had better days.

The scene was the Royal Oak bar in Nitshill, in the south of Glasgow. It was early in 2004 and The Licensee was there to invest in a slice of that part of the city. As far as he was concerned, there was a situation vacant.

The year before, the top man in the south side, Stewart 'Specky' Boyd, had died in a car crash in Spain. Two women and a young girl died with him. Tragic.

Boyd had been visiting Paul Johnston and his wife, Marie. Johnston, an ex-cop, was in self-imposed exile and on the run from charges in Scotland. The Johnstons and Boyd ran Guardion Security and Paul Johnston faced charges of brutality and corruption. Life in prison wasn't good for an ex-cop – not even for a bent ex-cop.

The last person to drive the death car before the crash was Paul Johnston. He claimed that he warned Boyd that the brakes seemed a bit dodgy but Boyd was a careful driver and had plenty of high-spec cars to choose from. Boyd would have used a safe motor for sure. His family, friends and many street players weren't convinced his death was an accident.

Back in Glasgow, the lucrative territory of the south side was up for grabs. Boyd's deputy, John McCartney, was known as the World's

Richest Dustbin Man because, for years, he kept working as a dustbin man while also working the streets in a much more sinister way. He was going to buy the Royal Oak, Boyd's symbolic HQ. With him, he had a new boy on the block, Craig Devlin. The pair were in cahoots with The Licensee who wanted a share of that scene. No problem. The Licensee would drive them there – and straight into hell.

The gunman knew McCartney and Devlin were due at the pub to discuss buying it. He quickly came through the door, marched straight up to the two and started blasting, firing low because he knew they'd be wearing bulletproof vests. If he had known The Licensee was there, the casualty rate would have been three that day.

The first the cops knew about the shooting was when they stopped The Licensee's jeep speeding down through the city streets. In the back were McCartney and Devlin, bleeding all over the upholstery, barely conscious.

The two men lived but at some cost. McCartney had been shot several times in the genitals and limps still. But he had worse than that to put up with because the street folk gave him a new nickname – No Balls.

A few weeks later, the Royal Oak was torched in a professional job and, a few days after that, it was razed to the ground and not a brick was left. It looked like an old trick – it looked like the time the cops were going to forensically check The Licensee's pub, The Caravel, and it disappeared overnight. What did they have to hide at the Royal Oak?

The Licensee had been close to coming a cropper – the closest he'd come in years. What was he doing driving his own car and without his usual minders?

Over the past year, his three main henchmen Trevor Lawson, Gordon Ross and Billy McPhee had all died bloodily. No one wanted their jobs – the wages weren't worth an early death. So The Licensee had had to drive himself. He was more vulnerable than he had ever been before.

His usual dose of paranoia was now mixed with self-pity. In recent months he has taken to drinking heavily and frequently. He was hanging around pubs and clubs trying to pick up young women. The love of his life, his wife Margaret, The Jeweller, and the real brains, had had enough and split with him. The Licensee was lonely and about to become lonelier.

Another of his top men, 'Fast' Eddie McCreadie, had been caught with a massive amount of drugs and jailed big time a couple of years before. Street players reckoned that McCreadie was set up by The Licensee – sacrificed in some deal with the cops. From prison, Fast Eddie contacted us, saying that he too thinks his boss stitched him up. Alive and kicking, McCreadie intends to reveal the lot about McGraw – his business practices over the past twenty years, his relationship with the cops, the deals struck, the bodies traded . . . the works.

Thomas McGraw is not a happy man – not on the street and not at home. The loss of his minders and his wife, Margaret, has made him shakier than ever and he has been far from happy. Mind you, she always played around with cop partners or young local men. McGraw knew about it and was often goaded mercilessly because of it but mostly he just put up with it. Margaret, The Jeweller, wasn't just the brains – she wore the trousers as well.

To be fair to McGraw, he has tried. In 2002, when I'd been recalled to prison, I had the minute consolation of knowing that he was in agony. The reason for his pain was nothing serious – he had just had all his teeth replaced by those fancy jobs they screw into the bone of your jaw. Since then, he's had a nip here and a tuck there, as if he's chasing his youth that's long gone. If you don't believe me, compare the picture of him being released from his drugs trial in 1998 with one of him now. One man looks old, worn out and ill. The other looks twenty years younger.

McGraw has tried hard all right but it hasn't worked.

Around Christmas 2004, he was nabbed by some traffic cop. He was well pissed in his jeep in the city centre, waiting for some young floozy to come out of a club. The old Licensee would have traded some guns and the charges would have been wiped from the police

344

computer. The new Licensee went to court in June 2005, got a heavy fine and lost his driving licence. In his business, that's like losing your legs. Has he lost all his friends – even the ones in uniform?

A few months later, he was spotted in the Black Bear pub, a nice wee place out by Glasgow Zoo in the east end of the city. On his own, he drank round after round of large vodkas and coke, staring into his glass as if hoping he'd find some answers there. Two young guys eventually came in and joined him. After a long confab in hushed voices, The Licensed One began to grumble then rose to his feet.

'IF THAT PLACE ISNAE TORCHED, THERE'LL BE FUCKING TROUBLE!' he screamed.

The two youngsters just shook their heads pityingly and quietly left the pub.

Things aren't working out for McGraw. He's lost his wife, lost his driving licence and lost his influence. But has he lost his other licence, the one to commit crime? No chance – he's just playing by different rules.

82

SEIZED UP
2005

'I need your help, Jamie,' the Asian businessman said.

'Whatever I can do,' replied Jamie Daniels. Jamie was one of the Daniels brothers, a family hated by the cops. Growing up in Possil, one of Glasgow's hardest areas, the Daniels Family had done all right. They were players and rumoured by everyone, from the cops to lazy journalists, to be big-time drug dealers. How else could they explain their wealth, went the argument, when all they seemed to do was run a scrap yard in downtown Govan? But the polis couldn't prove anything and that got their goat. That and the fact that one of the family had been jailed for killing a cop some years ago.

'I owe some money,' said the businessman,' to some heavy people. They know they'll get it but for some reason . . .'

'they want it now. Want it early,' said Jamie butting in.

'Aye, but how did you know?'

Jamie Daniels just smiled.

I knew what Jamie knew. Some guys in trouble with the cops had passed messages to me. They weren't wanted for crimes but had become targets of that new power – seizure of assets. Hit them where it hurts was the message from top cop Graeme Pearson who then set targets of many millions of pounds per year.

First they'd gone after my old pal Russell Stirton who was related to the McGovern Family who ran the north of the city. They'd never forgiven Russell for working a sting with me against the cops. They'd wanted him to plant smack on me. Instead, he and I had taped and filmed them talking about setting me up, talking about killing me.

Now the cops had gone after a load of other people. The strange thing was they didn't go after the one man everyone knew was one of the richest – Thomas McGraw, The Licensee. It's well recorded that McGraw is worth at least £20 million though we reckon that's closer to £30 million when you take his shenanigans abroad into account – not bad for a guy who hasn't held a job in decades. But, despite his wealth and its source being well known, the blue meanies, with their new power, hadn't gone near him. This just confirmed to me what I'd already been told by a rogue cop and a highly principled lawyer – on the sly, of course – that Pearson was now McGraw's handler. And he couldn't pull his own snitch now, could he?

According to the media, McGraw had had a lot of trouble. It started in Ireland when the authorities there investigated The Paradise Bar, a pub he owned. They seized the pub and load of dosh that couldn't be accounted for. What they didn't know was that it all belonged to an associate of his – ex-roofer Chic Glackin. A pal of McGraw's murdered lieutenant, Gordon Ross, Glackin felt well let down by The Licensee because of all the cash he'd lost. That was another pal lost.

Then McGraw did a sweetheart deal with the Inland Revenue, paying them something like £300,000. It sent the message that he was going straight but he paid buttons compared to what he should have coughed up. I was very, very suspicious.

When, in 2005, he was declared bankrupt over a few measly grand, I smelled a rat. He could have paid that out of only one of his smaller biscuit tins. Somebody had advised him that the bankruptcy was a good idea – as in bankrupt = got no dosh. Aye, right.

When I got the first message, it all made sense. McGraw was up to his old tricks and the cops were right on his side.

One player who'd had all his assets seized was invited to a meeting by a bloke called David Cassells. Known as Cass, he was a relative of McGraw. Along with him was James 'Mudsie' Mullen, also an associate of the snake. The idea was that Cass and Mullen would work out some deal for the bloke – a bit of funding upfront, a bit of business and some repayment arrangement.

When the guy arrived at the meeting place, there was Cass and Mullen and a third man.

'This is Tam,' said Cass.

McGraw had just invited himself in. The Licensee wanted to know how much the guy was hurting financially and he then went on to offer him work. Good offer? No. It was trafficking drugs and guess who took all the risks?

The same scenario was repeated for every major face whose assets were seized. McGraw was working for the cops, sussing out if they really had managed to grab most of these guys' money and then seeing how desperate they were.

No doubt, if any of them had taken up the offer of the drugs trafficking, some would end up getting nabbed – deliberately. McGraw had already done that to a bunch of guys – non-players every one – who were caught with millions of pounds' worth of cocaine hidden in bales of raw rubber. No wonder the police were leaving McGraw alone.

The Asian businessman owed the money to one Billy Mills. Upfront, Mills ran property schemes and small businesses, mainly in the trendy west end of Glasgow. In reality, he was McGraw's latest bitch. McGraw's great strength – his only strength – is that he's a fishwife gossip. Of course, this means that he knows who knows who and he was convinced the Asian businessman would go to Jamie Daniels for help. He would also have been advised by his cop pals that Jamie had just had his own assets seized. So McGraw would get Mills to call in the Asian bloke's loan with menaces as a way of getting to Daniels and testing out how much he was hurting.

But Jamie was not hurting enough to dull his thinking and he proceeded to give the Asian businessman some advice. A few days later, the businessman attended a meeting with McGraw and Mills. It was out in the open in an industrial estate they'd chosen and the place was crawling with CCTV cameras. The loan itself was illegal. They were about to threaten the man big time. So why did they want it all recorded? Because they had nothing to fear from the cops and no other player would chance being caught on camera so the Asian bloke would have no one to bail him out . . . or so they thought.

McGraw and Mills were deeply disappointed that Jamie Daniels hadn't turned up with the man and they were equally disappointed that the bloke didn't produce the money. They went from angry to furious and started making it plain that the guy would be eating his own testicles unless they got what they wanted and that's when they heard it. A scruffy old van came speeding into the estate heading straight for them. They dashed to their motor – Billy Mills's new high-spec Mercedes. He managed to get the engine started and had just hit the accelerator when the van went crashing at speed into the side of it. The Merc rocked. The van reversed and bumped it again and, this time, the driver held his foot on the gas and pushed the plush big motor all over the place. Message received – the snitch and his new bitch sped off.

The businessman hasn't heard from the two since and has taken it that his debt has been cancelled. McGraw, who loves money more than anything, will be heartbroken. But there was to be worse news for him – much worse.

This latest arrangement he had with the cops, under which he targets guys whose money has been seized, has angered and annoyed some serious people. A few of them have got together and have decided to sort this out once and for all.

A few years back, Frank 'The Iceman' McPhie, one of the most feared hit men in Britain, was taken out by a sniper as he stood at his own front door. It was a professional mob from outside and the cops admit they have no clue and no chance of catching them. The word is that the serious men who are so angry with The Licensee's latest business venture have hired this mob to see to him. The word is also that they agreed the deal for a cut price – the mob never liked The Licensee anyway.

Around good pubs in the east end and the city centre you'll catch McGraw, sitting on his own drinking vodka after vodka. He's a lonely man. Maybe he hasn't lost his licence to commit crime but maybe he realises he's in severe danger of losing more than that.

McGraw has dug his own hole and I'm happy to let him rot in it. But he isn't the only one licensed by the cops and with me in their sights. Ben Alagha was back.

83

NO ROOM AT THE INN

'He's done what?'

While Billy was on remand waiting for his trial for the murder of Jason Hutchison, I was visiting him in BarL and I couldn't believe what he was saying.

Ben Alagha had walked into Scotland Yard, asked for his handler by name and offered evidence implicating both Billy and me in the murder of Hutchison. Ben had no evidence because there was no evidence to be had but this was still dangerous – registered informants with a grudge, like him, always are.

In double-quick time, I got round to Billy's solicitor, John Macaulay, and offered him my portfolio on Ben – the affidavit, the smuggling papers, the sex slave evidence and the rest. If Ben Liar wanted to come ahead, then let him.

I hoped that Ben would take the stand at Billy's trial. Whatever he was claiming was untrue so surely we could counter that. But it would also present a chance to expose the raping, backstabbing, murderous bastard in open court – him and his cop chums. But John Macaulay and Donald Findlay QC took the opposite view and played safe. They quietly let the Crown know that, if they called Ben as a witness, they would shit on his credibility from a great height – one witness removed from the list, pronto.

While the chance to grill Ben had passed because the Crown had backed off using him as a witness, it was still revealing. If the authorities thought Billy's team were bluffing and that Ben was a credible witness, they would have called him in spite of the threats. They knew all about Ben – every damn thing – yet they still used him as witness and informant. It stank.

Even when Billy was sent to pokey for twenty-two years, Ben wasn't finished. He was obviously still working on that request from the cops and MI5 to get me. He was still trying to set me up so that he could avoid that deportation order hanging over his head like a hefty, razor-sharp chib.

Before I sussed Ben out for the rat that he is, I knew that large sums of money were mysteriously being moved about between bank accounts. We're talking hundreds of thousands turning up in some account, staying there for a while and being moved on. It had nothing to do with me and I wasn't interested to learn about the scam but now I wished I'd paid more attention.

At the beginning of 2005, cops from London accompanied by Glasgow polis turned up at my house with a search warrant. They took the strangest items like notes, copies of letters, bank statements. They didn't leave with much but I noticed that they did take correspondence I'd had with a guy called Paul McCusker who ran a security business. My habit of recording everything meant they not only had the letters I'd received from him but the ones I'd sent too. Strange one. I'd had some brief business with him through my security consultancy a couple of years before. The man treated his staff abysmally, getting them to claim benefits, then paying them tiny wages. He'd had an affair with one of his young workers and she'd had his baby but, although he was rich, the uncaring bastard wouldn't support that kid in any way. I didn't like him at all so he was doing no business with me.

A short while later, I realised why the cops had shown interest in McCusker when formal papers arrived from the Met. They were investigating a £3 million bank swindle and wanted to interview a long list of people. I ran down the names and recognised some from the papers I had on Ben's smuggling racket. The other thing that caught my attention was that there were only two Scots' names on the list – Paul Ferris and Paul McCusker.

It didn't take long to find out that Ben had gone to his handlers with these allegations. He had been running a big bank scam and was close to getting nabbed. So he did his usual and claimed he had only participated in it so that he could get information on the crooks. Christ knows how he came up with that list – probably the others named on it were as innocent as I was. And, as far as these claims were concerned, I wasn't just innocent – I was Persil white.

With nothing to fear, I made myself available in London to give a statement. Joey Pyle had fixed me up with his lawyer, a lovely and obviously very skilled bloke. One comprehensive statement later and the matter was dealt with. It was easy. I could prove that I only had one bank account and they'd obviously checked up on that. Banks these days have to cooperate with the dark forces to combat fraud and money laundering. A few years ago, that might have pissed me off but that day it suited me just fine.

Ben had also shot himself in the foot. As part of his statement he claimed that Billy and I met him on a certain date in 2002. There's just one problem with that, Ben – at the time, I was locked up in jail, my licence having been revoked after reports of golf clubs at dawn with The Licensee. If there is anything at all good about being sent back to jail, it's having the Home Office provide you with an alibi.

Then, of course, I gave Ben his colours by talking about all his shady dealings, the hot contracts, the double-crossing of pals and family. Well, he'd invited me to the party so he'd asked for it. By the time I had finished, Ben Alagha should have been in the shit but, then, he does have a licence to swindle. The authorities did sod all – as usual.

Back home, I forgot all about Ben's latest efforts to bring me down and got on with my life. Wanting to take the Glasgow film projects further, I went to open a bank account in the name of a company. Right from the start, I wanted everything to be well organised, legitimate and transparent but that was when the Royal Bank of Scotland refused to open an account. I had plenty of money. The security consultancy had been good to me and I'd just had a bit of unexpected good luck.

Before my last jail sentence, I had bought a share in a pub north of Glasgow, near Lenzie, overlooking the Campsie Hills. One of the partners ran it for a few years and it provided a very good income, thank you very much. Having lost a lot of even my legit money when I was jailed, I needed to cash in on this and discovered that the pub came with several acres of prime building land. After a tussle with Historic Scotland who had discovered a Roman burial plot on the land, we got a decent price. It meant that I got my original investment back and a very nice wee sweetener. Funnily enough, I still get invited there by the owners. They say it's good for business because the locals think that makes it a safe place and now it's popular with young courting couples wanting a peaceful, quiet night out – just the way it should be.

So, here I was, for the first time in my life, with plenty of dosh and no bad debts. The money was all legit and I wanted to use it as a hefty deposit to open a bank account but the bank said no – no account and no explanation. Then a pal phoned, a well-to-do businessman who has never been in trouble in his life, and the Royal Bank had just pulled the plug on him – again they offered no explanation. Next, someone who had connections with the security company, Frontline. A company run by honest businessmen, with proper books and very successful. Same drill. And it wasn't just the Royal Bank – it was all banks based in this country. There had to be a reason because these account closures weren't due to debt or lack of funds by any of these parties. It had to be the cops.

These days, seizure of assets is used as a major way to break organised crime. My pal Russell Stirton was the first big target when £3 million was grabbed. If they have not an iota of reason to seize your goodies, their next resort is to squeeze you out and that was the strategy they used on me. But, just as with seizure of assets, they also applied the move to other people I might have some business dealings with.

I withdrew from security consultancy some time ago, having taken advice from the body that will regulate the industry in Scotland. They told me that, when the rules come in, they wouldn't pass me as fit to be a consultant or an adviser because of my criminal record. So, rather than waiting to be pushed, I jumped. That meant my income would have to be earned entirely from other, creative projects. But how could I make films, support rock groups, run my website and write books if I had no bank accounts? I had rehabilitated myself and I was concentrating on honest endeavours but, despite this, the cops aren't content to leave me be. Even now the bastards come after me.

You either lie down and let these people walk over you or you keep fighting. Me? I'm for the latter. If you don't know how to do something, go to someone who does and that's what I did. It was simply solved in the end. Foreign banks don't let the British cops push them about so easily. So I went to them – problem solved.

Some problems aren't so easy to fix. Some things just aren't under my control. Some people . . .

84

GHOSTS

My past never seems to go away entirely – I suppose it never will.

As I'm leading my new life, William 'Tootsie' Lobban – the man who led my pals Bobby and Joe to their deaths – turned up in the papers, telling his story for a few quid. It was all lies and rubbish, of course, and he gave his bizarre, mental game away when he insisted on being photographed bowing in front of a picture of The Godfather – that's Marlon Brando, not Arthur Thompson.

Then, even as I was writing the end of this book, I heard from someone who wanted to help. After a phone call and a secret meeting, I was handed police documents all about Bobby and Joe's murders – new information, revealing information, information that has been kept from the public. In a shady pub, I was passed a thick file of formal reports that looked like they came from some official body. Then came the diamond – sketches of someone's impression of the murders. They looked too accurate in their minor details to be anything but genuine. They looked for all the world like a police artist's sketches.

If these details are true, the cops had a name for who bought the guns – the name of a good old pal of Arthur Thompson. William 'Tootsie' Lobban was there. Bobby was shot first and Joe next. One of the gunmen would appear to have been Billy Manson, Lobban's uncle and a good pal of Thompson. The guns were meant to have been disposed of by one Thomas McGraw, The Licensee. Maybe that's why they turned up later in a house in Blackhill? Who'd trust The Licensee with anything? Is all this what really happened? Who knows? But details from those drawings do match what I've been told by people who know the streets well. Also, after Bobby and Joe's murders, Billy Manson went into hiding in a caravan in Blantyre and that caravan was owned by Alex Morrison, boxing promoter and pal of Arthur Thompson. However, he didn't hide for long enough because, not long after Bobby and Joe died, he was stabbed to death.

I could go on but that's not my point. My point is that, if the cops did have this much detail, why don't the public know about it? And why are the murders of my two pals still unsolved? It's not my business or intention to solve Bobby and Joe's murders – that's for the cops to do. It's just like when TC Campbell was jailed wrongly for the Doyle murders – his job was to prove his innocence. But, now that he has done it, what have the cops done about finding the real killer? They now know that McGraw was in the Doyles' street that night, that he bought petrol nearby and that he asked someone to torch their door but what have they done with this knowledge? Fuck all. And that's what I expect from the police in solving Bobby and Joe's murders. Nothing. Two lost souls abandoned because of me – because they were my pals.

The sketches will go to Bobby and Joe's families, along with the letter from the cops about the murder guns. Maybe, just maybe, this will help to force the police into acting on their murders. Maybe they'll actually bother to do something – at least they might tell the families everything they know. Maybe.

Another good thing to come about over these sketches is that somebody, somewhere – maybe an ex-cop – has decided to help, even after all these years. Whoever you are, may you and yours have long and happy lives.

One night, someone torched the Provanmill Inn, the bar Arthur Thompson, The Godfather, frequented. At one time, what that place used to represent to me was that family and their betrayal of me. I have an image of Fatboy in there, just hours out of jail, reading out

357

his hit list with my name at the top and most of my pals' names underneath it. He was shot dead later that night. Yet, now, it doesn't matter to me any more if the Provanmill Inn is there or not. It had been torched over some business dispute or so the word is but it isn't in my world – not any more, not now.

Another ghost appeared – the last of the Thompson men, the runt Billy Thompson. Billy has been kicked out of the Ponderosa by his mum Rita. He's a junkie and brain damaged from a beating he got after demanding money from a couple of guys. Is he in an awful state? Yeah. Do I care? Do I fuck. How can I care about someone who beat up and hounded my old man when he needed two sticks to walk?

There's a view that, in life, you reap what you sow and, for me, that's just what Billy Thompson's doing – just like his father, Arthur.

There were those who intended to end Arthur's life and felt cheated when he died of a heart attack. But the night he died was the birthday of one of Bobby and Joe's wives and the day he was buried was the birthday of one of Bobby and Joe's sons. I like to think that as he lay dying – the pain crushing his chest, his throat choking with fluids – he saw Bobby and Joe standing at the bottom of his bed. It would have made a just and fitting end.

But, now, almost four years out of jail, I find myself not wasting my energy on arseholes like Lobban and Thompson any more. Why should I? They will dig their own graves and need no help from me. Besides, I have much better things to get on with and even better things to look forward to.

85

TOO MUCH TO LOSE

People have speculated about my whereabouts after leaving jail and, according to the grapevine, I have lived in big houses in every town in Scotland – every town, that is, except Stirling which is where I have been living for the past couple of years.

It's a nice, ordinary, quiet scheme with loads of old folk for neighbours. For the first year, every time I went home, I would follow the same route. Leaving the place, it would be the same process but in reverse. One day, when I had time on my hands, I decided to explore the area and that's when I realised that I lived fifty yards from a big, fuck-off cop shop. If you want some proof that I've changed, maybe that's just it – fifty yards from the polis and not knowing or caring. The old me wouldn't have done that.

But, as we write the last chapter of this book, I'm flitting from Stirling. It's not because of the cop shop – we've been neighbours for quite some time. It's the attraction of a new place and new scenery and it's also just because I can – the way you do when you're free.

In July 2005, the week of the G8 Summit, Stirling was taken over by protestors and some caused havoc, smashing up shops, pulling down signs and running through the scheme. My elderly neighbours were scared to leave their homes and I wanted to hit the streets and tell the anarchists to fuck off – to think of the people their actions were affecting as well as their principles and find other ways to protest without terrifying the frail and timid. Much as I agree with many of their aims, how they went about their business was little less than bullying. After all these years, bullying still angers me more than anything else. Inside, I felt like getting a group of the guys together and going out and having a word with the protestors – move them on and send them in the direction of the big boys, like the G8 mob themselves or their protectors, the cops. I wanted to but I didn't.

My own mother has had problems with junkies in her close and her upstairs neighbours, young folk, have been banging on the floor, playing loud music all night and fighting and squabbling. At times, it has left her fearful and I'll not stand for that. But now I go to the authorities, talk it through, reason and try to solve the problem. It takes time and patience and I can't help thinking that my old ways were quicker and more effective. But I've realised that staying clear of trouble and out of jail means that I can spend time with my mum. Too much time has been wasted in the past – time I should have spent with her and my two boys.

Young Dean is at primary school but still older than me in some ways. Are kids growing up faster? Or is it just that I've had a chance to grow up with him and he's grown up with me? – a chance I threw away with Paul, my oldest boy. He's a young man now and he's carrying a name that has meant trouble on Glasgow's streets – carrying my name with pride but not carrying my old lifestyle.

'I love you, Dad,' he said, when I had just left Frankland, 'but I don't love what you've done.' If I'm ever tempted to go back to the old ways, I just need to think of those words and remember the times we've had together – the three us of us, the Ferris boys. No way am I losing that again.

But why should I worry? There's my family, the feature film, the books, the website, the Glasgow films and more. It's the life I said I would live and I'm living it now.

The blue serge meanies will still come after me – try to fit me up, jail me, hurt me, tempt me into anger, violence or a lucrative scam. For the rest of my life, I'll need to be on my guard, on the lookout for trouble ahead – it's just one of the prices I pay for the life I led. But, be warned – follow me, harm me or mine, conspire against me, fight me and I'll fight you right back.

Yet I'm still here, still alive, still free and still going straight. That's the way it will stay. These days, I have too much to lose – it's called freedom.

WHERE ARE THEY NOW?

SAFFIA ABRAHAMS – is now known as Susannah York and lives abroad under protection.

JOHN ACKERMAN – though declared dead, was last heard of alive and well in Amsterdam.

JOHNNY 'MAD DOG' ADAIR – is held in prison in Ireland. His wife and followers have moved to Bolton, England.

JAMES ADDISON – is still at large.

BEN ALAGHA – is now known as 'Ben Laden' because he's committed such terrible crimes but he's never seen. He still lives in England in spite of the deportation order. Big-time grass.

MOHAMED AL-FAYED – is still a passport free zone but he's welcome in Scotland.

TAM BAGAN – is out of jail and has taken to a settled life of art, peace and the company of a good woman.

SIMON BAKERMAN – is still keeping bad company in Liverpool. He has since bought himself a new watch.

PAUL BENNETT – is still at large. He is last known to have been involved in setting up Spanish and English drug traffickers.

TOMMY BOURKE – is still in jail, fighting to prove his innocence of the murder of two Customs and Excise officers.

STEWART 'SPECKY' BOYD – two years after his death in a car crash, Spanish police are still investigating the cause. The last person to drive the death car, Paul Johnston, has since fled Spain.

CHARLES BRONSON – could have been free by 1980, still in jail in 2005.

KEN BUCHANAN – the former World Champ is still bobbing and weaving but now outside the boxing ring.

TC Campbell – has won his appeal against conviction of the 1984 murder of the Doyle Family. As this goes to print, he's negotiating compensation that will make him a millionaire but no amount of money can repay him for his lost years.

Rab Carruthers – free of drugs at last, Rab died in 2004 of lung cancer, resulting in Glasgow's biggest street funeral in many decades. Sadly missed.

Mark Clinton – is a good man and still free in spite of the cops trying to pin every hit on him.

Peter Cox – has parted company with the *Daily Record,* having successfully managed to piss off Rangers and Celtic supporters. Last heard of working at *The Sun.*

Kirsty Cunningham – is making ace films. Directed the documentary *Someone Stole My Foetus.*

Daily Record – under new editor, thank God.

Craig 'Hairy Hands' Devlin – since being shot at the Royal Oak, the snitch's bitch has been spending a lot of time at The Licensee's house in Tenerife.

Frankie 'Donuts' Donaldson – should have been a boxer. Last heard of, he put Grant 'Mr Paisley' McIntosh on the deck several times.

Doyle Family – their murders in 1984 remain unsolved.

Jeremy 'Jez' Earls – his death by shooting remains officially suicide.

Eatso – is hopefully free and happy and has found a cure for the farts.

Sam Emmery – is making great films – latest is *With Fran in Sudan.*

Billy Ferris – has launched legal action for an appeal against his conviction for the murder of fifteen-year-old Jason Hutchison. He was shanghaied from the cushy Induction Centre at Shotts Prison to the hell of sol con at BarL and then to an unofficial special unit at Glenochil Prison.

DONALD FINDLAY QC – is a bad singer but a great lawyer.

PINK FLOYD – reformed after twenty-four years for Live 8 and sang 'Wish You Were Here' two days after we wrote that chapter.

LISA FRENCH – is still a lawyer at Goldkorns, London, and a force to be reckoned with in every sense.

FRONTLINE SECURITY – is going from strength to strength despite efforts to tarnish its reputation. I wish I did own it.

WILLIE GAGE – has won the right to an appeal for his unjust conviction for the murder of Jason McAlroy. Free Willie Gage.

CHIC GLACKIN – another ex-pal of The Licensee, he's probably wishing he was still a roofer not a player. Maybe he is.

BOBBY GLOVER – his murder remains unsolved.

LANCE GOUDIE – is free under the witness protection programme but still peddling drugs and slashing himself.

LANCE GRAY – is a good man who's free at last. I owe you.

PAUL GRIMES – lives the lonely life of a supergrass. In spite of there being a £100K contract out on his life, he appeared on a Channel 5 documentary with Donal MacIntyre.

JOHN HAASE – is still held in top-security jails, fighting the system and spending a great deal of time in solitary.

JOE HANLON – his murder remains unsolved.

MICHAEL HOWARD – is about to resign as Tory leader. Where will he pop up again?

HUTCHISON FAMILY – several of them have been jailed for drug dealing since the murder of fifteen-year-old Jason.

GARY JACOBS – the former boxing champion was charged with drug dealing in 2004. All charges against him were dropped.

WHERE ARE THEY NOW?

PAUL JOHNSTON – after the death of Specky Boyd, Scottish cops suddenly did a deal with him, allowing him to end his Spanish exile. What did he trade with the cops?

PAUL KERR – is still lighting forest fires and negotiating deals. Watch this space?

WALTER KIRKWOOD – is not involved in gun dealing. Living near Dumbarton, he's earning a good living constructing decking.

KEVIN LANE – is still fighting against his conviction for murder. Check out www.justiceforkevinlane.com.

MARK LEECH – the cons' con, is now a human rights lawyer.

WILLIAM 'TOOTSIE' LOBBAN – who cares?

JOHN MACAULAY – is one of the best crime lawyers in Scotland and is particularly keen on fighting cases of unjust conviction.

DONAL MACINTYRE – is still throwing badminton matches against one-armed Colombian drug traffickers and making great TV.

IAN MCATEER – is still inside fighting for an appeal against his murder conviction.

JOHN 'NO BAWS' MCCARTNEY – has given up his cover as a dustbin man and is now paying young kids money to terrorise the residents of Barrhead.

GEORGE 'CRATER FACE' MCCORMACK – is still driving a taxi and taking the ugly pills.

IAN 'BLINK' MCDONALD – is out of prison and has gone very quiet.

MANNY MCDONNELL – the ex-IRA man teamed up with McGraw against all advice. In 2002, he had his house and car targeted by Billy McPhee and Gordon Ross, people he thought of as friends.

JOHN MCGLYNN – the young artist moved to Canada shortly after painting my portrait. Should I take that personally?

THOMAS 'THE LICENSEE' MCGRAW – has taken to booze and young women and is a pal-free zone.

JAMES MCINTYRE – watch out, watch out Tom Hagen's about! Writing for *River City* and *EastEnders*, he is contemplating a book on his exploits as a lawyer.

JAIMBA MCLEAN – is still taking the medication and living the quiet life with his family.

LENNY 'THE GUV'NOR' MCLEAN – has admitted accepting a hit contract on me from Arthur Thompson after I'd been found not guilty of killing Thompson's son, Fatboy. Before anything could happen, both Thompson and McLean died of natural causes.

BILLY MCPHEE – his murder remains unsolved.

FRANK 'THE ICEMAN' MCPHIE – his murder remains unsolved.

JOHN MCVICAR – the former armed robber and escape artiste is now well accepted as a writer and a commentator. Maybe I should move south?

BILLY MANSON – was stabbed to death as he sat in his car at traffic lights, shortly after Bobby Glover and Joe Hanlon's murders. His passenger was unhurt in the attack.

PAUL MASSEY – is in Frankland jail fighting for an appeal against his conviction.

PADDY MEEHAN – was freed by royal pardon. He wrote some books on the nature of crime then died a free but very bitter man.

STEVIE MOFFAT – his parole application is pending for his murder conviction – a murder he didn't commit.

DARREN MULHOLLAND – is still reading books for fun and hasn't forgotten about Fitzgibbon.

ALEXANDER NESS – is in jail, possibly forever.

RORY NICOLL – who ate all the pies? We know he's a player even if now he does the dishes and the hoovering.

GRAEME PEARSON – will take over the new Scottish Organised Crime Unit in the near future.

PROVANMILL INN – its ruins were torched for the second time in June 2005.

JOEY PYLE – the Don of Dons and his son go from strength to strength in legitimate business.

BRENDAN QUINN – is free at last, happy and in love.

KENNY RICHEY – has now been kept on Ohio's death row for almost twenty years. They plan to try him again for a crime he didn't commit – evil, bitter bastards that they are.

PAUL ROBINSON – the lawyer is still a good man but keeping some very bad company.

GORDON ROSS – his murder remains unsolved.

EVERTON 'ZB' SALMON – is still serving life. Respect to you and yours.

DAVID SANTINI – is still free and leading the quiet life. We've still to meet up since being released from jail.

ROY SHAW – is still as fierce as ever.

ARTHUR SUTTIE – is a good man and a good friend who is loved by many.

ARTHUR 'FATBOY' THOMPSON – his murder remains unsolved.

BILLY THOMPSON – sadly, The Godfather's son is now a homeless, brain-damaged junkie.

GRANT 'BASIL' TURNBULL – is waiting for his parole on compassionate grounds.

MR A VANNET – is now a Sheriff (a Scottish judge) in Airdrie.

DANNY VAUGHAN – is happy, free and breeding kids.

BERTI VOGTS – gave us all a break and left the Scotland manager's job. I still don't want to buy his house.

THE VULCAN – who knows? Who ever knows?

CURTIS 'COCKY' WARREN – is in jail in Holland, still fighting for his seized cash and winning battles worth millions of pounds.

ANN WIDDECOMBE – has reinvented herself as a novelist and an agony aunt for the very desperate indeed. She still knows nothing about any royal pardon.

DENNIS 'THE MENACE' WOODMAN – was last of heard of in hospital having had his throat slashed by some guy he'd cheated in a small-time deal.

INDEX

INDEX

INDEX

INDEX